DATE DUE

1 4 FEB 2002			
2 9 NOV 2002			

THE POLITICS OF SURVIVAL

J. L. Granatstein

THE POLITICS OF SURVIVAL

THE CONSERVATIVE PARTY OF CANADA, 1939-1945

University
of Toronto
Press

© University of Toronto Press 1967
Reprinted 1970
Printed in U.S.A.

SBN 8020–5192–8 (cloth)
8020–6109–5 (paper)

FOR ELAINE

Preface

Canadian political life during the Second World War was dominated by two major issues—conscription for overseas military service and the growth of socialism. These issues, one a throwback to the controversies of the Great War, the other seemingly a herald of things to come, shaped the conflict among the nation's political parties. Inevitably, internal struggles within the parties resulted as each attempted to plot its course.

The Conservative party underwent several changes in policy and leadership in its efforts to regain its strength after the *débâcles* of 1935 and 1940. The central contest within the party was between those who wished to make conscription and free enterprise the keystones of Conservative policy and those who feared that with such a restricted platform the Conservative party might again become a casualty of the war. This latter group, most of whose members favoured conscription and firmly believed in free enterprise, nonetheless believed that a new Conservatism, soundly based on a rational policy of social welfare, was a necessity if the party was to meet the challenge posed by the Co-operative Commonwealth Federation.

The dividing line between the protagonists in this Conservative controversy was not always a clear one. The militant conscriptionists united behind Senator Arthur Meighen and captured control of the party in November 1941. But after Meighen was defeated by a C.C.F. candidate in his bid to enter the House of Commons, the forward-looking Conservatives seized the initiative, held a conference, and propounded a new policy of progressive Conservatism. By December 1942 the party had a new leader in John Bracken, the long-time Liberal-Progressive premier of Manitoba, and a commitment to an advanced platform of social welfare measures. Bracken's selection had been engineered by Arthur Meighen with the tacit consent of both factions of the party, however, and until war's end, Bracken was tugged in two directions. The resulting compromises found the party entering the general election of June 1945 committed to conscription for the Pacific theatre and with an ambivalent attitude to social welfare. Well-organized and well-financed though it now was, the Conservative party emerged from the war—as it had entered it—in Opposition. Once again, Conservatism had been defeated by conscription.

This book is an attempt to detail the history of an important period in Canadian political life. It is based primarily on interviews with political figures and on examination of the very abundant collections of the letters and papers of politicians held by repositories and individuals across Canada. Unfortunately, French-Canadian primary sources for the period are almost entirely non-existent or closed to researchers, the sole exception being the Ernest Lapointe Papers at the Public Archives of Canada. Had the Conservative party not been so feeble in Quebec during the period under study, this lack would have been of greater consequence.

This work would have been impossible without the co-operation of many people. My greatest debt is to the Honourable R. A. Bell, P.C., M.P., Q.C., one of this country's first professional politicians, who opened his papers to me, granted me interviews, wrote letters on my behalf to others, and read the entire manuscript. If all men in public life were as co-operative, the task of the student would be much easier. Dr. C. P. Stacey, in 1965–66 Director of History at Canadian Forces Head-quarters, allowed me to use the Directorate files and the Crerar papers, helped in many other ways, and read the drafts of this manuscript. His assistance has improved the work substantially. I must also thank Miss Flora Macdonald, late of Progressive Conservative party headquarters, for her aid during my research there.

This work has been published with the help of a grant from the Social Science Research Council of Canada using funds provided by the Canada Council. Duke University's Commonwealth Studies Center provided a generous research grant without which I would have been unable to examine several manuscript collections. Messrs. Anthony and Agar Adamson, Mrs. H. A. Bruce, Mr. A. K. Cameron, the Honourable J. W. Gardiner, Mr. Terry Grier, Mr. H. A. Hanson, Q.C., Mr. W. R. Herridge, Mr. J. B. Lawson, Mrs. Albert Levitt, the late General the Honourable A. G. L. McNaughton, and Mrs. Stuart Ralston all per-mitted me to examine collections they control. The gentlemen who submitted to interviews were, almost without exception, completely frank and co-operative. Archivists across Canada assisted me in many ways. The entire staff of the Public Archives of Canada, that model public repository, was always especially helpful. My former colleagues in the Directorate of History in Ottawa, and particularly Lt.-Col. D. J.

Goodspeed, Dr. J. Mackay Hitsman, Thor Thorgrimsson, and Malcolm MacLeod, made many useful suggestions. The stylistic comments of Col. Goodspeed and Mr. Thorgrimsson, and Dr. Hitsman's knowledge of Canadian manpower problems were especially valuable. My friends, Robert Martin and Desmond Morton, and my colleagues, John Saywell, Peter Oliver, and Paul Stevens, also provided assistance.

Four acknowledgments remain. This monograph was originally presented as a dissertation in history at Duke University in May 1966, and I would be most remiss if I did not express my gratitude to the staff of that university for the courtesy and kindness with which I was received there. Professor Theodore Ropp, who supervised the dissertation, provided ideas, assistance, and criticism for three years. My debt to him is immense. The editorial staff of the University of Toronto Press, and particularly Miss Francess Halpenny and Mrs. Marion Magee, did not turn a sow's ear into a silk purse, but accomplished a small miracle all the same. Finally, my wife Elaine typed this work through innumerable drafts and helped in many different ways. With the exception of such errors or omissions as may remain, the final product is as much hers as mine.

J.L.G.

Contents

THE POLITICS OF SURVIVAL

1.   Introduction

The Tory tradition is to follow the British way of life. The Tory is British first, and secondly Canadian. The Liberal is Canadian first and a British subject afterwards—sometimes a long way afterwards. . . . The Tories put money and property first. The Liberals place humanity and equality of opportunity first. . . . The Tories are anti-Catholic—intolerant—and hate Quebec. The Liberals believe in freedom of worship, tolerance—and love Canada. . . . Toryism means reaction. Liberalism means progress.[1]

These well-worn slogans appeared in the reference handbook prepared by the Liberal party for its candidates in the general election of 1945. That such nonsense could still be peddled—and often accepted—as a realistic description of the Conservative party, its members, and its policies in 1945 is a testimony to the weaknesses of Conservatism both before and during the Second World War. And yet there were some elements of truth in the Liberal propaganda, elements which extended back in time to earlier crises and which hinged on the Conservative reactions to conscription and social welfare.

Conscription was the more perilous of the two issues. Canada had entered the Great War with enthusiasm, but the unity of the summer and fall of 1914 soon dissolved under the impact of casualties and a recurrence of the racial animosity that had cursed the nation since its birth. The English-speaking provinces, after some early hesitation, believed with a whole heart that England's cause was Canada's cause and that every fit man should serve. Quebec, on the other hand, had seen its initial urge to participate in the war disappear under the combined forces of government bungling and the attacks of the English majority.

The roots of Quebec's reaction went back into the history of New France. Hugh MacLennan captured the feeling of the *Canadien* in Père Beaubien, the rural priest in his novel *Two Solitudes*:

He thought of the war and the English with the same bitterness. How could French-Canadians—the only real Canadians—feel loyalty to a people who

[1]National Liberal Committee, *Reference Handbook, 1945* (Ottawa, 1945), p. 1–A6.

had conquered and humiliated them, and were Protestant anyway? France herself was no better; she had deserted her Canadians a century and a half ago, had left them in the snow and ice along the St. Lawrence surrounded by their enemies, had later murdered her anointed king and then turned atheist.[2]

"Je me souviens" was the motto of Quebec with good reason. The English overseas were the same to Father Beaubien and his compatriots as the English in Canada—the conquerers. The Boer War was still fresh in the memory; then English Canadians had demanded the right to help Britain crush a people very similar in some ways to the French Canadians. The 1914 war, too, was England's war, not Canada's, so let the English fight it. Attitudes of this sort were ineradicable, but the government of Sir Robert Borden compounded the problem by badly mismanaging recruiting in the province. No vigorous organization under French leadership was set up by Sir Sam Hughes, the anti-French, anti-Catholic Minister of Militia and Defence, and no intelligent effort was made to enlist the support of prominent public men. The failure to appeal to the pride and sentiment of the French Canadians played into the hands of the *nationalistes*, who increased their criticism of Canadian participation the more English Canada attacked Quebec for not providing her "fair share" of recruits for the carnage in Flanders. The political situation in Canada and the military situation on the Western Front had both reached the critical point by 1917.

"This year," said Père Beaubien, "the English provinces had imposed conscription on the whole country trying to force their conquest on Quebec a second time." Police and soldiers had conducted wide sweeps throughout the back country "and had taken young French-Canadians out of their homes like thieves to put them into the army."[3] Sir Wilfrid Laurier, who had welcomed a party truce in August 1914 and who had co-operated actively in the war effort throughout, was placed in an agonizing position, forced to choose between his origins and the national unity for which he had striven throughout his political life. If he joined Borden in a Union government, he would lose his Quebec following; if he did not, he would lose his English-speaking supporters. In the end, Laurier resolved his personal dilemma by refusing to enter a coalition and by affirming his belief that voluntary service was more efficient than conscription. His English followers deserted almost to a man, and a general election in December 1917 resulted in a Laurier-led Opposition that was almost wholly French-speaking and a Union government which contained scarcely a *Canadien* of stature.

[2]Hugh MacLennan, *Two Solitudes* (Toronto, 1945), p. 7.
[3]*Ibid.*

Although the Union government was composed of Conservatives and Liberals alike, it was the Conservative party that became a casualty of the war. The Conservatives had imposed conscription and had humiliated the great Laurier, and for what? The answer was evident to Quebec—for imperialism. The changes in leadership which followed the war emphasized the contrast between the two parties as between good and evil. Laurier was followed by William Lyon Mackenzie King, young and vigorous, although a platitudinous, circumlocutory speaker, and the one English-speaking Liberal of stature who had not declared against Laurier on conscription. Borden was succeeded as prime minister by Arthur Meighen, also young and vigorous, the ablest orator of his generation, and the minister who had steered the Military Service Act of 1917 through the House of Commons. With these men as leaders, conscription was sure to remain an issue of the postwar years, if only in the memory.

The Conservative party went into a prolonged decline in the West and in Quebec after 1921. The party thus fought every election faced with the necessity of sweeping Ontario and the Maritimes in order to have any chance of forming a government. Although this herculean feat was accomplished in 1925 and 1930, the rewards of victory were slim indeed. Under Meighen, the Conservatives won the largest bloc of seats in 1925, but King clung to power with the shaky support of the Progressives. The constitutional crisis of 1926 resulted in another election, and the Conservative party was defeated. This election was the last directed by Meighen. Brilliant and able as he was, Meighen never managed to lead his party to a clear victory over his despised rival. A controversialist, he revelled in argument. Instead of conciliating his opponents, he could only goad them on with his obstinacy, sarcasm, and self-assurance. These qualities did not make for successful political leadership in a country where conciliation and compromise seemed the great virtues.

Meighen was replaced by Richard B. Bennett, the choice of the first national convention of the Conservative party in 1927. In many ways Bennett was similar to Meighen. Like his predecessor, Bennett had gone west in his youth to make his fortune (but unlike Meighen, he had succeeded). He, too, was robust, extremely able, and a powerful speaker but, unlike Meighen who was a warm man in private, Bennett was an egotist who made enemies faster than he found friends. The new leader was to have no better luck than Meighen, although the Conservatives did win the election of 1930 after his strong campaign, regaining strength in the West and even breaking into Quebec for the first time since the war. The onset in earnest of the depression made this a hollow victory, however, and the Conservative party was destroyed for a generation.

There were limits to what any Canadian government could have done to overcome the paralyzing effects of the depression. Canada's dependence on foreign sales, particularly on the world wheat market, and her position as the weak corner of the North Atlantic triangle made her especially vulnerable. The situation was not eased by the balanced budgets, high tariffs, and faithful reliance on the rhetoric of free enterprise with which Bennett, as much the embodiment of capitalism as Meighen had been the symbol of conscription, first attempted to restore prosperity. Between one and two million Canadians in a population of ten million were on relief. The prairies were a parched dustbowl, the irreplaceable topsoil scattered by the wind. The social system of the nation was in upheaval. At last, by late 1934, the Conservative leader was ready to abandon orthodoxy, and the New Deal to the south provided a ready example. Under the influence of his brother-in-law, W. D. Herridge, the Canadian minister in Washington, Bennett proposed a sweeping programme of radical measures.[4] The depression-wracked electorate evidently regarded Bennett's sudden turnabout as a deathbed conversion, a desperate attempt to forestall certain losses in the election of 1935.[5] As a result, the Conservative party suffered its most crushing defeat, falling in strength from 137 to 39 members in the House of Commons of 245.[6] The Liberals again formed the government, not to be dislodged for twenty-two years.

[4]The W. D. Herridge Papers contain drafts of the radio speeches with which Bennett launched his New Deal, and there are unmistakable indications that Herridge pushed the Prime Minister faster along the new course than he would have liked. See also the discussion in J. R. H. Wilbur, "H. H. Stevens and the Reconstruction Party," *Canadian Historical Review*, XLV (March, 1964), 15–16.

[5]This may be an unfair judgment. Professor G. Horowitz has suggestively asked, "Why is it that the Canadian counterpart of Hoover apes *Roosevelt*? This phenomenon is usually interpreted as sheer historical accident, a product of Bennett's desperation and opportunism. But the answer may be that Bennett was not Hoover. Even in his 'orthodox' days Bennett's views on the state's role in the economy were far from similar to Hoover's; Bennett's attitude was that of Canadian, not American conservatism. . . . Bennett's sudden radicalism . . . may have been a manifestation . . . of a latent tory-democratic streak." G. Horowitz, "Conservatism, Liberalism and Socialism in Canada: An Interpretation," *Canadian Journal of Economics and Political Science*, XXXII (May, 1966), 157.

[6]Conservative results by province in 1935 (with 1930 results in brackets): Ontario—25 (59); Quebec—5 (24); Nova Scotia—0 (10); New Brunswick—1 (10); Manitoba—1 (11); British Columbia—5 (7); Prince Edward Island—0 (3); Saskatchewan—1 (8); Alberta—1 (4). There was also an Independent Conservative elected in the Yukon both times.

But the depression was not the sole cause of the Conservative *débâcle* of 1935. Bennett's New Deal legislation had provoked a fierce reaction from the merchant class and from the old guard of the party. The prominent Liberal industrialist and fund-raiser, Vincent Massey, jeered in a letter to a friend that Bennett was "a self-appointed St. George . . . out to slay the dragon of 'uncontrolled capitalism,' of which until a few months ago he was the leading defender."[7] Understandably, the dragon's reaction was to withhold the contributions without which the Conservative campaign could not function. Financial problems were compounded by the collapse of the party organization. There was not a single Conservative government in office in any of the nine provinces in 1935; two years earlier there had been six.[8] The superb electoral machine that had won the 1930 election was no more. The offices had been closed, the files allowed to become outdated. Attempts to begin organization in late 1933 and early 1934 failed, and as Dr. R. J. Manion, Bennett's Minister of Railways and Canals, put it, "all we receive from the Chief [is] a stare. . . . So far, this Great Conservative Party, which is supposed to be the friend of big business, has not one dollar in its treasury." The belatedly resurrected organization had had no chance.[9]

The party was also weak internally. Eight of the eighteen members of Bennett's cabinet retired from active politics before the election. There had been a noisy break in 1934 with H. H. Stevens, the Minister of Trade and Commerce, who had attacked business from his position as chairman of the Price Spreads Inquiry of 1934.[10] Defeatism was rife within the cabinet. "For a year or more before the election," Manion wrote, "I was so sure of a grand-slam defeat that I prepared myself financially so that I could take a much-needed rest for a year. . . ."[11] The cabinet, the party, and the nation were apparently united in the belief that the driving, efficient, dictatorial Bennett was not the man to be prime minister during the depression.

[7]Massey to Lord Howard of Penrith, Feb. 22, 1935, in Vincent Massey, *What's Past is Prologue: The Memoirs of the Right Honourable Vincent Massey, C.H.* (Toronto, 1963), p. 220.

[8]In Ontario, Nova Scotia, New Brunswick, Prince Edward Island, British Columbia, and Saskatchewan.

[9]Manion to his son, James, Jan. 12, 1934, quoted in Wilbur, "Stevens and the Reconstruction Party," p. 6; Arthur R. Ford, *As the World Wags On* (Toronto, 1950), pp. 145–6.

[10]See J. R. H. Wilbur, "H. H. Stevens and R. B. Bennett, 1930–34," *Canadian Historical Review*, XLIII (March, 1962), 1, 9, 16n.

[11]Manion to C. H. Dickie, Jan. 2, 1936, quoted in Brian J. Young, "C. George McCullagh and the Leadership League," unpublished M.A. thesis, Queen's University, 1964, p. 62.

Bennett solidified the impression in the popular mind that the Conservative party was reactionary. The first four years of his administration remained in the memory, the last year and the New Deal did not. The people apparently believed that like all Tories Bennett favoured a high tariff; that like all Tories he favoured big business. But like all Conservatives, too, Bennett wanted the continuation of an independent British Canadian nation. In an effort to counter the assimilative effect of American radio stations, the "reactionary" Bennett had established a state-owned broadcasting system in 1932. Bennett abhorred the concept of public ownership, but once convinced that the choice lay between "the State or the United States," he had acted.[12] Borden had not liked the idea of a state-owned railway system either, but he had established the Canadian National Railways in 1918. The New Deal of 1935 was further evidence that in unusual circumstances the Conservatives could take radical steps. By 1935, however, the depression had spawned other parties that had no qualms whatsoever about radicalism.

"Third" parties had won more than 20 per cent of the popular vote in the election of 1935. The Progressives were gone, but the shattered political structure they had left in western Canada gave ample room for new movements of protest. The Co-operative Commonwealth Federation, a democratic socialist party, had been formed in 1932 from intellectuals, workers, and the die-hard remnants of the Progressive party. In their first election, the C.C.F. won 400,000 votes and elected seven Members of Parliament. This was a modest start, but the socialists would gain strength rapidly a few years hence. The Social Credit party, which had burst into prominence with its capture of the province of Alberta earlier in 1935, returned seventeen members to the House of Commons, all but two from Alberta. The Social Crediters were exponents of the "funny money" doctrines of the fascistic Major C. H. Douglas, but their success in Alberta was attributable to the leadership of the remarkable William "Bible Bill" Aberhart, a school teacher turned radio revivalist. The third of the minor parties to contest the 1935 election was the Reconstruction party, founded and led by the dissident Conservative, H. H. Stevens. Although Stevens' candidates won almost 400,000 votes, the new party elected only a single member—Stevens himself— and disappeared with scarcely a trace. Reconstruction's main effect was to siphon off desperately needed Conservative voting strength. In at least forty-five constituencies, the combined Reconstruction and Conservative vote would have won the seat. Thirty-six of these constituen-

12Margaret Prang, "The Origins of Public Broadcasting in Canada," *Canadian Historical Review*, XLVI (March, 1965), 1, 3, 31.

cies had been Conservative in the last parliament.[13] A more skilful Conservative leader than Bennett would never have permitted Stevens to break away.

Bennett was to remain Leader of the Opposition until the summer of 1938. The party he would turn over to his successor in that year was at its lowest point, sneered at as reactionary, imperialist, and anti-French. If its fortunes were ever to be restored, it would have to select a new type of leader. It was with this thought in mind that the majority of the delegates to the second national convention of the Conservative party travelled to Ottawa in July 1938.

[13]A redistribution between the elections of 1930 and 1935 makes it difficult to be exact about the total effect of the Reconstruction party. The forty-five constituencies were distributed as follows: Ontario—24 (of which 21 had been Conservative in 1930); Nova Scotia—5 (4); Quebec—7 (5); Manitoba—4 (3); New Brunswick—3 (3); British Columbia—1; Saskatchewan—1. Based on A. L. Normandin, ed., *The Canadian Parliamentary Guide, 1936* (Ottawa, 1936).

2. The Conservative Setting

Despite the party's difficulties, the convention of 1938 met at a time of potential opportunity for the Conservative party. The depression showed few signs of abatement, and the Liberal government of Mackenzie King, as concerned with balanced budgets and *laissez-faire* as the Bennett government had ever been, seemed ineffectual in dealing with the problems of human misery. In addition, acute tensions were developing within the Liberal party between King and provincial premiers like Dufferin Pattullo of British Columbia and Mitchell Hepburn of Ontario.[1] Quebec, too, seemed ripe for exploitation. The leader of the Union Nationale government, Maurice Duplessis, had been provincial Conservative chief early in the 1930's. Since winning power in 1935 at the head of his new party, a coalition of reform groups, Duplessis had consolidated his hold on the province, had driven anyone with liberal tendencies from his government, and had adopted the role of a militant autonomist. His antipathy to the federal government had led him to ally himself with the Ontario premier, forming the "Duplessis-Hepburn axis." The worsening international situation, resulting in fears of a new war, also seemed to create an opportunity for the Conservative party in Quebec, but only if it could shed its conscriptionist, imperialist reputation. A new leader, free of the stereotyped Tory views of the past, was necessary if the opportunity was to be exploited. Was there such a man in the Conservative party? And if so, would the party allow him the manoeuvrability he would need to fight and defeat Mackenzie King?

Dr. Robert J. Manion was the one avowed candidate for the leadership who seemed to satisfy the new requirements of the party. A 56-year-old physician from Fort William, Ontario, Manion had first been elected to parliament as a Liberal Unionist in 1917. Unlike many others, he had not returned to the Liberal fold after the war but had become a minister

[1]Margaret A. Ormsby, "T. Dufferin Pattullo and the Little New Deal," *Canadian Historical Review*, XLIII (Dec., 1962), 277–97; Richard M. Alway, "Hepburn, King, and the Rowell-Sirois Commission," *Canadian Historical Review*, XLVIII (June, 1967), 113–41.

in both of Meighen's short-lived governments. He had served as Minister of Railways and Canals in the Bennett administration and had lost his seat in the election of 1935. Manion was an Irish Roman Catholic, and although he was not fluent in French himself, his wife was a French Canadian and his children were bilingual. During the Great War, he had served as a medical officer with an infantry battalion until injured and invalided home, and he had received the Military Cross for heroism in the field. An outgoing, delightfully personable man and a highly effective, if unpolished, platform speaker, Manion had substantial and vocal support from rank and file delegates, particularly among the French-speaking who had apparently forgotten his wartime advocacy of conscription. His character and record, however, gave rise to opposition to his candidacy from certain powerful party figures.

"The Doctor is undoubtedly a very strong candidate," wrote Senator Arthur Meighen, one of those most strongly opposed to Manion, some months before the convention,

. . . and there is no one I would feel more like working with and working for than Bob Manion, at any time. On the score of loyalty, courage and long service he is the best entitled. At the same time I have very serious question whether he can win, and have still graver questions as to how he could handle the job after he did win. With all his ability, he lacks a certain deftness of utterance—the capacity to formulate his pronouncements along definite and well-considered lines, to make them forcible and at the same time well fortified and defensible. This is very vital in a Leader.[2]

Meighen's assessment was undoubtedly partly correct. A certain rashness, a certain Celtic volubility, was one of Manion's predominant traits. Manion did not measure up to the standards of a Meighen or a Bennett, noted R. B. Hanson, once Bennett's Minister of Trade and Commerce but, he asked, who did?[3] Hanson also noted that one of the objections raised against Manion was his religion. The Conservative party had not had a Catholic as leader since 1894, and Manion himself had long believed that he could not be chosen "short of the absence of any other good (Protestant) candidate. The word in brackets is regrettable," he wrote to his son, "but very strongly felt by the majority in my opinion, an opinion formed more by deduction than direct evidence."[4] Manion's supposed lack of leadership ability and his religion were doubtless

[2]Public Archives of Canada (P.A.C.), Arthur Meighen Papers, M.G. 26, Meighen to H. R. Milner, April 14, 1938.

[3]R. B. Hanson Papers, Personal Correspondence, Hanson to H. R. Milner, May 9, 1938.

[4]P.A.C., R. J. Manion Papers, M.G. 27, Vol. 16, Manion to his son, James, Oct. 20, 1936.

important factors motivating those opposed to his selection, but even more important were his views on the issues of the day. As Minister of Railways and Canals, Manion had occupied one of the hottest seats in the government, and in the opinion of the Canadian Pacific Railway, he had been found wanting.

The railway question had bedevilled Canadian politics since Confederation. One of the greatest achievements of Sir John A. Macdonald's long career had been the construction of the Canadian Pacific Railway; his greatest humiliation had been the earlier Pacific scandal caused by the revelation that his party had accepted substantial campaign funds in the election of 1872 in return for the promise of the transcontinental charter. The Dominion had experienced a tremendous boom in railway construction in the last decades of the nineteenth and the first decades of the twentieth centuries, but the expansion had been shakily financed. The inevitable collapse could be postponed, but the railroads, particularly vital for Canada, could hardly be allowed to go out of business. Consequently the Canadian National Railways had been formed from a group of insolvent lines during and immediately after the Great War. The expansionist 1920's had seen heavy expenditures by both the C.N.R. and C.P.R., and the onset of the depression placed the two railways in difficulties. Revenues fell by more than one-quarter, and the annual deficit of the C.N.R. twice exceeded $60 millions. The burden of the C.N.R.'s losses fell on the government; the losses of the Canadian Pacific had to be borne by its shareholders. This was an unsatisfactory situation, and throughout the 1930's Sir Edward Beatty, the President of the C.P.R., had proposed that the management of the two roads be unified, a solution that would supposedly produce yearly economies of $75 millions, sufficient to wipe out the losses of the Canadian National and to ease the plight of the C.P.R.'s investors.[5] But the Bennett government had gone on record in 1933 as being opposed to the unification of the railways, and one of Bennett's campaign slogans in the 1935 election was "amalgamation never, competition ever."

Manion's assessment of the railway situation, characteristically propounded with more vigour than tact, was that Beatty "desired to unload the C.P.R. on the people of Canada before it came crashing down

[5]Canada, Parliament, Senate, *Debates*, Report of Special Committee on the Railway Situation, May 11, 1939, pp. 354–8. The Committee pointed out that the C.N.R. deficit was not incurred because of operating losses, but pertained "entirely to interest charges due public investors and relate for the most part to former privately-owned lines which the government took over and continued in operation in the national interest." Beatty's life has been unsatisfactorily treated in D. H. Miller-Barstow, *Beatty of the C.P.R.* (Toronto, 1951). See also Roger Graham, *Arthur Meighen*. III. *No Surrender* (Toronto, 1965), 38–43.

around his ears," and he favoured a policy of "cooperation" between the two great railway corporations. Unification, he insisted, "would mean complete monopoly in the hands of one company of Canadian railway transportation. It would mean the building of huge voting power under one management. . . ."[6] In view of the sums involved (the operating revenue of the C.N.R. approximated $250 millions in 1929) and of the tight little circle of interlocking directorates that made up the Canadian "corporate élite," feelings on this issue ran high.[7]

The extent of the role played by the Canadian Pacific in the pre-convention leadership manœuvrings is difficult to determine. Certainly Manion believed that Sir Edward Beatty was doing everything in his power to block his selection,[8] and there can be no doubt that at least one aspirant for the leadership carried on extensive conversations with Beatty in the hope of winning his support.[9] As this prospective candidate was H. H. Stevens, who had broken with the party in 1935 because of his radical attitude to business, it seems evident that Beatty was exploring every possible alternative to Manion. There can be very little doubt that the C.P.R. president hoped to discover a friendlier candidate.

Whether they were in league with Beatty and the C.P.R. or not, many others were looking for a candidate able to stop Manion. In April 1938 Arthur Meighen proposed the name of Sidney Smith.[10] President of the University of Manitoba, the 41-year-old Smith was able and friendly but a novice who had never been involved in anything more than faculty politics. Despite this large drawback, an informal campaign sprang up[11] to garner support for Smith (who was willing to accept a unanimous

[6]Manion Papers, Vol. 45, Memorandum of meeting with Meighen, May 8, 1939; Progressive Conservative Party Files, Manion File, "Press Release of Hon. R. J. Manion's Speech, Smith Falls [*sic*], Ontario, July 24, 1939," p. 3. Manion expressed similar views in his autobiography, *Life is an Adventure* (Toronto, 1936), pp. 350–1.

[7]The C.P.R., it should be noted, was also a contributor of some importance to the campaign coffers of the Conservative party. For the election of 1930, for example, it had contributed at least $50,000 and was the largest corporate contributor. Manion Papers, Vol. 11, List of contributors as of September 2, 1930.

[8]*Ibid.*, Vol. 16, Manion to his son, March 26 and June 19, 1938.

[9]P.A.C., H. H. Stevens Papers, M.G. 27, Vol. 150, Warren Cook to Stevens, May 6, 1938; Stevens to Cook, May 11 and June 24, 1938; Stevens to D. F. Glass, May 12 and May 21, 1938; Glass to Stevens, June 14 and June 28, 1938.

[10]Meighen Papers, Meighen to H. R. Milner, April 14, 1938. Meighen, perhaps, did not originate the Smith campaign. Manion wrote his son in March that he had been approached by a prominent senator and asked to go to Manitoba to sound out a university professor of whom he had never heard for the leadership (Manion Papers, Vol. 16, Manion to his son, March 26, 1938).

[11]Hanson Papers, Personal Correspondence, H. R. Milner to Hanson, April 29, 1938; J. T. Hackett to Hanson, May 14, 1938; Hanson to George Black, M.P., June 3, 1938; Meighen Papers, Henry Borden to Meighen, May 4 and June 6, 1938; Stevens Papers, Vol. 154, Stevens to F. E. Dorchester, June 3, 1938.

offer of the leadership[12]), only to collapse when Meighen concluded that he could not even win the Manitoba convention delegates.[13] Meighen himself was the choice of many prominent Conservatives, including Bennett,[14] and even Manion indicated at one stage that he would be willing to step aside for the former prime minister.[15] Meighen was not interested,[16] however, and as a result, efforts were made to induce Bennett to reconsider his resignation and to persuade other candidates to withdraw in his favour. "I got the idea in Ottawa," wrote John Dafoe of the *Winnipeg Free Press,* "that the drive for R.B. to succeed himself is now on with his connivance and assistance. . . ." What was bringing about the campaign for Bennett, he added, was the "chilling fear" that the only alternative was a Manion-Duplessis combination.[17] If this was the plan, Bennett soon talked himself out of contention: "I know you will realize how impossible it is for me to continue as Leader of the Party," he wrote to R. B. Hanson. "I have almost broken my health as it is and certainly I am informed that I am taking too great a risk at the present time by devoting myself to my work in the manner which I have."[18] With time running out before the convention, the search for an acceptable candidate became desperate. Some members of the old guard apparently turned to "their last shot," J. Earl Lawson, the 47-year-old member for the Toronto riding of York South and one of Bennett's last appointees to his cabinet.[19] Lawson was made the Opposition

[12]Douglas Library, Queen's University, Norman Lambert Papers, Diaries, April 5, 1938, regarding a conversation with Gratton O'Leary.

[13]Meighen Papers, Meighen to H. R. Milner, May 26, 1938.

[14]H. A. Bruce Papers, clipping from *Financial Post,* July 30, 1938, letter to editor from Bennett. (This letter was not intended for publication.)

[15]Manion Papers, Vol. 16, Manion to his son, March 26, 1938; Meighen Papers, Meighen to J. A. Clark, April 30, 1938.

[16]Graham, *Meighen,* III, 77.

[17]P.A.C., J. W. Dafoe Papers, M.G. 30, Microfilm roll M-78, Dafoe to George Ferguson, June 9, 1938; The Hon. R. A. Bell Interview, July 15, 1964; Arthur R. Ford *As the World Wags On,* p. 110; Manion Papers, Vol. 16, Manion to his son, June 19, 1938; Bonar Law-Bennett Library, University of New Brunswick, R. B. Bennett Papers, Notable Persons File, Norman MacLeod to Bennett, Jan. 30, 1940.

[18]Hanson Papers, Personal Correspondence, Bennett to Hanson, June 20, 1938; R. K. Finlayson Interview, July 6, 1963; Ford, *As the World Wags On,* p. 110; Stevens Papers, Vol. 154, Stevens to A. L. Burrows, May 12, 1938. Apparently Bennett changed his mind again during the convention proceedings and decided to try to retain his position; he had waited too long, however, and could find no support (Graham, *Meighen,* III, 82–3).

[19]Stevens Papers, Vol. 154, Stevens to Col. R. H. Webb, M.L.A., June 24, 1938; H. R. Jackman Interview, Sept. 8, 1964. "Their last shot" was Manion's description of the Lawson campaign (Manion Papers, Vol. 16, Manion to his son, June 19, 1938).

financial critic in the Commons, an event that immediately sparked speculation that he was Bennett's anointed choice for the succession,[20] but he lacked Manion's experience, magnetism—and delegate support.

Manion was the overwhelming choice of the French-Canadian delegates to the convention,[21] and this was likely an additional spur to those opposing him. Perhaps because he was of Irish Roman Catholic descent, perhaps because of his Liberal past, or perhaps because his wife was French Canadian, Manion was suspected of being somewhat less loyal to the empire than a leader of the Conservative party should be. In 1933, he had been heard to remark that he was a pacifist, and he himself had written privately that he was "not madly Imperialistic."[22] The propaganda put forward by his friends in support of his candidacy had stressed his acceptability to Quebec. One pamphlet stated that the issue confronting the Conservative party was to find a man "nationally known and respected in the English provinces and [with] reasonable prospects of gaining substantial support from Quebec." Manion was an ideal choice, the leaflet stated, as he "has associations with Quebec . . . that no other eligible Conservative possesses and that are capable of becoming decisive factors under reasonably favorable conditions."[23] Certainly French-speaking Conservatives, starved for a victory in their province, believed Manion to be the most acceptable candidate. According to one probably apocryphal story, Georges Héon, Manion's leading Quebec supporter, approached key Conservative Orangemen, seeking support for his candidate and holding out the prospect of fifty Quebec seats. The Orange leaders, the story went, were willing to support a Catholic "but just this once."[24] The bitterness aroused by this issue inevitably was felt on the convention floor.

On the first day of the convention,[25] the war cry was raised. Meighen,

[20]E.g., Norman MacLeod, "Today in Ottawa," *Windsor Star*, June 20, 1938, clipping in J. Earl Lawson Scrapbooks.

[21]The Montreal *Gazette* (July 5, 1938) estimated that Manion had the support of 90 per cent of the Quebec delegation.

[22]James Eayrs, *In Defence of Canada*. I. *From the Great War to the Great Depression* (Toronto, 1964), 282; Manion Papers, Vol. 16, Manion to his son, Oct. 1, 1936.

[23]Circular letter (printed) by C. G. Dunn, *Quebec Chronicle-Telegraph*, n.d., in Stevens Papers, Vol. 154.

[24]John W. Lederle, "The National Organization of the Liberal and Conservative Parties in Canada," unpublished Ph.D. dissertation, University of Michigan, 1942, pp. 90–2; Finlayson Interviews, June 1 and July 6, 1963. Cf. Manion Papers, Vol. 16, Manion to his son, July 10, 1938.

[25]The organization of Conservative conventions will be examined in connection with the 1942 convention (*infra*, pp. 136–7). The best study of the subject to date is Ruth M. Bell, "Conservative Party National Conventions, 1927–1956: Organization and Procedure," unpublished M.A. thesis, Carleton University, 1965.

the Conservative party's incomparable orator, swept the English-speaking delegates out of their seats and into "wild outbursts of cheers and applause" with an impassioned appeal for the empire and an attack on the defence and foreign policies of the isolationist King government. "Have we come to the point where we will lock the gates against Great Britain?" he shouted, excoriating the government's alleged refusal to permit the British to train pilots in Canada. "If we call ourselves partners in the Empire, let us behave the way partners behave. . . . I want this country to play an honorable and worthy part, and to stay within the British Empire."[26] Meighen's inflammatory speech drove the Quebec delegates into "open rebellion," and Héon is reported to have said that his province's delegates would stay at the convention only if "the threat that was boomed yesterday" was "removed." Meighen did not represent public opinion, the Quebec Conservative said, and the Conservative party would be better served if he "shut up."[27] Manion believed that Meighen's speech was a deliberate provocation to French-Canadian delegates, a calculated attempt to "smash the convention by the war cry." He wrote to his son of Meighen's attempt, either as a dupe for the C.P.R. and Bennett or in co-operation with them, to force the French from the convention or to drive the Ontario vote away from him. It was, he stated flatly, "a real conspiracy of the filthiest type."[28] If this was Meighen's intention, it was unsuccessful. The Quebec delegates remained at the convention, assuaged by a virtually meaningless compromise defence resolution in the party platform calling for "consultation and co-operation between all the members of the British Commonwealth of Nations."[29]

Another resolution in the platform declared the party to be against "any plan of unification or amalgamation of the great railways of Canada" and instead pledged support for a policy of co-operation. This was a setback to the Canadian Pacific, but one with which Manion

[26]*Toronto Daily Star*, July 5, 1938, p. 1. On the British-Canadian discussions of 1938, see James Eayrs, *In Defence of Canada. II. Appeasement and Rearmament* (Toronto, 1965), 91–103.

[27]Toronto *Globe and Mail*, July 6, 1938, p. 1; July 7, 1938, pp. 1, 8.

[28]Manion Papers, Vol. 16, Manion to his son, July 10, 1938. Cf. Graham, *Meighen*, III, 80–3; Meighen Papers, Meighen to Bennett, July 12, 1938.

[29]National Conservative Party, *Resolutions Passed at the National Conservative Convention, July 5, 6, 7, 1938* (n.p., n.d.), p. 3. "I suppose you are receiving a number of letters as I am," wrote Bennett to Meighen, "complaining bitterly of the terms of the resolutions passed by the Convention. I think there is . . . great resentment as to the methods employed by Héon and others at the Convention . . ." (Meighen Papers, Bennett to Meighen, July 22, 1938). See the discussion in F. H. Soward *et al.*, *Canada in World Affairs: The Pre-War Years* (Toronto, 1941), pp. 103–5.

apparently had little to do. Hanson, the chairman of the resolutions committee, wrote that "no one could have got a resolution through the Committee or through the Convention, in favour of unification." The fact is, he added, "that the great mass of Canadians . . . are against this proposal and to advocate it in our party platform is only to commit suicide."[30] The stage was now set for the final act of the convention.

Manion was the clear favourite in the struggle for the leadership, and his election seemed a certainty until the nomination speeches. However, Murdoch MacPherson of Regina, a former attorney general of Saskatchewan but virtually unknown outside his province and a late entry in the race, almost captured the convention with a magnificent fighting speech. The old guard, some hitherto pledged to Lawson, some still at loose ends, quickly united behind MacPherson. Lawson's supporters deserted him *en masse*, even the mover and seconder of his nomination switching to the unknown prairie lawyer. "I learned I was betrayed," a bitter Lawson told the press, "but it was too late to do anything about it."[31] Despite the sudden rush of support for MacPherson, Manion's delegates held fast, and he won the leadership handily on the second ballot.

Manion's successful capture of the leadership had been accomplished in the face of the determined resistance of important elements of the party. Meighen, Bennett, and their old guard supporters had tremendous influence, particularly in business and financial circles, and their disorganized performance at the convention was no measure of their strength. The Canadian Pacific and its satellite interests similarly were important for the Conservative party. If he was to succeed, Manion would have to resolve his differences with the Montreal and Toronto wings of Conservatism. Manion's religion, too, was an important and possibly critical factor. Some Liberals believed Manion would cut into the Catholic vote, but some Conservatives thought his selection would provoke an Orange reaction.[32] In addition, the new leader would have to deal with Quebec; he would have to show his party and the nation that there were real prospects of success in French Canada and yet not

[30]Manion Papers, Vol. 6, Hanson to Manion, July 11, 1938. Manion wrote to Beatty that the delegates had passed the resolution "without consulting me" (Vol. 2, Manion to Beatty, Aug. 18, 1938).

[31]*Ibid.*, Vol. 16, Manion to his son, July 10, 1938; Jackman Interview, Sept. 8, 1964; Lou Golden, "From Out of the West," *Saturday Night*, LV (March 9, 1940), 5; Toronto *Globe and Mail*, July 8, 1938, p. 3; *Toronto Daily Star*, July 9, 1938, clipping in Lawson Scrapbooks.

[32]Saskatchewan Provincial Archives, J. G. Gardiner Papers, R. F. Hogarth to Gardiner, July 15, and reply, July 25, 1938; Hanson Papers, Hanson to the Hon. R. Morand, July 12, 1938.

appear to be too conciliatory lest he alienate English Canada. The problems confronting him were enormous, and Manion would have to demonstrate his mettle from the start.

His first task was to re-enter the House of Commons from which he had been absent since his defeat in 1935. In November 1938 he easily won a by-election in London, Ontario, defeating a C.C.F. candidate, "the Liberal Party extending the usual courtesy to a newly-elected Party Leader" by not opposing him.[33] His second task, to rebuild the party organization, was far more difficult of solution.

Manion's immediate efforts to restore the position of the Conservative party were unpromising. Because he warned in one of his first speeches as leader that the reform of the social order was the only alternative to "wreck, anarchy and revolution," he was assailed by the Conservative press of Montreal and Toronto. The Toronto *Evening Telegram* branded his attitude as "tripe,"[34] while the *Montreal Star* sarcastically chided (on August 11, 1938): "Revolution! Tush, tush, Dr. Manion. Turn over. You are sleeping on your back." But it was the Montreal *Gazette*, widely believed to be the representative of St. James Street financial interests, which expressed itself most pointedly (August 12):

If the new leader has any inclination to move to the left he can, of course, indulge it, but he cannot take the Conservative party with him. In his own interest he should be warned against a false step which may lead him away from the great political element in this country upon whose support he must rely, a step which may conceivably compel that element to seek a new allegiance.

The warning could not have been more pointed.

Manion noted the criticism but refused to alter a course which he felt was well received elsewhere in the country. "My terrible crime," he wrote his son, "has been that I have pointed out that if our system is to endure, we must give opportunity to youth and work and wages to people willing to take them." He was privately convinced that the attacks had been made because of his stand on the railway issue, but he apparently felt it necessary to assert his conservatism. "I am just as orthodox as anyone in my desire to preserve our economic system," he wrote to H. R. Milner, a leading Alberta Conservative and a key figure in party

[33]*The Canadian Annual Review of Public Affairs, 1937 and 1938* (Toronto, 1940), p. 58. The Lambert Diaries, August 15, 16, 1938, indicate clearly that Manion and the Liberals agreed on London: "Saw Dr. Manion re by-elections. 1) He said London appeared to be the most desirable place so far as he was concerned. I said that London would be more convenient for us. . . ." The next day the Prime Minister was told that "London was acceptable" to Manion.

[34]Ross Harkness, *J. E. Atkinson of the Star* (Toronto, 1963), p. 261.

fund-raising, but "[I] believe that action is necessary at the present time to cure the blot of unemployment and to bring a greater measure of social justice to all our citizens."[35] Manion was no radical, but to certain elements in the party he seemed so.

The problems of financing the party were not eased by Manion's first key appointment. As his national organizer, the leader had selected Dr. John Robb, a physician from the tiny Northern Ontario village of Blind River and a personal friend who had nominated Manion when he had first tried for the Conservative leadership in 1927. Robb had some experience of Ontario politics and had been provincial Minister of Health from 1930 to 1934 but, as Manion knew, he was not a national figure. Moreover, he had no wide acquaintance among the business and financial interests that might have served to circumvent the hostility already evident toward Manion.[36] At approximately the same time as Robb was appointed in late July, Manion set up his financial organization, naming Allan Ross and Harry Price, two Toronto businessmen, to work with Robb in looking after party funds.[37] Significantly, perhaps, none of these three important appointees was from Montreal.

Manion realized that the opposition to him in Montreal might make it more difficult to get the money needed for organizational work but doubted that this would be impossible. However, he added with a momentary and uncharacteristic flash of pessimism, "quite frankly, we have not had much evidence to the contrary, as yet."[38] The root cause of the difficulties was Manion's attitude to the railway question. "Being as I am, profoundly in disagreement with your views and those of the delegates to the convention, as expressed on the question of railways," Beatty wrote the newly elected leader, "you will not expect me to congratulate you on the railway plank in the Party platform. For many years," he continued with no attempt at subtlety, "I have been hoping that it would be to the Conservative Party we should look for a solution of this important national problem. . . . Apparently that hope is deferred. . . . I have talked with many Conservatives," he concluded, "who are now—much against their inclinations—Liberals."[39] Further correspondence and meetings between the Conservative leader and the

[35]Manion Papers, Vol. 16, Manion to his son, Aug. 3, and Aug. 26, 1938; Vol. 9, Manion to Milner, Sept. 26, 1938.
[36]John R. Williams, *The Conservative Party of Canada, 1920–49* (Durham, 1956), p. 126; Manion Papers, Vol. 7, Manion to D. M. Hogarth, Aug. 4, 1938. Cf. *ibid.*, Vol. 8, J. M. Macdonnell to Manion, June 21, 1939.
[37]Manion Papers, Vol. 5, Manion to V. M. Drury, Sept. 30, 1938.
[38]*Ibid.*, Vol. 16, Manion to his son, Oct. 16, 1938.
[39]*Ibid.*, Vol. 2, Beatty to Manion, July 8, 1938.

railway president followed, but Manion refused to give ground in his opposition to unification.[40] As a result, Beatty could write Bennett, who needed precious little convincing, that "I had quite a chat yesterday with your successor in Ottawa, and it only served to confirm my previous impression that he will not measure up to the office and lacks both the ability and wisdom to succeed men like Sir Robert, Arthur Meighen and yourself."[41]

The pressures on Manion to be more flexible increased. Letters from Members of Parliament and from friends in late 1938 and 1939 urged him to reach an accommodation with Beatty and business.[42] Among these friends was Major-General Donald M. Hogarth, a mining promoter of substance, Manion's mentor on the stock market, and an influential figure in Conservative fund-raising. In an extraordinarily frank letter,[43] Hogarth assessed the attitude of the "money-bags" to the Manion party:

As things stand whilst they are almost unanimously against King this element will be unanimously for him with their money and influence in preference to you and the Conservative party. . . . I believe with all my heart and soul that this means disaster at the polls and that as time goes on many [illegible] who are presently behind you will be influenced by this element and you will be left holding an *empty* bag. You can't compete with the C.C.F. . . . Even if you should . . . King and laissez-faire will be seized upon as the house of refuge and security. I beg you to heed this warning in shaping your course of action.

The Railway problem is of course the key to the situation—The Montreal Gang through various ramifications will freeze up the financial channels right across the country. . . . The strange part of it is that they *do not want King.*

Hogarth went on to suggest a procedure which could resolve the problem. "Despite your differences with A[rthur] M[eighen]," he wrote, "he is the man to use for the purpose of developing a formula. He has the confidence of this crowd, loathes . . . King and has a profound respect and liking for Bob M[anion]. . . ." If Manion would only consent to talk to Meighen and to appear on the same platform with him, he would win the next election without doubt "and be certain of the wherewithal with which to fight it." Unfortunately, by June 1939 when this letter was apparently written, Manion was already out of patience

---

[40]*Ibid.*, Manion to Beatty, Aug. 25, 1938.

[41]Bennett Papers, Notable Persons File, Beatty to Bennett, Oct. 1, 1938.

[42]Manion Papers, Vol. 11, Stevens to Manion, June 6, 1939; Vol. 12, W. A. Walsh, M.P., to Manion, Sept. 22, 1938; Vol. 8, J. M. Macdonnell to Manion, June 28, 1939; Vol. 2, Manion to C. C. Ballantyne, July 20, 1939; Vol. 8, Hogarth to Manion, Jan. 20, 1939; Hanson to Manion, July 31, 1939.

[43]*Ibid.*, Vol. 8, Hogarth to Manion, Wednesday [June 7, 1939?].

(and probably out of favour) with the former prime minister. As Leader of the Opposition in the upper chamber, Meighen had served on the Special Senate Committee on Railway Conditions and had been instrumental in producing a minority report calling for unification.[44] After this embarrassing episode, Manion had met with Meighen in his chambers in the Parliament Buildings, had called him a "tool of the C.P.R.," and had told him to emphasize in the future that he spoke only for himself and not for the party.[45] With this in mind, Manion refused Hogarth's suggestion that he appear with Meighen, stating that if he did so he could only be regarded as a traitor to the party's convention resolution against railway unification. The doughty Conservative leader concluded his reply with a firm declaration of principle:

> You may be right regarding the impossibility of getting financial support with Beatty and his crowd bucking us but whether we get financial support or not I intend to possess my own soul and not be merely the hireling of Beatty and his little coterie. I had hoped that there were enough independent Conservatives to stand by the party . . . but if I am wrong . . . I and the party will have to face the consequences.[46]

The first instalment of the consequences was reflected on the party's balance sheet. Some $35,000 was still owing from the 1935 general election,[47] and the Conservative financial apparatus was meeting difficulty collecting sufficient funds to pay for the widespread organizational effort needed to build the party into a contender for power. From August 1938 to October 1939 the party spent $94,000, or a little less than $6,500 a month, hardly enough to create an organization from the ground up across a country the size of Canada.[48] Nonetheless, some progress was made. Financial representatives were appointed on the prairies and in the Maritimes, contacts were explored, and arrangements were made for Manion to meet informally at dinners with groups of business leaders.[49] The results of these meetings, at which Manion showed to his best advantage, gave some grounds for hope. "I imagine that I had been painted by our big business friends who are opposed to us as such a complete nitwit," he wrote of one Toronto gathering,

---

[44]The minority report is found in Senate, *Debates*, May 24, 1939, pp. 416–22. The differences between Meighen and his leader were the subject of much speculation ("Backstage at Ottawa," *Maclean's*, LII (Aug. 1, 1939), 8).

[45]Manion Papers, Vol. 45, Memorandum, May 8, 1939.

[46]*Ibid.*, Vol. 8, Manion to Hogarth, June 20, 1939.

[47]*Ibid.*, Vol. 5, Bennett to G. B. Foster, Jan. 28, 1939 (copy).

[48]From September 1938 to July 1939 the party collected $43,000 in contributions (*ibid.*, Vol. 14, Miss J. E. Denison to Manion, Dec. 31, 1939; Vol. 11, financial statement, n.d. [December, 1939?]).

[49]*Ibid.*, Vol. 10, Harry Price to Manion, March 17, 1939, April 27, 1939; Vol. 5, G. B. Foster to Manion, Aug. 24, 1939.

"that they were somewhat surprised to find that I was presentable at all."[50]

Despite his problems with the business wing of the party, Manion was still optimistic about his chances. He was convinced that the country was dissatisfied with the Liberal government and Mackenzie King, and reports from his organizers confirmed this belief. "Things continue to look splendid for us," he wrote in April 1939. The size and spirit of the crowds that cheered him on a tour in the summer were "symtomatic [*sic*] of the general discontent against the Government."[51] "If we can only avoid some big issue coming up that may completely befuddle the minds of the electorate," he said to his son, "I feel convinced that King is on the way out. . . ."[52] The one issue certain to befuddle the voters, however, was completely beyond Manion's control.

The threat of war—and the question of Canadian involvement— placed Manion's whole plan in jeopardy. With few exceptions, English-speaking Conservatives believed that when England was at war Canada was at war, and the most vocal among them favoured conscription and a large expeditionary force. On the other hand, Manion's *Canadien* followers generally would have preferred to see Canada stay neutral in any European conflict, but recognizing the virtual impossibility of this in light of the three-to-one English-speaking majority in Canada, they accepted the necessity for a "limited liability" war. Canada could send economic aid and volunteers, most French Canadians of all political parties maintained, but there could be no conscription for overseas service under any circumstances.[53] Manion's dilemma was all too clear: if he attempted to appease French Canada by pledging the party against conscription and a full-scale war effort, he would be attacked by Anglo-philic Tories, led by Meighen, Bennett, and the metropolitan Conservative press; if he refused to make the concessions demanded by Quebec, he stood no chance whatsoever of gaining seats there, so strong were the memories of 1917. He might be able to walk the tightrope for a

50Hanson Papers, file P-450-M, Manion to Hanson, Aug. 26, 1939.
51Manion Papers, Vol. 16, Manion to his son, April 10, and July 18, 1939.
52*Ibid.*, Jan. 18, 1939.
53Other assessments of the national mood differ. Sir Herbert Marler, the Minister in Washington, told Sumner Welles, "that if Great Britain undertook to maintain . . . Czechoslovakia and as a result found herself in a war with Germany it would have the gravest repercussions in Canada. He said that certainly not more than ten percent of the Canadian people would be willing to find themselves in [such] a war. . . . He said that the sentiment for keeping out of war and for self-defense was quite as strong in Canada as it was in the United States, and that under no conditions would the Canadian people be willing to take part in another world war which had its origins in Central European problems." F. D. Roosevelt Library, F. D. Roosevelt Papers, Memorandum of conversation by S. W[elles] with Canadian Minister, Sir Herbert Marler, March 15, 1938.

short time, but he would eventually have to jump one way or the other. His final choice was scarcely in doubt. Manion had been selected because it was believed that he would appeal to the *Québecois*, and the French-Canadian delegates to the convention had been his strongest backers. In addition, he sincerely believed that a second conscription crisis would be disastrous to Canadian unity. "Apparently you do not see the need of trying to keep Canada from splitting down the middle," he wrote one vociferous Vancouver correspondent. "I do. I cannot see for the life of me what good it would do to the Empire for Canada to get into a sort of semi Civil War of its own."[54] Manion would have to choose Quebec.

Less than three months after he assumed the leadership, the Munich crisis faced Manion with his first test. Emulating the British Opposition, his reaction was to do and say nothing until the government reacted. In part, this was a patriotic desire to spare the Prime Minister domestic embarrassment in a difficult international situation, but Manion's action was also based on his feeling that King, too, was in a corner, boxed in by the French and English wings of the Liberal party. Mackenzie King was probably waiting for him to come out with a flag-waving imperialist statement, Manion said, and he had no intention of accommodating him. "Why help him out when anything anyone else says can do the Empire no good?"[55] Only on September 28 did Manion venture a comment, limiting himself to agreeing with Mackenzie King's statement of support for Chamberlain issued a day earlier.[56] If Manion had not previously realized the shape of the dilemma confronting him, he did so after reading the mail and the editorials that this first statement produced. The flag-wavers in Toronto and Montreal—"the usual crowd of old bachelors and childless parents"—had attacked his statement for not being imperialist enough, he said, while Ottawa's *Le Droit* had criticized it as too imperialist.[57]

Manion did not make his next major move into the delicate area of imperial relations until after the destruction of Czechoslovakia in March 1939. Then he acted only after he had been "tipped off on

[54]Manion Papers, Vol. 13, Manion to J. A. Clark, Sept. 13, 1939. As recently as 1936, however, Manion had written in his autobiography (*Life is an Adventure*, p. 224) that "the only fair and just method of raising men for the army during war is by conscription. . . ." Needless to say this was used against Manion with great effect by his Liberal opponents.

[55]Manion Papers, Vol. 13, Manion to R. H. Saunders, Sept. 17, 1938 (page headed "confidential, not sent").

[56]*Ibid.*, press release, Sept. 28, 1938; Soward *et al.*, *The Pre-War Years*, pp. 114–17.

[57]Manion Papers, Vol. 16, Manion to his son, Oct. 7, 1938. See the correspondence in Vol. 13.

Sunday night [March 26] that King was coming out anti-conscription and Lapointe [King's French-Canadian lieutenant] was coming out in support of the idea that there could be no neutrality" in a war in which Great Britain was involved. "It was my idea of a proper compromise policy," he said, "and I gave an interview to the press on Monday which covered the points . . . as I felt if [the Liberals] beat me with this proposal I would be just trailing along behind."[58] "I do not believe Canadian youth should be conscripted to fight outside the borders of Canada," Manion told the press in Ottawa. "Canada can play her part in the empire and in support of our democratic institutions by full co-operation with Great Britain through volunteer units, through supplying munitions, foods and other necessities to our allies, and by fully protecting Canada's own territory."[59] Manion's information about the Prime Minister's intentions proved correct, for on March 30, Mackenzie King came out flatly against conscription for overseas service.[60] Both great parties were now on record against conscription and in favour of voluntary participation— the policy that, in the final result, Canada was to pursue for the first five years of the war. Considering the past history of his party, and considering that Conservatism's strength was concentrated in English-speaking Canada, it is remarkable that the Conservative leader was the first to take a stand on this issue. Many in his party, however, were most dissatisfied.

"I may say personally that I am very disappointed in Manion's leadership," wrote Colonel H. A. Bruce, a Toronto surgeon recently retired as Lieutenant Governor of Ontario, even before his leader's declaration against conscription, "because he will not take a stand without first considering what the attitude of Quebec will be, so that in essence he allows Quebec to determine his policy and in this respect is following the lead of King. . . ."[61] At the same time, Manion's French-Canadian followers were urging him to go further than King, demanding in fact that he declare against any automatic commitment by Canada in the event of England's becoming involved in war.

The attitude of Quebec Conservatives puzzled Manion. "I do not see any reason," he wrote Héon,[62] the sole French-speaking Conservative Member of Parliament, "why I must, every time I open my mouth, talk

[58]*Ibid.*, Manion to his son, March 31, 1939.

[59]*Toronto Daily Star*, March 28, 1939, p. 1. See also C. P. Stacey, *The Military Problems of Canada* (Toronto, 1940), p. 146. Stacey cites a slightly different version of the interview from the Toronto *Evening Telegram*.

[60]Canada, Parliament, House of Commons, *Debates*, March 30, 1939, p. 2426. Manion then repeated the substance of his press interview in his speech (pp. 2428–42).

[61]Bruce Papers, Bruce to Lord Beaverbrook, Feb. 27, 1939.

[62]Manion Papers, Vol. 6, Manion to Héon, Aug. 1, 1939.

of this damned issue, which stirs up trouble in both [Ontario and Quebec]; and, quite frankly, I don't see why so many of you chaps down there find it necessary to talk all the time on questions of this kind. . . . Why," he asked with pardonable exasperation, "must it always be the subject in Quebec?" The pressure on him to outdo the Liberals was unfair, Manion maintained, especially when there was such a good opportunity to attack the Liberals at hand:

Here is the Liberal Party, which for years attacked us for being the Imperialist group, for spending too much money on defence, for preparing for war. They attacked us in the House and they carried on a whispering campaign as well as openly attacking us on conscription, defence, and everything of that sort in the Province of Quebec. . . . They won two or three elections on the conscription issue, on the betrayal of Laurier, and so forth. . . . Now the same Liberal party is spending four times as much as we spent on defence; and in addition . . . King . . . quoted Sir Wilfrid Laurier's statement of 30 years ago: "If England is at war we are at war and liable to attack."

. . .

Surely, in view of all these facts, we are in a splendid position. Surely I having beaten them to the no-conscription idea and they taking exactly the same attitude as I did puts us in the very best position to attack them. Then why . . . expect me to take a more extreme position against participation than the Liberals take?

Manion's exposition of his stand did little to mollify Héon. It seems clear that neither really understood the position and problems of the other. Manion's attitude was already an extraordinary one for the leader of Canadian Conservatism to take and one which threatened to destroy the foundations of his support in Tory areas. On the other hand, Héon faced the herculean task of persuading French Canada that the Conservative party had changed and that Manion was not Meighen. He was in difficulties, he wrote his leader with emphasis, because of the Liberal line:

(A) MANION BETRAYED LAURIER.
(B) HE CAME BACK FROM OVERSEAS TO VOTE FOR CONSCRIPTION.
(C) MANION IS FOR CONSCRIPTION. HE SAYS SO IN HIS BOOK.
(D) HE VOTED AGAINST BILINGUAL MONEY. HE HATES THE FRENCH LANGUAGE.
(E) LAPOINTE WILL KEEP YOU OUT OF WAR. HE SAID SO AND SAID HE WOULD FIGHT AGAINST PARTICIPATION.

After consulting a number of Quebec cabinet ministers, deputy ministers, and legislators, Héon continued, he had come to the conclusion that the only way Quebec Conservative candidates could overcome the effective Liberal propaganda would be to state that Canada's "obligations to the

Commonwealth should be limited to securing the inviolability of our territory."[63] Manion probably objected to this line, but as he was on the verge of a clear breakthrough in the province of Quebec, it is not unlikely that he would have gone along.

Early in August, Manion and Duplessis had arrived at an agreement which guaranteed the Conservative leader the full support of the Union Nationale organization. The Conservative leader and the Quebec premier had met at the Chateau Frontenac in Quebec in December 1938.[64] Subsequent negotiations had been secretly carried on by T. H. Onslow, private secretary to William Tremblay, the Quebec Minister of Labour, acting for Duplessis, and Dr. Robb, acting for Manion. In a letter to Robb confirming the agreement, Onslow affirmed that he was authorized to state that "we are prepared to do the following just as soon as the date of the Federal Election is finally announced":

Conservative Organization—Quebec's 65 Counties
Without advertising it in any way, each Quebec member of the National Union (they now hold 74 seats out of 90) will be requested and instructed to help and cooperate only with the Conservative candidate in his county. Our Deputies will be assured that in return for their full cooperation, the Conservative Party promises to cooperate fully with the Quebec Provincial Government in starting, immediately after the election, extensive unemployment relief works in all the Counties of the Province of Quebec, where help is needed. . . . you will be getting the entire support of the Duplessis Government without even having to spend one cent for travelling expenses.[65]

If this was a genuine offer, and Manion apparently believed that it was, the Conservative party was sure to win substantial representation in Quebec. His reply—"that your Government can count on 100% cooperation from me when the time comes"[66]—must have been written with jubilation. The agreement with Duplessis was his vindication, his reward for sticking to the tortuous course he had maintained since winning the leadership. With the assurance of support in Quebec, he was certain to win the election, and in these circumstances the business and financial interests would come back to his camp. "No group," he had written Hogarth, "are quicker to climb on the bandwagon than they are once they think things are looking like victory."[67] Perhaps Manion was right in his assessment, perhaps not. The question became an academic one on the morning of September 1 when the first reports of the Nazi invasion of Poland reached Canada.

[63]*Ibid.*, Héon to Manion, Aug. 21, 1939.
[64]Information from the Hon. R. A. Bell, Feb. 6, 1967.
[65]Manion Papers, Vol. 15, T. H. Onslow to Manion, Aug. 5, 1939, enclosing Onslow to Robb, Aug. 4, 1939.
[66]*Ibid.*, Vol. 15, Manion to Onslow, Aug. 9, 1939.
[67]*Ibid.*, Vol. 8, Manion to Hogarth, Jan. 23, 1939.

3.   The War, the Election, and the Defeat of Manion

In his fourteen months of leadership, Manion had made sincere and determined efforts to rid the Conservative party of its imperialist, conscriptionist heritage, but the outbreak of the war increased the opposition to him within the party ranks. This vocal antagonism could serve only to reinforce the latent fears of Quebec voters: What assurance was there that Manion could maintain his position throughout the war? And if he went, what guarantee was there that conscription would not be advocated by his successor? In such circumstances, Quebec might better stay with King and Lapointe. Worse yet, the Conservative arrangement with Premier Duplessis became a dead letter within the first six weeks of the war. These factors destroyed the *raison d'être* of Manion's selection and, combined with the continuing hostility of powerful forces within and without the party and the superior tactical skills of Mackenzie King, rendered Manion's position untenable.

The outbreak of the war in Europe was a heavy blow to Manion's hopes of victory in the federal election due within a year. The Prime Minister, he wrote, "certainly has the luck of the very devil—just as he was on the verge of going out, this crisis comes along and allows people to forget his past sins. . . . Of course," he added, "it all depends on how he carries on; and I cannot imagine that he will do very well."[1] But the skill with which Mackenzie King managed the opening days of the war and the special session called to determine Canada's course belied Manion's words.

King's grasp of political tactics was never better demonstrated than in the first ten days of September 1939. For all practical purposes, Canada's defensive preparations in the years immediately prior to 1939 had been predicated on the assumption of a united imperial war effort in the event of a new European conflict.[2] Since Munich, King had been convinced

[1]Manion Papers, Vol. 12, Manion to Lt.-Col. R. H. Webb, Sept. 4, 1939.
[2]Kenneth W. McNaught, "Canadian Foreign Policy and the Whig Interpretation: 1936–1939," Canadian Historical Association, *Report*, 1957, p. 52. For details of the limited rearmament programme of the 1930's, see C. P. Stacey,

that Canada had no feasible alternative other than to participate at Britain's side,[3] but he had pledged that parliament would decide on peace or war.[4] His motives for such a course varied scarcely at all from Manion's. Both leaders were attempting to appeal to French Canada, but while Manion was hoping to build anew, King was trying to keep his strength intact. There were also some persons in the English-speaking provinces, led by a tiny but vocal group of academics and with some supporters in parliament, who believed that Canada should remain neutral in any foreign war.[5] Mackenzie King's task was to reconcile these neutralists and nationalists to Canadian participation, and yet to take measures forceful enough to satisfy those demanding immediate aid to the Allies. He accomplished this task with supreme skill.

King had announced on August 25 that "all possible precautionary measures" were being taken to meet "whatever eventuality may arise," and later on the same day he had authorized the calling out of militia units to guard vital points.[6] On September 1, the government ordered the mobilization of a "Canadian Active Service Force," and two days later, after Britain had declared war, "all necessary measures which would be required in a state of war" were taken.[7] But still the nation was not at war with Germany. A special war session of parliament met on September 7, and the assembled members and senators heard the Governor General declare that they had been called together "in order that the government may seek authority for the measures necessary for the defence of Canada, and for co-operation in the determined effort . . . to

---

The Official History of the Canadian Army in the Second World War. I. *Six Years of War* (Ottawa, 1955), 7–37; James Eayrs, *In Defence of Canada*, II, *passim.*

[3]Douglas Library, Queen's University, Charles Dunning Papers, King to Dunning, Sept. 3, 1938; R. MacGregor Dawson, *Canada in World Affairs: Two Years of War, 1939–1941* (Toronto, 1943), p. 10; J. W. Pickersgill, *The Mackenzie King Record.* I. *1939–1944* (Toronto, 1960), 12.

[4]House of Commons, *Debates*, May 24, 1938, p. 3183, and radio broadcast, Sept. 3, 1939, quoted in Pickersgill, *Mackenzie King Record*, I, 16.

[5]E.g., "Keep Canada Out of War," *Maclean's*, L (May 15, 1937), reprinted in F. H. Underhill, *In Search of Canadian Liberalism* (Toronto, 1960), pp. 183–91; J. T. Thorson, M.P., in House of Commons, *Debates*, March 31, 1939, pp. 2483–9.

[6]Stacey, *History of Second World War*, I, 40–1.

[7]*Ibid.*, pp. 42, 46. Colonel Maurice Pope, Secretary to the Chiefs of Staff Committee, was told by the Minister of National Defence, Ian Mackenzie, "to convey to the Chiefs of Staff that they were to give effect to all the defence measures . . . and to fire on any blinking German who came within range of our guns—but that we were not at war. This instruction amused me greatly and I exclaimed, 'You are certainly trying to have it both ways,' and Ian, chuckling, replied, 'Of course we are.' " Maurice A. Pope, *Soldiers and Politicians: The Memoirs of Lt.-Gen. Maurice A. Pope, C.B., M.C.* (Toronto, 1962), p. 140.

resist further aggression. . . ."[8] On the next day, the Prime Minister reiterated his pledge that conscription for overseas service would never be enacted by his government, but it was not until September 9 that King made it clear that if the Address in Reply to the Speech from the Throne was approved by the House of Commons, the government would "immediately take steps for the issue of a formal proclamation declaring the existence of a state of war between Canada and the German Reich."[9] An amendment to the Address, moved by Liguori Lacombe, an isolationist Liberal from Quebec, that "Canada should refrain from participating in war outside of Canada,"[10] was rejected without a vote being recorded, and the Address was also adopted without a vote. "La discipline de parti," Robert Rumilly wrote, "jugule la masse des libéraux canadiens-français."[11] A formal submission to the King was dispatched to London by cable, and the next morning, Sunday, September 10, exactly one week after the British declaration, Canada was at war.[12]

There were heated objections to the Prime Minister's course from both imperialists and Quebec nationalists. "No vote is necessary [to declare war]," T. L. Church, a true blue Toronto Tory, told the House of Commons, "because it is well known that when Britain is at war Canada is at war."[13] *Le Devoir* (2 septembre 1939) insisted on the other hand that "Le Canada n'est pas pays d'Europe" and demanded neutrality. Long after the war, there were still traces of this attitude in French Canada. "Rétrospectivement," André Laurendeau said, "nous pensons la guerre de 1939–45 comme un conflit mondial: elle l'est devenue. En 1939, elle était européene, exclusivement européene, sauf dans la mesure où la Grande-Bretagne et la France y entraînèrent leurs empires."[14] Canada went to war, many French Canadians believed, only because Great Britain was at war. Despite these attacks, King's policy had obviously followed the middle way. As the Governor General, Lord Tweedsmuir, wrote, "My Prime Minister has succeeded very skilfully in aligning Canada alongside Britain with a minimum of disturbance. He, of course, is being criticized for not declaring himself roundly and clearly, but in my view his policy has been the right one."[15] Mackenzie King's calculated policy of refusing to commit the country to any course

[8]House of Commons, *Debates*, Sept. 7, 1939, p. 1.
[9]*Ibid.*, Sept. 8, p. 36, and Sept. 9, 1939, p. 51.
[10]*Ibid.*, Sept. 9, 1939, p. 73.
[11]*Henri Bourassa* (Montréal, 1953), p. 768.
[12]The Royal Proclamation is in Dawson, *Two Years of War, 1939–41*, pp. 285–6.
[13]House of Commons, *Debates*, Sept. 9, 1939, p. 73: cf. Arthur Meighen in Senate, *Debates*, Sept. 9, 1939, p. 8.
[14]*La Crise de la conscription, 1942* (Montréal, 1962), p. 36.
[15]Janet A. Smith, *John Buchan, A Biography* (London, 1965), p. 458.

without the approval of parliament had secured almost unanimous support for the nation's entry into the war.

The Prime Minister had dealt with the crisis so effectively that the Opposition had little choice other than to follow his lead. On September 1 Manion had issued a statement that affirmed that "there can be no neutrality for Canada while Britain is engaged in a war of life and death."[16] He was supported in this position by all members of his party, including, with some minor reservations, Georges Héon.[17] While Héon, however, was declaring himself against the sending of an expeditionary force abroad,[18] the first rumblings of conscriptionist sentiment became audible.[19] "I can understand men like Lapointe taking this stand [against conscription]," wrote Brigadier-General J. A. Clark of Vancouver, one of the Conservative party's more vocal and persistent advocates of compulsory service, "but I cannot understand my own Party falling in line. It may be that the Party could not declare for conscription at the particular moment but it did not need to declare against it. I may add that I have been severely rebuked by the Party leader for these thoughts."[20] For the moment at least, Manion controlled his party.

The coming of war had one additional effect on the Conservative party. When King and Manion met on September 6, the day before the opening of the hastily called war session, the Prime Minister told the Leader of the Opposition that "there would be no general election certainly until after the next session—that is, the January session." Manion gladly accepted this and proposed that any necessary by-elections should not be contested, but should go by acclamation to the party previously holding the seat.[21] A political truce—and one without stated duration— was in effect. This cease fire was taken very seriously by the Conservative leader. All organization was stopped, and the party offices in Ottawa were rented to the High Commissioner for Eire.[22] Unofficially, some local organization was continued throughout the country,[23] but when Dr. Robb, the national organizer, submitted a plan for a reduced head-

[16]Progressive Conservative Party Files, Manion File, press release.

[17]House of Commons, *Debates*, Sept. 9, 1939, p. 81.

[18]*Ibid.*, p. 83.

[19]Manion Papers, Vol. 10, Harry Price to Manion, Sept. 9, 1939; Vol. 13, J. A. Clark to Manion, Sept. 11, 1939; Vol. 10, E. E. Perley, M.P., to Manion, Oct. 10, 1939; *Toronto Daily Star*, Oct. 2, 1939, p. 6.

[20]Bennett Papers, Series H, Miscellaneous 1937–1946, Vol. 3, J. A. Clark to Bennett, Sept. 25, 1939.

[21]Manion Papers, Vol. 45, Memorandum of meeting with King, Sept. 6, 1939.

[22]Progressive Conservative Party Files, File PEI-Q-la, Robb to J. P. Callaghan, Sept. 14, 1939 (form letter); File M-M-4, Robb to Errick Willis, Sept. 15, 1939; "Backstage at Ottawa," *Maclean's* , LII (Oct. 15, 1939), 10.

[23]E.g., Manion Papers, Vol. 15, A. Kendall to Manion, Sept. 25, 1939.

quarters establishment, Manion told a supporter that if Robb wanted to keep the organization functioning, he would have to pay the costs from his own pocket.[24] In part at least, as Manion's words indicate, the total cessation of organization was the result of the party's inability to raise money. As soon as the war broke out, Manion wrote, "those who were kind enough to help us simply told us: 'Well there is a war on now and we will not assist political organizations' and they have stayed by that resolution—so much so that, confidentially, we have not been able to pay off the money we owe. . . ."[25] But with the organization closed down and a political armistice in effect, the Conservative leader travelled in September to Atlantic City, New Jersey, for his first holiday since assuming the leadership. While he was at the shore, however, Premier Duplessis called an election in Quebec, and the carefully constructed Union Nationale-Conservative alliance was destroyed.

Secure with his seventy-five members in the provincial legislature of ninety, the Quebec premier had remained silent throughout the first weeks of September, but evidently he had been taking soundings around the province. On September 23, Duplessis summoned his cabinet, and to a bare quorum he announced his intention of going to the electorate.[26] Presumably, he viewed the war as an excellent election issue, for he had two years remaining in his term, and earlier in the year he had told his caucus that he had no intention of holding an election until 1940.[27] Duplessis' plan, as revealed in his election manifesto, was to fight the election against the Mackenzie King government, attacking Ottawa for using the war as an excuse to destroy provincial autonomy:

Depuis plusieurs années, une campagne a été conduite et des tentatives directes et indirectes ont été faites, en vue d'amoindrir considérablement et même d'anéantir l'autonomie provinciale dans le but de ne former qu'un seul gouvernement dirigé par Ottawa.

L'Union Nationale considère que l'autonomie provinciale, garantie par le pacte fédératif, est essentielle aux meilleurs intérêts de la province, conforme à ses traditions, à ses droits et à ses prérogatives indispensables.

Invoquant le prétexte de la guerre déclarée par le gouvernement fédéral, une campagne d'assimilation et de centralisation manifestée depuis plusieurs années, s'accentue de façon intolérable.

The Union Nationale, Duplessis' manifesto concluded roundly, "a travaillé sans cesse et travaillera toujours à des œuvres de construction et

---

[24]*Ibid.*, Vol. 10, Manion to Harry Price, Sept. 15, 1939.
[25]*Ibid.*, Vol. 13, Manion to A. L. Hanna, Nov. 4, 1939.
[26]Leslie Roberts, *The Chief* (Toronto, 1963), p. 51.
[27]Manion Papers, Vol. 4, the Hon. T. J. Coonan, M.L.A., to Manion, May 1, 1939.

de réconstruction, mais jamais à des œuvres de déstruction."[28] The gauntlet had been thrown down, and the federal government, despite Duplessis' great strength, could hardly ignore a challenge which threatened to split off Quebec from the rest of the nation and cause the very breach that Mackenzie King had so deftly prevented only two weeks before.

"I don't see how anyone can minimise the importance of the Quebec elections," wrote Brooke Claxton, a brilliant Montreal Liberal lawyer, in a letter that was circulated within the cabinet.

They may mean the first shot in a Canadian civil war, or the break-up of confederation, or they may even be the first serious rebuff to the nationalist movement in fifty years. . . .
    In this election, I think that the colours should be nailed to the mast without compromise. If the P.M., Lapointe . . . and every other minister join in . . . they should get a majority of the popular votes. . . . If, however, the P.M., and the Federal Liberals do and say little or nothing then they will not only lose Quebec in this election and in the Federal election, but they will also lose the other provinces in the next election and the party will disappear with extreme rapidity.[29]

Similar views had already been expressed within the cabinet by the Postmaster General, C. G. "Chubby" Power. With some difficulty Power persuaded his senior colleagues from Quebec, Ernest Lapointe, the Minister of Justice and King's chief aide, and P. J. A. Cardin, the Minister of Public Works, that Duplessis' challenge had to be met by federal intervention in the provincial election.[30] As a result, the three ministers announced on September 26 that they were entering the fight, and over the initial objections of the Prime Minister, they declared that if Duplessis were re-elected they would resign from the federal cabinet. The strongest argument against Duplessis, the three ministers told King, was the public knowledge that if he was not defeated the Quebec ministers would resign and thereby open the door to a conscriptionist government in Ottawa.[31] Elect Duplessis, the *Québecois* would be warned, and you will have conscription; elect the Liberals, and we— Lapointe, Cardin, and Power—will protect you.[32] The issue was clear,

[28]Printed in Michel Brunet, *Histoire du Canada par les textes*. II. *1855–1960* (Montréal, 1963), 128–9. See Herbert F. Quinn, *The Union Nationale: A Study in Quebec Nationalism* (Toronto, 1963), p. 105.

[29]P.A.C., Ernest Lapointe Papers, M.G. 27, Vol. 49, extract from a letter by Claxton, Sept. 27, 1939.

[30]Norman Ward, ed., *A Party Politician: The Memoirs of Chubby Power* (Toronto, 1966), p. 347. Cf. Norman Lambert Diaries, Sept. 25–27, 1939.

[31]Pickersgill, *Mackenzie King Record*, I, 35; Dafoe Papers, Microfilm roll M–79, Grant Dexter to Dafoe (describing interview with Lapointe), Oct. 25, 1940.

[32]Manion Papers, Vol. 15, Frédéric Dorion to Manion, Nov. 7, 1939, indicates the effectiveness of this Liberal line.

and to ensure the success of provincial Liberal leader Adélard Godbout's campaign, the federal party took complete control of the election fight.[33] Initially money was scarce because Norman Lambert of the National Liberal Federation refused to release any national party funds for the election, but these difficulties were soon overcome. The Minister of Agriculture, J. G. Gardiner, loaned $25,000 in Saskatchewan party funds and undertook to raise money in Toronto. Cash began to come in from Quebec sources, and Lambert, pressed hard by Gardiner, Power, and Mackenzie King, relented and loosened his purse strings.[34] At the end of the election, Power said of finances, "we were in no great difficulties on that score."[35]

The Quebec election faced Manion with a calamitous choice. The party needed Duplessis' support to have a chance of making gains in Quebec, but if it supported him in his campaign against participation, the effects would be disastrous in English Canada. "I see Lapointe's statement re Duplessis," he wrote from Atlantic City to his private secretary, Richard A. Bell. "I may be asked to back the latter. If so, it might be very awkward. Feel around—tho [*sic*] do no suggesting that I take part, as I feel it much safer to be silent. Yet if I could *safely*," Manion added, "I'd like to hit Lapointe and his gang. But it might do great harm outside Quebec."[36] The only motive for the Liberal intervention in Quebec was "politics," Manion believed. "Why they should resign because of a Provincial result no one knows; but, of course, their purpose was to try and frighten the French-Canadians into voting against Duplessis and give Lapointe and his gang a chance to get their filthy machine back in power down there, then perhaps pull an election up here in the hope of sweeping the country."[37] Although H. H. Stevens, for one, agreed with this interpretation,[38] Manion's position illustrates clearly the extent of the difference in outlook between the leader and many of his followers. Either he did not see the implications for the nation and the war effort in a Duplessis victory or, if he did see them, Manion chose to subordinate them to his own partisan considerations.

The more Manion pondered the Quebec situation, the more difficult he found it to keep silent.[39] On October 16, less than ten days before the election, he was on the verge of making a statement attacking the

[33]Ward, ed., *Power Memoirs*, p. 347.

[34]Lambert Diaries, Sept. 25, Oct. 3, 1939; Gardiner Papers, Gardiner to C. L. Burton, Oct. 27, 1939; Gardiner to J. S. McLean, Oct. 27, 1939; Ward, ed., *Power Memoirs*, pp. 128, 349; Lambert Diaries, Oct. 18, 1939.

[35]Ward, ed., *Power Memoirs*, p. 349.

[36]Manion Papers, Vol. 2, Manion to Bell, Sept. 30, 1939.

[37]*Ibid.*, Vol. 16, Manion to his son, Oct. 18, 1939.

[38]*Ibid.*, Vol. 11, Stevens to Manion, Oct. 6, 1939.

[39]*Ibid.*, Vol. 66, Diary, Oct. 17, 1939.

Lapointe intervention when he received a telephoned message from Georges Héon:

> . . . it had more effect on me than all the other arguments which our crowd were making against my giving out a statement [he wrote to Héon the next day]. I really felt that I should, in view of the fact that my name is being bandied about down there. . . . However, because of what you say and the probability that any statement of mine, even attacking them without mentioning Duplessis would be taken in Quebec as my endorsement of Duplessis and perhaps hurt him among the voters, I decided that I should keep quiet.[40]

In Héon's opinion, Manion's support would hurt Duplessis at the polls. If this was so, and Manion evidently agreed that it was, what conceivable chance was there for any gains in Quebec in the coming federal elections?

Duplessis' interjection of war issues had revived the memories of 1917 with a vengeance, and the intervention of the Liberal cabinet had turned the mighty force of the conscription issue against the Quebec premier. There was nothing Duplessis could do to counter the Liberals' pledges against conscription. The promises were clear and explicit. Adélard Godbout, for example, had stated in a radio address at the opening of the campaign that he would leave his party if conscription was ever enforced: "Je m'engage sur l'honneur, en pesant chacun de ces mots, à quitter mon parti et même à le combattre si un seul Canadien français, d'ici la fin des hostilités en Europe [*sic*], est mobilisé contre son gré sous un régime libéral ou même un régime provisoire auquel participeraient nos ministres actuels dans le cabinet du très honorable M. King."[41] Duplessis would be able to cash this blank cheque in 1944, but in 1939 his party was destroyed at the polls, thus ensuring that Conservatism once again would be shut out in Quebec. "Duplessis overwhelmingly defeated," Manion noted glumly as the Liberals took 53 per cent of the popular vote and sixty-nine seats in the legislature. "Another example of a dictator who has antagonized everyone. Lost his head like R.B.B[ennett]."[42] The Union Nationale leader had handed the election to the Liberals "on a platter," Manion believed, by getting involved with war issues and giving Lapointe a chance.[43] But Manion did not make the error, common across the English-speaking provinces, of assuming that the Quebec vote meant that French Canada solidly backed the war effort.[44] Rather, the Liberal vote represented the belief that conscription could be avoided more surely under the Liberals than

[40]*Ibid.*, Vol. 6, Manion to Héon, Oct. 17, 1939.
[41]Brunet, *Histoire du Canada par les textes*, II, 130.
[42]Manion Papers, Vol. 66, Diary, Oct. 25, 1939.
[43]*Ibid.*, Vol. 16, Manion to his son, Nov. 6, 1939.
[44]E.g., Toronto *Globe and Mail*, Oct. 26, 1939, p. 6.

under Duplessis.[45] At the same time, the election had divided Quebec Conservatives into two hostile groups. "The Conservatives who opposed Duplessis are bitterly resentful toward those who supported him," wrote one English-speaking Quebecker to Manion, and it is impossible, this same correspondent added in reference to a prominent French-Canadian Conservative who had worked for Duplessis, "for us to ally ourselves in the future with a man whose stand is so much at variance with our sincere beliefs."[46] The October provincial election had shattered Manion's dreams about Quebec, and for the duration of the war the Conservative party virtually ceased to exist there.

Despite the Quebec setback, the Conservative organization remained dormant through November and December of 1939. The cause of the delay in resuming operations was now frankly admitted to be the party's desperate financial position,[47] and it was not until early in the new year that Manion agreed that "small scale" organization could begin in February.[48] Meanwhile, Manion was attempting to make use of his time in preparing for the session of parliament due to begin on January 25[49] and for the election to follow. But once again he began to encounter obstacles within his party. Some of his more restive followers, perhaps foreseeing a *débâcle* or perhaps from objections to wartime elections in general, began urging him to avoid an election if possible, or at the least to suggest a one-year extension of the life of parliament to Mackenzie King.[50] Manion disagreed with these suggestions, stating the obvious fact that if he sought to postpone the election, he would inevitably be accused of being afraid to face the people. Furthermore, as he wrote to Meighen, "I must confess quite frankly that I hardly understand the reasoning of Conservatives who have an utter contempt for King and yet who seem to think if there is an election he would sweep the boards. On the contrary, my conviction is he would do nothing of the sort, especially if our Party stands loyally behind its leader."[51]

There were some elements within the party, however, who were not

[45]Houghton Library, Harvard University, J. P. Moffat Papers, Vol. 47, Memorandum of conversation with J. W. Pickersgill, Nov. 26, 1941; F. R. Scott, "The Real Vote in Quebec," *Canadian Forum*, XIX (Dec., 1939), 270; Roberts, *The Chief*, pp. 59–62.

[46]Manion Papers, Vol. 11, J. G. Ross to Manion, Oct. 27, 1939.

[47]*Ibid.*, Vol. 14, Manion to Robb, Nov. 30, 1939; Progressive Conservative Party Files, File M-M-6, Robb to W. C. Miller, Dec. 13, 1939.

[48]Manion Papers, Vol. 14, Manion to Robb, Jan. 3, 1940.

[49]E.g., *ibid.*, Vol. 14, Manion to J. Earl Lawson, Jan. 24, 1940.

[50]*Ibid.*, Vol. 15, Hogarth to Manion, Jan. 24, 1940; Vol. 12, Brig. J. S. Stewart to Manion, Dec. 27, 1939.

[51]Meighen Papers, Manion to Meighen, Jan. 23, 1940. Cf. *ibid.*, Meighen to Clark, Jan. 15, 1940.

prepared to stand behind Manion. In a front-page editorial on December 28, 1939, the Montreal *Gazette* urged that Bennett return to parliament to revitalize the Conservative party. With Bennett in the House again, the editorial argued, the Opposition would speak with a more authoritative voice and would be in a good position to give constructive co-operation to the Government. Since his retirement from the leadership the former prime minister had been living in England, but at the time of the *Gazette* editorial he was in Canada to raise money for the British Red Cross and to address a Toronto meeting of the Empire Club. Apparently he had not been consulted about the newspaper's suggestion, but there are indications that he was not totally averse to the idea. "I saw Mr. Bennett while he was here," wrote Colonel H. A. Bruce, "and he was strongly of the opinion that there should be no war-time Federal election. I approached him on the possibility of his return, explaining the weakness of his successor, and while he vouchsafed no answer to this suggestion, I am of the opinion that if the demand was strong enough he would consent. . . ."[52] Manion's reaction to this Bennett "boom" was to see in it "some sort of a linking up of some of those who opposed me at the Convention for the purpose possibly of trying to shoulder me out if I do not come to terms. . . ."[53] The hostility to the party leader in Montreal circles, so evident throughout his first year of leadership, had shown few signs of decreasing with the passage of time. Another threat to Manion's position was developing in Toronto, and here the contender was the Leader of the Opposition in the Ontario legislature, George Drew.

Probably the most physically attractive politician in the Dominion, Lt.-Col. George Drew had been in the public eye for a number of years. As a soldier, as a lawyer, and as a popular journalist, he had quickly established both a reputation and a following. He had resigned from his position as chairman of the Ontario Conservative campaign committee in 1937 as a result of differences with provincial leader W. Earl Rowe on the party's labour policy. In the next year, however, he had been selected as leader, largely on the strength of his instigation of the sensational Bren Gun Contract Inquiry in the fall of 1938.[54] He and his backers now believed that he was ready for national politics.

[52]Bruce Papers, Bruce to George McCullagh, Dec. 28, 1939. Also Manion Papers, Vol. 4, Clark to Manion, Jan. 3, 1940.
[53]Manion Papers, Vol. 16, Manion to his son, Dec. 28, 1939.
[54]The Bren Gun Contract Inquiry was, perhaps, the most contentious issue in Canada's prewar rearmament. The contract for the production of the Bren light machine gun had been let under suspicious circumstances, and Drew had revealed the scandal in a magazine article. See the discussion in Stacey, *The Military Problems of Canada*, pp. 128–33.

Manion was fully aware of Drew's magnetic appeal. "I entirely agree with you that George Drew makes a very fine impression wherever he goes," he wrote. "He has a splendid appearance and is an excellent speaker, added to which he can discuss military questions from a wide personal knowledge of such matters." But, he added, "quite frankly, he is not an easy man to cooperate with."[55] There were some grounds for Manion's reservations. Shortly before Christmas 1939, he had heard of a speech delivered by Drew to the Conservative Progress Club, an organization of young Toronto businessmen. According to J. Earl Lawson, the Ontario leader had said "that the Conservative Party was at the lowest ebb it had ever been in its history and that unless new life blood was enfused it would die of anemia. He then proceeded to outline a robust constructive policy for the rehabilitation of our railways. . . . then took occasion to point out that what was needed for the Conservative Party was courageous, instructive leadership."[56] Apparently this talk of Drew's did not worry Manion. What did bother him, however, was Drew's penchant for commenting forcefully on matters of federal concern.

Manion believed that it was essential that he and the Ontario leader meet to discuss their respective and proper spheres. In a letter to Drew early in January, Manion asked for a meeting and added that he was avoiding speech-making until the opening of parliament "because I am afraid of merely putting King on his guard and permitting him thereby to get better prepared for the session. I am even going so far as to hope," he continued, perhaps thinking of his truce with the Prime Minister, "that you chaps who have been cracking him will ease down for the next three weeks."[57] The confrontation requested by Manion was held on January 8 and was a great success. "We got along swimmingly," wrote Manion to one of his loyal supporters:

I suggested to him, and he concurred in it at the time apparently, that until the House opened he might refrain from discussing Federal matters—that I felt discussion by him or others at the present time was placing King on guard and, naturally, therefore putting me at a disadvantage when the House met. He seemed to wholly agree, merely saying that he would discuss the matter, say, of guarding Provincial works . . . and with that I agreed entirely.[58]

Within a week of their meeting, however, Drew had renegued on the agreement. "I think it is clear," he wrote Manion, "that I cannot possibly

[55]Manion Papers, Vol. 14, Manion to Milner, Jan. 2, 1940.
[56]*Ibid.*, Vol. 5, Earl Lawson to Manion, Dec. 21, 1939.
[57]*Ibid.*, Vol. 5, Manion to Drew, Jan. 2, 1940.
[58]*Ibid.*, Vol. 14, Manion to Karl Homuth, M.P., Jan. 16, 1940.

avoid extensive references to the situation as it exists, particularly so far as it affects the province of Ontario." Manion could do nothing to stop the Ontario leader, and within a few days Drew had joined Premier Hepburn in a scathing attack on the war policies of the King administration.[59]

Mitchell Hepburn had been feuding with Mackenzie King for several years.[60] "Shrewd, single-minded, with a dominant will,"[61] Hepburn had swept into office in December 1934 on a platform of reform and economy.[62] Within a few years, however, the aura of office transformed him into a staunch defender of the *status quo*, and he used the full power of his government to battle the Committee for Industrial Organization in its attempts to organize the workers at the General Motors Corporation plants in Oshawa. "I can speak only for Ontario," he said in June 1937 of his attempts to defeat the American labour "agitators." "I cannot speak for Canada because we have a vacillating Government at Ottawa. . . . I am a reformer, but I am not a Mackenzie King Liberal any longer."[63] Hepburn's stand on the C.I.O. was endorsed by George Drew, and the informal alliance between the two was strengthened after Drew became leader of the Ontario Conservatives. As Drew wrote to Manion in the summer of 1939, the resulting situation was unique in Canadian political history. He would attack Hepburn if it served the interests of the national party, Drew said, but he believed that there was much to gain by letting the Ontario premier devote his energies to attacking Mackenzie King.[64] Manion shared this belief and even cherished the hope that Hepburn could be brought to assist the Conservative party in the federal election.[65] What Manion had not banked on, it was all too evident, was that Drew and Hepburn would unite their forces for an all-out attack on the federal government.

The Ontario premier launched his assault in mid-January. The King government was guilty of slipshod measures; there was, despite the despatch of a division overseas and the inauguration of the British

[59]*Ibid.*, Vol. 5, Drew to Manion, Jan. 15; Manion to Drew, Jan. 16, 1940.
[60]For details, Peter Regenstreif, "The Liberal Party of Canada: A Political Analysis," unpublished Ph.D. thesis, Cornell University, 1963, pp. 246–9; Douglas Library, Queen's University, Norman McL. Rogers Papers, Rogers to Hepburn, Feb. 27, 1939 (draft), and Memoranda, "Giving aid and comfort to the enemy," n.d.
[61]Moffat Papers, Vol. 46, Notes on trip to Toronto, n.d.
[62]*The Canadian Annual Review of Public Affairs, 1934* (Toronto, 1935), pp. 174–80; Neil McKenty, "Mitchell Hepburn and the Ontario Election of 1934," *Canadian Historical Review*, XLV (Dec., 1964), 293–313.
[63]*Canadian Annual Review, 1937–1938*, p. 166.
[64]Manion Papers, Vol. 5, Drew to Manion, Aug. 3, 1939.
[65]*Ibid.*, Manion to Drew, Aug. 8, 1939; Vol. 9, Manion to J. R. MacNicol, Nov. 29, 1939.

Commonwealth Air Training Plan, a lack of energy in the prosecution of the war; and, furthermore, the Prime Minister had shown a positive hatred for the province of Ontario.[66] Spurred on by the Toronto *Globe and Mail*,[67] Hepburn introduced a resolution of censure "regretting that the Federal Government at Ottawa had made so little effort to prosecute Canada's duty in the war in the vigorous manner the people of Canada desire to see,"[68] and with the eager aid of Drew's Opposition, this measure was passed by a vote of forty-four to ten on January 18.

The Hepburn-Drew resolution, Mackenzie King quickly observed, gave him the opportunity of avoiding "all the contention of a session known to be immediately preceding an election." Before the day was out, therefore, he had decided to hold the election as soon as possible.[69] There was, of course, that unfortunate promise to Manion that a session would be held before the dissolution, but in King's opinion, the extraordinary Ontario resolution justified its abandonment.[70] The Prime Minister believed that his government was "in a very strong position from one end of the country to the other":

That Hepburn's action is on all fours with Duplessis'. That he has been living in an atmosphere of groups around him in Toronto; is filled with his own prejudice and hate; and is entirely blind to the sentiment in other parts of Canada. I believe an appeal to the country will bring us back as strong, if not stronger, than we are at present.

King's judgment was correct, as was his following comment:

. . . the greatest relief of all is the probability of having the election over before the worst of the fighting begins in Europe. I have dreaded having to choose the moment for the campaign and specially to choose it at a time when human lives are being slaughtered by hundreds of thousands, if not by millions. In this way, we can probably have the election over before the spring campaign in Europe begins.[71]

---

[66]Hepburn was particularly incensed about army conditions. After a visit to a Toronto camp in December 1939 he wrote of the "most deplorable condition of affairs one could imagine. Men without uniforms, proper underwear and shoes. . . ." Ontario Department of Public Records and Archives (P.A.O.), Prime Minister's Office, M. F. Hepburn Papers, Supplementary Files (private), 1939, Hepburn to W. M. Southam, Dec. 1, 1939.

[67]E.g., Toronto *Globe and Mail*, Jan. 17, 1940, p. 6.

[68]*Ibid.*, Jan. 19, 1940, p. 1.

[69]Pickersgill, *Mackenzie King Record*, I, 62. C. G. Power, for one, had been urging King for some time to dissolve parliament regardless of his commitment to Manion (Ward, ed., *Power Memoirs*, p. 352).

[70]King was capable of believing even his own worst sophistries, but in this instance he apparently felt that he had acted somewhat unfairly to Manion. J. W. Pickersgill, "Mackenzie King's Speeches," *Queen's Quarterly*, LVII (autumn, 1950), 310; House of Commons, *Debates*, Jan. 25, 1940, pp. 2–4.

[71]Pickersgill, *Mackenzie King Record*, I, 62, 63.

Characteristically, however, King said very little on the subject of an immediate dissolution, informing only the War Committee of the cabinet and his party organizer of his intentions.[72] On the morning of the day parliament was to meet, the Prime Minister was still making changes in the Speech from the Throne, and it was only then that he finally decided on a dissolution that day. The Governor General was informed of the changes in his speech, and at three o'clock when parliament assembled, Mackenzie King found Tweedsmuir "immensely pleased that the secret of the dissolution had been so well kept."[73]

The announcement that the government had decided on an "immediate appeal to the country" stunned the assembled legislators. "The result," Tweedsmuir noted, "has been such a buzzing in political circles as to resemble nothing so much as a bee-skep which has overturned."[74] In his brief speech of explanation, King placed the blame squarely on the action of the Ontario legislature in censuring the conduct of the war effort. Then, in a passage with which Manion must secretly have agreed, King added:

What is the cry already? Already after this resolution is passed, the leader of the Conservative party in Ontario, at a political meeting, tells the meeting, and through the meeting the province, and through the province the country, that the election must start at once; and he gives them the slogan, "King must go." That is to be the slogan. . . . How can I be expected to do what is expected of me by this country . . . if all of my time and thought is to be surrounded by the animosities of political opponents who are seeking to undermine every effort. . . .[75]

When, at last, Manion managed to get the floor, there was little he could do other than to state that he—if not his nominally subordinate Ontario leader—had kept his pledge of non-partisanship and co-operation in the war effort.[76] Although King noted smugly that Manion "was particularly bitter and nasty,"[77] the Conservative leader had ample grounds for protest.

Why call a snap election [he asked] on this group of two hundred and forty-five members . . . who have come here from all parts of Canada, at great expense in many instances? . . .

---

[72]*Ibid.*, p. 63; Lambert Diaries, Jan. 23, 1940. Cf. Gardiner Papers, "Address of J. G. Gardiner, 1940 Election Campaign," n.d.: ". . . rather unexpected calling of the election. Those of us who have been associated with the government were probably not so surprised as those of you who were not. We were all united in the decision reached and took some part in reaching that decision."

[73]Pickersgill, *Mackenzie King Record*, I, 64.

[74]House of Commons, *Debates*, Jan. 25, 1940, p. 2; Smith, *Buchan*, p. 469.

[75]House of Commons, *Debates*, Jan. 25, 1940, p. 5.

[76]*Ibid.*, p. 11.

[77]Pickersgill, *Mackenzie King Record*, I, 64.

. . . The understanding was that the House of Commons would be called in regular session and that we would discuss the activities of the government. . . . If we had come here, as we have, and gone on for a few weeks, the Prime Minister might have decided that an election should be called; but to put over a political trick of this kind I say is disgraceful and is sneering at the political traditions of Canada and the British Empire.[78]

King had broken his pledged word, and in so doing he had caught the Conservative party without organization, without funds, and without the political ammunition sure to have been unearthed by a full session of parliament. It was small comfort to Manion that he had been right in his advice to Drew, for there was no time for gloating.[79] Drew's help, as well as that of every Conservative in the Dominion, would be needed if anything was to be salvaged in the election on March 26. The reaction of the daily press to the dissolution, however, gave little promise of a rallying to the Tory banner.

Although only a few days before on January 22 it had urged that no election be called, the Montreal *Gazette* rapidly changed its tune. "In the circumstances," the lead editorial of January 26 pontificated, "this exceptional procedure is not without justification. . . . A short campaign and a definite mandate will best serve the interests of the country. . . ." In the light of the newspaper's past performance, it is hardly surprising that there was no mention whatsoever of Manion in this editorial. The Toronto *Globe and Mail*, still not definitely aligned with the Conservative party, was harsher in its judgment of King, calling his ploy good politics, but not good war service. "Premier Hepburn and Colonel Drew and the Ontario Legislature do not represent the country, not even Ontario in this case," the *Globe and Mail*'s editorial added, "and have had a distinction thrust on them they are not likely to welcome." The traditionally Conservative *Ottawa Journal* agreed with King's reasoning but objected to his "incomprehensible action" in dissolving parliament so suddenly. This did not suggest "democratic or British practice."[80] Most of the remaining Tory papers were similarly mild in their reaction,[81] and this reflected their mistrust of Manion far more than their love for Mackenzie King. "I doubt if any Leader in our political history has had

[78]House of Commons, *Debates*, Jan. 25, 1940, p. 10.

[79]Manion evidently believed that Drew "had engineered the Ontario House attack, Drew hoping thereby to usurp Manion's Dominion leadership" (Bruce Papers, Mrs. Bruce's Diary, Jan. 29, 1940).

[80]Toronto *Globe and Mail*, Jan. 26, 1940, p. 6; *Ottawa Journal*, Jan. 26, 1940, p. 4.

[81]The question of press reaction is discussed in "Canada's War Effort," *Round Table*, XXX (March, 1940), 425. The *Winnipeg Free Press*, a strongly Liberal newspaper, had published an editorial a few days before the dissolution urging against an election. "The words had hardly been printed," wrote G. V. Ferguson,

the same discomfiting experience that Dr. Manion now is having," a veteran Ottawa correspondent wrote to Bennett in England, "in being forced to eat the bread that has been returned to him upon the waters. I refer, of course, to his policy of catering to French and Catholic sentiment in Canada, instead of following the traditional Conservative course of militant imperialism."[82] In January 1940, however, there was little evidence that any Conservative Members of Parliament wanted a policy of militant imperialism in the party platform.

The Conservative caucus met to discuss the party's strategy on January 26, the day following the abbreviated session. With the sole exception of J. Earl Lawson (who had already indicated that he would not contest his seat) the members unanimously endorsed Manion's policy against conscription for overseas service.[83] This could hardly be interpreted as an appeal to Quebec, for after the Duplessis defeat few Conservatives could have held illusions about party strength there; it can only be interpreted, therefore, as reflecting a Conservative desire to maintain national unity and as a reaction to what was believed to be the mood of the electorate. At the same caucus, as Manion later recalled it, Earl Rowe, formerly Ontario Conservative leader and then member for Dufferin-Simcoe, "without previous consultation with me—arose and proposed that in the ensuing election we stand on a national government platform. There was wild and enthusiastic acclaim and not one word of opposition."[84] Accordingly, Manion released a statement after the caucus, advocating "a truly national government in the sense that the very best brains obtainable among our people are drafted to serve in the Cabinet." If elected, he stated, "I shall form such a government."[85] Certainly none could have expected this pledge of national government to be hailed in a French Canada where the Union government of 1917 was as hated a memory as the conscription with which it was inextricably linked. Most likely, the national government policy was shaped in an

---

the editor at the time, "before Mr. King had dissolved the House, and that evening . . . the *Free Press* war council decided to throw what weight it could in favour of Mr. King's decision. As a close friend of us all remarked, you could hear a very long way from Winnipeg the squeal of tires taking the sharp corner." George V. Ferguson, *John W. Dafoe* (Toronto, 1948), p. 108.

[82]Bennett Papers, Notable Persons File, Norman M. MacLeod to Bennett, Jan. 30, 1940.

[83]*Ottawa Journal*, March 20, 1942, p. 10. This is in a statement released by Manion in explanation of his reasons for advocating national government.

[84]*Ibid.*; cf. Politicus, "Who Did Support National Government?" *Saturday Night*, LVI (April 12, 1941), 8.

[85]Clipping from Saint John *Telegraph-Journal*, Jan. 27, 1940, in Manion Papers, Vol. 61.

effort to win back to the Conservative party the business and financial element of the nation.

National government had been a subject of speculation for some years in Canada. Many businessmen apparently regarded it as the panacea that would end needless party bickering and thus would get the country moving again. Sir Edward Beatty evidently viewed a national government as being more likely to implement railway unification than a party government, and there is an unconfirmed rumour that he had offered $3 million for a national government campaign in 1935.[86] Other groups had toyed with the idea as well. In 1935, the League for National Government was formed by a group of Toronto businessmen, and there were persistent reports in that year that Prime Minister Bennett was leaning to some form of coalition.[87] These rumours proved false and the subject of national government remained dormant until the last summer of peace. Then Manion had attacked the notion in a speech in July 1939 that was to be used against him in the 1940 election campaign. "I say to you," he declared at Port Stanley, Ontario, "no hope for Canada lies in that path, but a very real menace to democracy lurks in any fusion of Conservative and Liberal forces. Under our system, there must be a government and an opposition. Were the suggested union to take place," he warned, pointing to the socialist C.C.F., "the opposition must of necessity be formed by another party in the House. . . ."[88]

The outbreak of war resulted in new pressures on Manion to come out for national government, but the Conservative leader remained adamant in his opposition to the scheme. ". . . I have no desire to have a proposition put up to me that I would have to accept," he wrote to his son. "Indeed, I doubt, confidentially, if any proposition could be put up to me that I would accept."[89] Nonetheless, throughout September 1939 he was consulting provincial leaders and prominent Conservatives as to their views on the subject.[90] "My own feeling," he said to R. B. Hanson, "would be that we could not even look at the question unless we got nearly a fifty-fifty break in the portfolios."[91] By this date, however, Manion's objection was apparently not to national government

[86]Ernest Watkins, *R. B. Bennett* (Toronto, 1963), p. 224.

[87]Young, "C. George McCullagh and the Leadership League," pp. 148–50; Meighen Papers, "Loring C. Christie" Folder.

[88]Address, July 26, 1939, quoted in Saskatchewan Liberal Association, "National Government Menace to Democracy. . ." 1940 election pamphlet, copy in Gardiner Papers.

[89]Manion Papers, Vol. 16, Manion to his son, Sept. 11, 1939.

[90]E.g., *ibid.*, Vol. 15, Manion to P. C. Black, Sept. 20, 1939.

[91]Hanson Papers, File P-450-M, Manion to Hanson, Sept. 20, 1939.

as such, but only to serving in a government led by Mackenzie King.[92] There are strong indications that Manion would willingly have joined a coalition headed by J. L. Ralston, King's Minister of Finance, and while it would appear that confidential conversations were held with Ralston on this possibility, nothing came of the matter.[93]

In any case by the end of October Manion had concluded that national government would be a successful campaign issue—a "ten-spot,"[94] he called it. The proposal, as Hanson understood it after discussing the idea with Manion, was "that sometime previous to the next General Election you should come out with a Manifesto saying in effect to the Canadian people that they are not getting the right Leadership from King, that if elected to office you will form a National Government of the best brains available in the Country, and win the war."[95] Apparently the subject was also discussed and approved by a special caucus committee early in December.[96] It seems highly probable, therefore, that national government would have been a major Conservative programme whatever the date of the election.

Immediately he had declared for national government, demands and suggestions flew thick and fast at the Conservative leader. George McCullagh, the mercurial publisher of the *Globe and Mail*, indicated that he would support national government if Manion could get "Bennett and Meighen and bring in good men from across Canada."[97] Manion was all for bringing in good men, "but became almost violent when H[erbert Bruce, who was acting as intermediary between McCullagh and Manion] suggested the calling of Bennett from England," Mrs. Bruce recorded in her diary. "He said he would only come out and knife him."[98]

[92]Manion Papers, Vol. 10, Manion to W. H. Price, Oct. 18, 1939.

[93]Harry Price Interview, Sept. 8, 1964. Mr. Price was one of the key financial figures in Manion's party. He stated that he, representing Manion, had several discussions with Ralston, but he also adds that Mackenzie King knew of the meetings. The importance attached to these conversations by both sides may be doubted, however. The Hon. J. W. Pickersgill, author of the *Mackenzie King Record* and King's secretary at the time, has stated that the fact "that the subject is not dealt with in the diary is a pretty conclusive piece of evidence that Mr. King attached very little importance to it in his own mind" (letter to author, Oct. 6, 1964). Similarly, the Hon. R. A. Bell, then Manion's private secretary, who was normally aware of all the leader's transactions, knew nothing of these conversations, and he has said that he doubts any conversations were of serious nature (letter to author, Sept. 14, 1964). P.A.C., J. L. Ralston Papers, contain no information on this point.

[94]Hanson Papers, File P-450-M, Manion to Hanson, Nov. 2, 1939.

[95]*Ibid.*, Hanson to Manion, Oct. 3, 1939.

[96]Politicus, "Who Did Support National Government?" p. 8.

[97]Bruce Papers, Mrs. Bruce's Diary, Jan. 26, 1940.

[98]*Ibid.*, Jan. 29, 1940.

Financial problems, too, were pressing in on the harassed Manion. From New Brunswick, Hanson gloomily wrote that "I feel sure you will have great difficulty in getting funds together. In Montreal, the people who usually do for the party want a National Government and they want something done about the Railway question."[99] Manion had now declared for national government, but it was highly unlikely that he would or could modify his forcibly expressed views on railway amalgamation. At this point he was offered a packaged solution to all his problems.

On January 28, only three days after the dissolution, Manion came to Toronto at the request of a former cabinet colleague, the Hon. Wesley Gordon of Haileybury, Ontario. Gordon proposed that Manion issue a statement—and he produced a draft in his own handwriting—to the effect that after the election the Conservative leader, if successful, would permit the elected representatives chosen to support national government to select the man to form the government. If this were done, the implication was clear, financial difficulties would vanish overnight. In effect, Manion was being asked to fight the election, win it, and then step aside. Of course, Gordon said, it was unthinkable that the caucus would spurn the victorious leader, but Manion did not believe this. "I went into a rage," he later recorded, "telling him that this was merely a scheme to get rid of me should I win, that it was another move of the Montreal gang to get me out of the way. . . . I talked pretty rough . . . and of course I refused point blank."[100] This rejection did not stop a deluge of similar pleas in the next ten days. His friend, Don Hogarth, sent a letter urging support for the plan—"There is *positively* nothing on the ball but what is stated," he said, *"to ensure the defeat of King throu [sic] the leadership of Bob Manion"*—and he enclosed a long memorandum from Meighen warmly endorsing it.[101] According to Colonel C. E. Reynolds, the president of the Canadian Corps Association and another of those who called upon the hardpressed Manion at this time, Mitchell Hepburn also agreed with the proposal.[102] In addition, Manion's two principal money-raisers, Harry Price and Allan Ross, perhaps concerned

[99]Manion Papers, Vol. 6, Hanson to Manion, n.d.

[100]*Ibid.*, Vol. 45, Memorandum, March 27, 1941; Vol. 14, Memorandum, n.d. The Bruce Papers contain a letter (Bruce to McCullagh, Jan. 31, 1940) which indicates that Bruce, at any rate, believed Manion would agree to the proposal. This surmise was based on conversation with the leader.

[101]Manion Papers, Vol. 7, Hogarth to Manion, n.d., and enclosure. Part of Meighen's memorandum and Manion's response is in Graham, *Meighen*, III, 92–3.

[102]Manion Papers, Vol. 15, Manion to Hepburn, Feb. 7, 1940. I am indebted to the Hon. R. A. Bell for sending me a copy of the memorandum Reynolds left with Manion (letter to author, April 14, 1965).

with the difficult task they faced, joined with several other Toronto Conservatives in pressing the scheme upon him.[103] "I told them, among other things," Manion later noted, "that if I did not get a vote at all I should rather own my own soul than follow this stupid course."[104]

The inventor of this truly extraordinary plan is unknown, but certainly the idea was a foolish one. Manion believed that he was being asked to act as "a sort of front man" for Bennett or Meighen.[105] Howard Ferguson, the former premier of Ontario who had also urged the plan, was told by Manion that "I would at once be accused by the liberals . . . of promising such things as no conscription . . . and that I was to be bought out immediately after . . . to allow Bennett or Meighen or some other to do things I had promised I should not do."[106] It is impossible to judge the accuracy of Manion's assessment, but in the Byzantine atmosphere of intrigue which characterized Conservative politics at this time, it would seem unlikely that he was too far off the mark. Certainly if he had agreed to the proposal, he would have been devastatingly attacked by the Liberals.

As it was, the national government campaign was encountering difficulties. Did all candidates have to be good Conservatives—or was there room for the dissatisfied from the other parties? Was the Conservative party still the Conservative party—or was it now the National Government party? Within a week of the national government statement, there were demands that party nominating conventions be opened to all comers.[107] At first, Manion demurred, stating to one correspondent "that under any circumstances probably seventy-five to eighty-five per cent of our vote will be a Conservative vote anyway."[108] It soon became clear, however, that influential newspapers considered the national government plank to be "a cloak for the Tory Party,"[109] and strong efforts were made to secure some genuinely non-Conservative candidates. These efforts, almost without exception, foundered in the constituency associations on the "deep-rooted objections by unreasonable Tories to anything but a straight Tory convention."[110] The problem was compli-

[103]Bruce Papers, Mrs. Bruce's Diary, Feb. 6, 1940.

[104]Manion Papers, Vol. 45, Memorandum, March 27, 1941.

[105]*Ibid.*, Vol. 7, Manion to Hogarth, Feb. 2, 1940; Vol. 66, Diary, Feb. 1, 1940.

[106]*Ibid.*, Vol. 45, Memorandum, March 27, 1941.

[107]*Ibid.*, Vol. 14, Clark to Manion, Feb. 3, 1940; Progressive Conservative Party Files, File BC-B-1c, R. L. Maitland to Manion, Feb. 5, 1940; Bruce Papers, Mrs. Bruce's Diary, Feb. 6, 1940.

[108]Manion Papers, Vol. 14, Manion to Clark, Feb. 5, 1940.

[109]*Ibid.*, Earl Lawson to Manion, Feb. 13, 1940.

[110]Progressive Conservative Party Files, File BC-B-1c, Maitland to Robb, Feb. 8, 1940; File BC-B-1a, Robb to A. C. Des Brisay, Feb. 9, 1940.

cated further when Manion was cornered by the press on his campaign train and asked to state his preference for the party name—Conservative or National Government? Manion knew, as his private secretary later noted, "that if he issued a statement that all candidates supporting him were to be designated Conservative he would not succeed in appeasing— as he was seeking to do—certain influential newspapers and certain other influential interests who could not be persuaded that the National Government policy was anything but a hypocritical camouflage."[111] Eventually the Conservative leader issued a statement that he personally would prefer to use the term National Government in describing his candidates.[112] The change did nothing to help Manion's cause; instead, it angered many who believed that to throw away the honoured name of Conservative was going too far.[113] The futility of the entire exercise became apparent when both Mackenzie King and J. S. Woodsworth, the C.C.F. leader, indicated that none of their followers would join a national government led by Manion.[114] The Conservatives, one writer noted at the time, "appear to be all dressed up for coalition and to have nowhere to go to coalesce, not to add having no particular purpose to coalesce about."[115]

National government had not developed into the effective issue Manion had hoped, and he was having great difficulty in finding a stick with which to beat the government. "The general criticism of Dr. Manion's campaign," one unfriendly Conservative wrote, "is that he has been too diffuse instead of centering upon the war as his issue, plus the magnificent constitutional issue Mr. King gave him when he ran away from Parliament. Can you imagine a party leader talking about tariffs, about a ministry for youth, about port administration and about the Bennett government's wheat policy, when he has these other issues placed in his lap?"[116] This was an understandable criticism, perhaps, but it is difficult to see what else Manion could have done. The constitutional issue had been defused almost immediately by the action

[111]Hanson Papers, File P-450-M, Bell to Hanson, April 16, 1941.
[112]Politicus, "Who Did Support National Government?" p. 8.
[113]E.g., Hanson Papers, Hanson to T. Cantley, April 1, 1940.
[114]W. L. Mackenzie King, *Mackenzie King to the People of Canada* (Ottawa, 1940), radio address, Feb. 23, 1940, pp. 36–53.
[115]B. K. Sandwell, "The Federal Election," *Queen's Quarterly*, XLVII (spring, 1940), 93.
[116]Bennett Papers, Notable Persons File, Norman MacLeod to Bennett, March 9, 1940. Cf. Dafoe Papers, Microfilm roll M-79, Dafoe to Grant Dexter, Feb. 23, 1940. These proposals were lifted from a draft election platform prepared early in 1939 in anticipation of a peacetime election. The platform in several versions is in P.A.C., R. A. Bell Papers, M.G. 27, Vol. 1.

of the daily press in condoning King's actions, and there seemed little to be gained in attempting to press this point. The war issue was more complex. The phoney war, as it then was, was not rousing the people against the government, and most seemed satisfied with Mackenzie King's "limited liability" policies.[117] There was no popular support for conscription anywhere in the Dominion, Manion later recalled, and "before every meeting . . . the first demand by our candidates was that I make it very clear I was opposed to conscription for overseas service."[118] Despite Manion's repeated pledges against compulsory service,[119] however, the mood of the nation was such that the most effective weapon against him was the belief that his party, if elected, was more likely to implement conscription than were the Liberals under Mackenzie King.[120] Any remarks on the war, therefore, except perhaps charges of Liberal inefficiency could only reinforce the fear that the Conservatives were too aggressive, too imperialist, too likely to press for conscription as in 1917. Paradoxically, apparently few Canadians believed that King's Liberals favoured a massive war effort, and as a result the Liberals were able to stress the war more than their opponents.[121] *"There* is only *one outstanding issue,"* Norman Rogers, the Minister of National Defence, told a radio audience. "It is the choice of those to whom you are prepared to commit the direction of the Canadian war effort during the critical years that lie ahead of us."[122]

When Manion turned his attention to other areas of public concern, however, he was instantly attacked for neglecting the war, the central issue. Promises to increase the price of wheat by 40 per cent were met by sardonic calls for the Conservative leader to increase the price of fish at the same time.[123] The Montreal *Gazette* in an editorial on

[117]"It is a fantastic situation," wrote W. D. Herridge of his attempts to shape a war party out of Social Credit and other motley groups. "We try to form a war party in a country which scarcely realizes it is at war. All we hope to do now could be done with ease six months hence." Saskatchewan Provincial Archives, G. H. Barr Papers, Herridge to Barr, Feb. 5, 1940.

[118]Memorandum by Manion quoted in *Ottawa Journal*, March 20, 1942, p. 10. Cf. Herridge Papers, Herridge to Bennett, May 24, 1941; F. A. Brewin, "Conscription in Canada," *Canadian Forum*, XIX (Feb., 1940), 342.

[119]R. J. Manion, "The Issue as I See It," *Maclean's*, LIII (March 15, 1940), 53.

[120]E.g., Manion Papers, Vol. 16, Manion to his son, March 4, 1940; Vol. 66, Diary, March 26, 1940; Hanson Papers, Hanson to A. Davidson, March 25, 1940. Cf. *National Government Publicity News* in Manion Papers, Vol. 61, for Conservative efforts to counter this Liberal line.

[121]E.g., advertisements in the *Halifax Chronicle-Herald*, March 25, 1940.

[122]Rogers Papers, 1940 Election Speeches, Address, Feb. 19, 1940. Cf. Douglas Library, Queen's University, C. G. Power Papers, [Norman Lambert?] Memorandum re 1940 Election Campaign, Feb. 1, 1940, which details Liberal thinking.

[123]*Halifax Chronicle-Herald*, Feb. 20, 1940, p. 8. See also Gardiner Papers, Election Material, Address, "Manion at Brandon," n.d.

February 20 entitled "Is it a War Election?" criticized Manion for not sticking to war issues and then blasted the unfortunate leader for his position on railway unification. In a national broadcast, Mackenzie King also drew attention to this issue. Manion had left a path "strewn with promissory notes," the Prime Minister declared. "At no place has he enunciated a war policy. At every place he has left behind him a peace promise. Nearly every promise has been designed to influence unduly the community in which it has been made. Nearly every promise has been a promise to spend the tax-payer's money . . . on something which has nothing to do with the winning of the war. . . ."[124]

When Manion attempted to point out inefficiency and alleged corruption in the Department of National Defence, he was hampered by a lack of concrete evidence. If there was corruption and inefficiency, it had not, thanks to King's tactics, been aired in Parliament, and the Liberals easily squelched most charges by demanding that the Conservatives cite specific instances.[125] Manion knew, for example, that a British Columbia infantry battalion had gone overseas without winter underwear, but for several weeks his source for this information, General J. A. Clark of Vancouver, refused to allow him to make details public.[126] Frustrated and angered by the Minister of National Defence's denials,[127] Manion allowed his Irish temper to run loose, and he called Norman Rogers an "irresponsible little falsifier" and an "unscrupulous little man" with a "contempt for truth."[128] Manion overstepped the bounds in this instance, and many Conservatives were greatly perturbed. "One can expect personal vindictiveness, spite and venom from certain elements of the population," a prominent Conservative wrote to Rogers, "but when the lead is given by the party leader I turn in disgust."[129]

The disgust with Manion's campaign, whether motivated by distaste for his policies or for his tactics, made itself felt most sharply in its effect on the party finances. The problem still was centred in Montreal. The attitude of the *Gazette* and the *Star*, both traditionally Conservative and both more or less hostile to the leader if not to the party, was symptomatic of the reaction to Manion's fund-raisers in the Quebec metropolis. As Montreal and Toronto provided the money for the party's central fund, the effects of the drought were felt across the country.

[124]King, *Mackenzie King to the People of Canada*, radio address, March 21, 1940, pp. 77–8.
[125]Rogers Papers, 1940 Election Speeches, Address, March 14, 1940.
[126]Manion Papers, Vol. 14, Manion–Clark correspondence, Feb. 2, 3, 5, 6, 1940. Cf. Toronto *Evening Telegram*, March 9, 1940.
[127]Rogers Papers, 1940 Election Speeches, Address, n.d.
[128]Clipping from *Windsor Star*, March 18, 1940, in Manion Papers, Vol. 61.
[129]Rogers Papers, Correspondence 1940, Henry Borden to Rogers, March 19, 1940.

New Brunswick had always received its funds from Montreal, Hanson wrote Meighen in a letter pleading for his intervention in that city, but nothing was forthcoming this time. "I could handle my own position," he wrote, "but no other candidate in New Brunswick can do this and we have got to have money for them." The tragedy, Hanson added, was that prospects were excellent in New Brunswick.[130] Meighen's reply, while indicating that he had made some quiet efforts in Montreal, was hardly hopeful. With J. W. McConnell and his *Montreal Star* opposed "and the others quite frigid toward our present leader," he said, "I don't think we can get anywhere there."[131]

The financial situation did not ease as the campaign progressed. In March, the election was being financed on a day-to-day basis and current accounts were in arrears.[132] Candidates who had been promised financial support from the central fund either received less than pledged or, in some cases, nothing at all. Less than $100,000 was available for the 82 seats in Ontario, the area in which party hopes were brightest.[133] Throughout the nation as a whole, one of Manion's fund-raisers later recalled, the Conservative party spent only some $470,000 to $500,000, ending up $25,000 in debt.[134] In 1930, by way of comparison, the Canadian Pacific Railway and the Bank of Montreal had each contributed $50,000 to the party's election coffers, eight additional firms had donated $25,000 or more, and the Conservatives had raised $500,000 in Montreal alone.[135] In 1940, apparently without exception, these large donors withheld their support from Manion. Exact Liberal expenditures are unknown, but Senator Norman Lambert, president of the National Liberal Federation in 1940, was quoted as saying that his party spent $1 million in the election.[136] This is almost certainly a low estimate. Liberal fund-raising was decentralized, making it difficult to determine the total expenditure, but Senator Lambert's diaries indicate beyond any doubt that the Liberals had all the money they needed. No candidate in any province went short,[137] a striking contrast to the unhappy plight

130Meighen Papers, Hanson to Meighen, Feb. 24, 1940.

131*Ibid.*, Meighen to G. B. Jones, Feb. 26, 1940.

132Manion Papers, Vol. 14, Allan Ross to Manion, March 7, 1940.

133*Ibid.*, Bell to R. H. Wilson, April 29, 1940.

134Harry Price Interview, Sept. 8, 1964; Manion Papers, Vol. 11, Ross to Manion, April 29, 1940; Hanson Papers, File O-160-F, W. H. Price to Hanson, Nov. 27, 1940.

135Manion Papers, Vol. 11, List of contributors to Sept. 2, 1930. The 1940 list is in *ibid.*, April 22, 1940.

136Eugene E. Harrill, "The Structure of Organization and Power in Canadian Political Parties: A Study of Party Financing," unpublished Ph.D. dissertation, University of North Carolina at Chapel Hill, 1958, p. 180.

137Lambert Diaries, January 23–March 29, 1940.

of many Conservatives. Manion's "radicalism" and his unfriendly attitude to business had cost him and his party dearly.

The gruelling winter campaign ended on March 26, 1940. As late as March 12, Manion foresaw gains in the Maritimes, Quebec, and Ontario.[138] Other observers shared his optimism. Hanson looked for five seats in New Brunswick and at least six seats in Nova Scotia; Robb, the Dominion organizer, expected eight seats in British Columbia; and the party organizer in Saskatchewan promised eight seats.[139] Two capable political reporters predicted that Manion would be returned with at least ninety seats, and with strength in Ontario, the Maritimes, Manitoba, and British Columbia.[140] These predictions only made the shattering defeat all the more unpalatable for Manion. "We are swamped . . . ," Manion wrote in his diary on election night.[141] The rout was complete. Only 40 Conservatives were elected to the House of Commons as opposed to 184 Liberals, the largest parliamentary majority thus far achieved in Canada. Manion himself lost his seat, and his party garnered barely 30 per cent of the popular vote. Twenty-five of the party's forty members came from Ontario constituencies, and only one was from Quebec.[142] Only three members of the new caucus had cabinet experience—Hanson, Grote Stirling of British Columbia, and W. Earl Rowe—and none of these had served even as long as one year in the Bennett government. The Conservative party in parliament was left even weaker than it had been after the defeat of 1935.[143]

Manion's immediate assessment of the reasons for his defeat was

[138]Manion Papers, Vol. 14, Manion to Ross, March 12, 1940.

[139]Meighen Papers, Hanson to Meighen, Feb. 24, 1940; Progressive Conservative Party Files, File Y-Y-1a, Robb to Mrs. Black, March 16, 1940, and File S-S-7, A. Kendall to Robb, March 23, 1940.

[140]*Winnipeg Free Press*, March 22, 1940, p. 5; "Backstage at Ottawa," *Maclean's*, LIII (March 1, 1940), 10.

[141]Manion Papers, Vol. 66, Diary, March 26, 1940.

[142]The antipathy to Manion in Montreal was such that even anti-Manion Conservatives lost their seats. One of the victims, C. H. Cahan, an M.P. for fifteen years, wrote to Lapointe protesting the Liberal tactics. Although everyone knew he was anti-Manion, Liberals had tried to smear him by saying he was against the woman's vote, relief, and old-age pensions. In French-speaking districts, Liberals said his name was Cohen; to Protestants, they said he was Catholic. Lapointe Papers, Vol. 11, Cahan to Lapointe, May 17, 1940.

[143]Conservative representation was as follows (1935 results in brackets): P.E.I., 0 (0); N.S., 1 (0); N.B., 5 (1); Que., 1 (5); Ont., 25 (25); Man., 1 (1); Sask., 2 (1); Alta., 0 (1); B.C., 4 (5); Yukon, 1 (1). The Quebec Conservative listed himself as an independent Conservative. Three Liberals included in the total of 184 were listed as Independent Liberals and three were listed as Liberal-Progressives. The C.C.F. returned eight members, and New Democracy (Social Credit) ten. Two Independents and one Unity party member completed the House of Commons of 245.

that "anti-war sentiment across Canada thinks King less aggressive. . . ."[144] The results of a survey of Conservative candidates taken in April provided little evidence to force the Conservative leader to alter his appraisal. People were afraid of conscription, he believed, and they were certain King would never implement it. "Undoubtedly," he added, "the big item was the fact that I had with me most of those who are sometimes called the ultra-Imperialists and the people largely felt that King is doing enough."[145] There were other reasons for the defeat, but fear of conscription was high on almost every list. In the constituency of York West, on the outskirts of Toronto, for example, the successful Conservative candidate, Rodney Adamson, asked his association members for their opinions as to the cause of the party's defeat:[146]

When the ballot boxes were opened, they contained two hundred and eighty opinions . . .

Reason	%
Conscription	20.6
Religion of leader	19.9
Change of party name	12.1
Lack of policy	10
Wrong leader	8.9
Etc.	

Similar opinions were expressed in other areas of the country.[147]

Many, however, disagreed with these assessments and placed the blame squarely on the party leader. "Now [Manion] is saying that it was the anti-conscription vote that defeated him," a Conservative jounalist wrote to Bennett.

I do not think he is on sound ground in this assertion. The explanation of his monumental failure, I am convinced, is simply the fact that he did not inspire confidence in any quarter in himself as a possible war-time Prime

---

144Manion Papers, Vol. 66, Diary, March 26, 1940.

145*Ibid.*, Vol. 17, Manion to his son, April 18, 1940. Curiously, the C.C.F., the only party to take a stand against full participation in the war, suffered at the polls. The C.C.F. were hurt for being against the war, while the Conservatives, Manion said, were hurt for being pro-war. Evidently the Liberals straddled the middle of the road very effectively. P.A.C., C.C.F. Records, M.G. 30, Vol. 77, H. Gargrave to David Lewis, April 3, 1940.

146A. Rodney Adamson Papers, Election Correspondence 1940, Memorandum, n.d. The effect of Manion's religion on the electorate is difficult to determine. Both press and politicians seem to have avoided the subject but, to judge by the voters of York West, his Catholicism may have been damaging. In a campaign that ran into difficulties from every quarter, however, it is impossible to isolate one factor.

147Progressive Conservative Party Files, File PEI-Q-1a, Robb to P. W. Turner, April 4, 1940; Hanson Papers, Hanson to C. D. Gordon, April 5, 1940; Meighen Papers, E. N. McGirr to Meighen, June 22, 1940; Manion Papers, Vol. 14, L. H. Snider to Manion, May 3, 1940.

Minister. . . . By [his campaign of promises], he simply gave Mr. King and the Liberals an excuse for claiming that he was running away from the war issue, and that the Government alone was confining its case to an appeal for a mandate to prosecute the war successfully. While I do think the anti-conscription vote went with the Government, I also think that Dr. Manion failed to get the vote of the imperialistic and loyal section of the electorate.[148]

The Conservative press adopted a similar view. The *Gazette*, of course, blamed the defeat on Manion, urged the party to go to the right of the Liberals, and called for a re-dedication to Conservative principles "adapted but not distorted" to fit changes in the economy,[149] while the Vancouver *Province* stated that there was nothing in Manion's record to cause the electorate to believe that he would co-operate more enthusiastically with the empire than would Mackenzie King.[150] In these circumstances, it was almost certain that Manion's position as leader would be placed in jeopardy.

The first reaction of Manion himself to the election results was that he should give up the leadership. "I still anxious to quit," he scrawled in his diary early in April. "My energy all used up."[151] There were few visible signs of a popular movement for his resignation, however ("though of course there is the little group who opposed me right from the beginning and who have already shown signs of desiring me to quit"[152]) and Manion began to reconsider his course. His friends urged him to stay—"must think of country and party—would smash party," he wrote of their arguments[153]—and he did not want to create the impression that he was running away.[154] He continued to agonize over his decision throughout April 1940, but he took no positive action other than to call a caucus of the members for May 13, four days before the opening of the new session.

Strong opposition to the leader was developing within the parliamentary party. "I think, between ourselves," wrote Herbert A. Bruce, newly elected for Parkdale (Toronto), "considering the result it is just as well that Bob went down with the others. If he resigns as I presume he will . . . it will relieve the party of a very weak leader."[155] R. B. Hanson, returned to the House of Commons after an absence of five years, held similar views. "I do not see how Manion can stay," he wrote to a Saskatchewan member. "I have not told him this, but without a

[148]Bennett Papers, Notable Persons File, N. MacLeod to Bennett, April 8, 1940.
[149]March 27, 28, 1940, p. 8.
[150]March 27, 1940, p. 4.
[151]Manion Papers, Vol. 66, Diary, April 6, 1940.
[152]*Ibid.*, Vol. 17, Manion to his son, April 18, 1940.
[153]*Ibid.*, Vol. 66, Diary, April 20, 1940.
[154]*Ibid.*, Vol. 14, Manion to Stevens, April 22, 1940.
[155]Bruce Papers, Bruce to McCullagh, April 3, 1940.

seat in the House and with such a small party . . . I would not think he will want to stay. . . ."[156] In another letter, he stated the situation as he saw it in blunter terms:

I think we should keep an open mind in regard to your question of the leadership. I have heard from Manion once or twice. He is non-committal, but personally I do not see how he can stay. Of course he was caught unprepared and had not had time to sell himself to the country, especially to those who have usually helped us financially in Montreal. They looked very coldly on his election from the very beginning and the lack of money down here was terrible. We had difficulty in selling Manion to the rank and file of the Party and I think we have got a fairly full support from the extremely Protestant element, but not 100%. Over and above, he failed to attract any appreciable Roman Catholic vote in this part of the country and it is a potent factor against us. I personally do not see how he can stay, but it may be that . . . he will make the attempt, and we may have trouble.[157]

Apparently Manion was unaware of these cross-currents within the caucus, for he wrote to a friend that the "Members who have spoken to me have all taken a [favourable] attitude, with the exception of one who was non-committal. . . ."[158]

As the conflicting pressures on Manion continued, he attempted to evade his decision as long as possible. "Have about decided to offer my resignation," he wrote in his diary on April 29. "Then let [the caucus] do as they wish—*and take the responsibility*. Personally I hope they accept. Would like to be free."[159] Several days later, Manion wrote to his journalistic friends advising them of his decision to submit his resignation, and he even leaked a delphic statement to the Canadian Press wire service:

In unusually well-informed Conservative circles on Parliament Hill, the opinion is expressed that at the Caucus of Conservative Members of Parliament on Monday, the 13th, the present leader, Dr. Manion, will submit his resignation to caucus. If the caucus accepts the resignation, that would mean the retirement of Dr. Manion as leader. If, on the contrary, they refuse to accept it, it would be a vote of confidence in the present leader and a request that he continue in his position.[160]

Clearly Manion had not decided that he wanted to surrender his job. "It may be absolutely as you say in regard to my sticking," he wrote a confidant on May 9, "and I am ready to do it but only on the condition that the elected Members of the House, by a good majority if not

156Hanson Papers, Hanson to E. Perley, M.P., April 8, 1940.
157*Ibid.*, Hanson to J. R. MacNicol, April 11, 1940.
158Manion Papers, Vol. 14, Manion to Hogarth, April 30, 1940.
159*Ibid.*, Vol. 66, Diary, April 29, 1940.
160*Ibid.*, Vol. 14, Manion to J. Bird, C. G. Dunn, etc., May 9, 1940; Vol. 61, press release, May 10, 1940.

unanimously, show some confidence in me. If they do this, it will be a reply to the groups . . . who have been gunning for me for so long." On this same day, however, the wavering leader wrote in his diary that "[I] have decided to put in my resignation. . . . Hope they accept it!"[161] In these circumstances, the final decision could only be made by the caucus.

The first task of the caucus when it convened was to select the man who would act as Leader of the Opposition in the first session of the new parliament, for even if Manion remained as party leader he would be out of the House of Commons until he won a seat in a by-election. Polite jockeying for the opening had been going on throughout April and May, and five contenders were nominated for the post: R. B. Hanson; Howard Green, the representative from Vancouver South; A. C. Casselman, party whip and M.P. for Grenville-Dundas; Joseph Harris, Toronto member and unsuccessful candidate for the leadership at the convention of 1938; and Grote Stirling, Minister of National Defence in the last year of the Bennett administration. Stirling dropped out of the race after one ballot, and he was followed by Green and Casselman. In the last of the five ballots, Hanson (who had, as he wrote Bennett, "made it quite plain that I was not seeking [the post] but if I could be of service and the Party wanted me unanimously I would serve until my successor was appointed"[162]) won narrowly over Harris.[163]

Late in the afternoon the caucus turned to the main business of the day. Manion, after assessing the causes of the election disaster, turned to his own position:

> In politics, success is the criterion by which leadership is judged. It is true that Tupper, Borden and Meighen all experienced more than one defeat before success or retirement; but after full deliberation I feel that there are certain circumstances having a strong bearing on my own case which influence me to take the course of laying in your hands, for your considera-tion and action, my resignation from the position of Leader of the Con-servative Party, at this first Caucus of Conservative Members since the election.
>
> My election as Leader took place at a National Convention; but a Con-vention is not a continuing body, the only group who at the moment have any authority to speak for our Party from a Federal stand point, are the Conservative Members of the House of Commons.
>
> If you accept my resignation I shall be quite content, for my personal wish is to retire. But I realize that my first obligation is to the Party, as is

---

[161]*Ibid.*, Vol. 14, Manion to C. G. Dunn, May 9, 1940; Vol. 66, Diary, May 9, 1940.

[162]Bennett Papers, Notable Persons File, Hanson to Bennett, July 4, 1940.

[163]Hanson Papers, File P-200, Hanson to L. L. Golden, June 17, 1940; clippings from *Windsor Star* and *Ottawa Citizen*, May 14, 1940, in Manion Papers, Vol. 61.

yours. Therefore, if you decide that *in the best interests of the Party*, you cannot accept my resignation, my duty will be to return to the House of Commons as soon as possible to render the highest possible public service of which I am capable.

In order not to embarrass discussion, I shall now leave the Caucus, merely suggesting to you that it might be advisable not to come to a final conclusion until perhaps Wednesday [May 15]. . . .[164]

After Manion left the meeting, discussion began with a motion that the resignation be accepted. The mover and seconder of this motion, Earl Rowe and Herbert Bruce, had met with Manion before the caucus at his request. They had been shown the speech Manion proposed to deliver and had been informed that it was his desire that the resignation be accepted. Many years later, Rowe stated that he would never have taken the initiative had Manion not indicated that he wanted to be released.[165] Many of the members did not favour an immediate decision, however, and a delegation was sent out to see Manion: ". . . they seemed in a hurry [Manion noted in his diary]—met me by their request . . . at 7:30 asking me if I did not favor a conference of all the members, cand.'s, sen.'s, prov. leaders, etc. They thought 'caucus not sufficiently representative' etc. I assented. Told them conference must be within 6 wks. to 2 mos. They said even sooner."[166] The idea of a conference was dropped shortly after the delegation returned to caucus, however, when Douglas Ross, a Toronto M.P., seconded by Harry Jackman, another Toronto member, moved again that Manion's resignation be accepted.[167] This time, there was no long discussion, and, as Hanson later wrote, "the conclusion reached by the large majority was that it was impossible ever to build him up, and that, while we liked him personally, it was better for the Party that he should go, and go now."[168] The vote in the caucus was twenty-six to five in favour of the motion,[169] and only the formalities now remained. A committee of three was appointed to prepare a formal letter of appreciation to Manion,[170] and the leader was notified of the result.

[164]Manion Papers, Vol. 65, Speech to caucus, May 13, 1940 (typed copy).

[165]The Hon. Earl Rowe Interview, Sept. 9, 1964; Bruce Papers, Mrs. Bruce's Diary, May, 1940.

[166]Manion Papers, Vol. 66, Diary, May 13, 1940. Cf. Bruce Papers, Mrs. Bruce's Diary, May, 1940.

[167]Jackman Interview, Sept. 8, 1964; clipping from *Vancouver Sun*, May 23, 1940, in Manion Papers, Vol. 61.

[168]Bennett Papers, Notable Persons File, Hanson to Bennett, July 4, 1940.

[169]The five M.P.s who voted for Manion were Green, Desmond, Diefenbaker, Homuth, and Harris (Manion Papers, Vol. 66, Diary, May 14, 1940).

[170]Bruce Papers, Bruce to Hogarth, May 16, 1940. The letter of appreciation is in Manion Papers, Vol. 61, J. R. MacNicol to Manion, May 14, 1940.

"It was damned rotten of them to do it in the insulting manner in which they did it," a bitter Manion wrote after his resignation had been accepted. "Seemed almost indecent haste." "As usual," he recorded in his diary, "I find that some who owed me much and other supposed friends *were* the men who hurried acceptance of my resignation. . . ."[171] And yet, although he had been prepared to stay on as leader, Manion was not entirely sorry to take his leave of the Conservative party. He had seen his policies destroyed more by bad luck than by bad management. His plan of seeking an accommodation with Quebec had been an early casualty of the war and of Duplessis' schemes. The chances of defeating King in the election were wiped out by the war and by the memories of conscription. With the collapse of his policies, Manion was exposed to the full force of the hostility of the Montreal interests, and his replacement was inevitable.

It has become fashionable for both historians and politicians to write off Manion as a lightweight of little consequence.[172] This is grossly unfair. He did not have the intellectual force of a Meighen or a Bennett, but he did have integrity, intelligence, and political courage. His one great mistake, and it was the error which ultimately lost him the leadership, was in opposing, rather than appeasing, the party's powerful business and financial supporters. But this was an error of principle, and Manion had acted on his belief that he was serving the best interests of his party and his country. Who can say that he was wrong? Similarly, his attitude to Quebec was based on principle. After Duplessis' defeat in October 1939, he could easily have changed course and launched an appeal aimed exclusively at English-speaking Canadians. That he did not was possibly a political error, but it was certainly in the national interest. Manion made mistakes, to be sure, and he had the misfortune of facing Mackenzie King, the greatest political tactician in Canadian history, but he was not a nonentity. The forces that defeated him were entrenched within the Conservative party, and only a full-scale assault could drive them out. Manion had lacked the necessary firepower, but other challengers would follow him. In the meantime, however, with great events portending, the Conservative party was in its weakest condition in history.

[171]Manion Papers, Vol. 8, Manion to C. D. H. McAlpine, May 25, 1940; Vol. 66, Diary, May 13, May 14, 1940.
[172]". . . the honest, lightweight Manion," Bruce Hutchison, *Mr. Prime Minister, 1867–1964* (Don Mills, 1964), p. 262; Graham, *Meighen*, III, 84–94; the Hon. T. A. Crerar Interview, July 17, 1964; the Hon. M. J. Coldwell Interview, July 6, 1963.

4.   The Plight of the Party

R. B. Hanson succeeded to the Conservative leadership three days after the German armies flung themselves upon the Low Countries and France. Within five weeks, most of western Europe was in the grasp of Hitler's new order, Great Britain was seriously threatened, and Canada had become England's ranking ally. The impact of these events upon Canada and Canadian politics was profound. The limited liability policies of the phoney war period were tossed aside, the armed forces were rapidly strengthened, and an alliance was concluded with the United States. The Conservative party—disorganized, without funds, and with a new, untried, temporary leader—was also affected by the startling events of the early summer of 1940. Conscription became a respectable topic for the first time in the war, and Mackenzie King was again plagued with demands for national government. In the months that followed, however, differences on war policy developed within the Conservative party, and the growing ascendance of the conscriptionists became evident.

Hanson, the man selected by his peers to lead the Conservative party in the House of Commons through the critical days of the war, was not "a politician of brilliant abilities or any high debating powers," the *Round Table*'s Canadian correspondent reported, "but he is an able lawyer and has, along with a judicial temper and an agreeable personality, a vein of shrewdness and an instinct for parliamentary strategy. . . ."[1] Born in 1879, Hanson built a large, prosperous legal practice in the small New Brunswick capital of Fredericton, twice was elected mayor of his town, and represented the constituency of York-Sunbury in the House of Commons from 1921 to 1935. In 1934, Prime Minister Bennett named him to the cabinet as Minister of Trade and Commerce, and although he performed his duties competently, he was engulfed in the Liberal landslide of 1935. Hanson had little if any personal ambition, but after regaining his seat in 1940, he was not averse to accepting the post of Leader of the Opposition and, indeed, in May 1940 he was

[1]"A New War Effort," *Round Table*, XXX (Sept., 1940), 894.

probably the best qualified member of the caucus. Immediately caucus had selected him, however, Hanson and Herbert Bruce approached Arthur Meighen and asked him to leave the Senate, return to the lower chamber, and again become leader of the party.[2] "They really thought that he would agree," Mrs. Bruce noted in her diary, and for a time Meighen seriously considered the suggestion.[3] But, "largely I think because he thought he could not accomplish the desired result," Hanson said, "and also I believe because of his abhorrence at getting back into the political maelstrom,"[4] he declined. In the meantime, Hanson was left to determine the party's policy in the entirely new situation created by the collapse of the Allied position in Europe.

". . . I believe our position has immeasurably improved," wrote the new leader of his party, "not so much because of any actions on our part but because King's stock has gone down in a most surprising and astonishing manner. It should not be surprising or astonishing either," he added, "because there has been masterly inactivity in their war effort."[5] Hanson's assessment of the situation was probably correct, for King's domestic position had been weakened by the reverses at the front. Demands were made in the House of Commons for his resignation. "In this dreadful hour of crisis," one platitudinous Conservative M.P. stated, "when the very existence of everything we hold dear, hangs by a thread, I solemnly implore the Prime Minister, for the good of his country, to emulate the example of Mr. Chamberlain, who, with much less reason to do so than he has, resigned his office in the interest of sustaining public confidence in the ability and determination of the government to carry the war to a successful conclusion." "The greatest contribution you can make towards winning this war, Mr. Prime Minister," another Conservative said, paraphrasing a speaker at Westminster, "is for you to hand in your resignation."[6] Mr. King was not Mr. Chamberlain, however, and as M. J. Coldwell of the C.C.F. reminded the House, "whether we . . . like it or not the Prime Minister less than two months ago received the largest endorsation [*sic*] that a government has ever received in the history of Canada."[7] However

[2]Bruce Papers, Mrs. Bruce's Diary, May 1940; Hanson Papers, File O-160-F-1, Hanson to G. B. Foster, June 19, 1940; Meighen Papers, "Conservative Party leadership, 1940" Folder; Graham, *Meighen*, III, 94.

[3]Bruce Papers, Mrs. Bruce's *Diary*, May, 1940; Meighen Papers, Meighen to Willie Juneau, May 21, 1940.

[4]Hanson Papers, File O-150, Hanson to D. C. Coleman, June 11, 1940.

[5]Bennett Papers, Notable Persons File, Hanson to Bennett, July 4, 1940.

[6]House of Commons, *Debates*, May 21, 1940, p. 108 (Mr. Cockeram); May 23, 1940, p. 161 (Mr. J. A. Ross).

[7]*Ibid.*, May 30, 1940, p. 354.

extreme its tenor, the Opposition criticism nevertheless did reflect a popular disquiet, a feeling that not enough was being done.[8] With the fall of France the demands for action became more insistent.

The French capitulation spurred Hanson to action. ". . . I thought the matter over all night," he wrote to Bennett,

feeling that something drastic had to be done to stir [the government] out of their inertness and complacency. I finally decided on three things—(1) that [the Prime Minister] should declare a state of national emergency; (2) that he should pass legislation putting at the disposition of the State all the man-power and material resources of the nation; and (3) that in order to effectively carry out (1) and (2), especially (2), he would have to have a National Government. . . .

Accordingly, I sought an interview, taking Stirling [his seat-mate and the Minister of National Defence, 1934–1935] with me.

I prefaced my remarks by stating that I believed the position demanded immediate action, that I was not actuated in any degree by political or partisan motives, but that I felt I had to insist that steps be taken at once to meet the situation. I was laying down principles to him rather than details of any measures, and I placed before him my proposals.[9]

"They asked me," King recorded in his diary on June 17, "for the sake of the country, would I not feel that I could change my view on conscription." There was absolutely no chance of this. "In the first place," the Prime Minister said, "I believed it would create a worse situation in Canada than it would remedy." If it ever became necessary to impose conscription for overseas service, King added, "I would be ready to step out."[10] In addition, the Prime Minister also stated that conscription would produce "civil war in Quebec," or so Hanson said.[11] Perhaps to his surprise, Hanson found Mackenzie King not unwilling to consider compulsory service for home defence, and within a few days of the fall of France, therefore, the National Resources Mobilization Act, which authorized "special emergency powers to permit of the mobilization of all the effective resources of the nation, both human and material, for the purpose of the defence and security of Canada," was law.[12]

[8]E.g., Clifford Bowering, *Service: The Story of the Canadian Legion, 1925–1960* (Ottawa, 1960), p. 107; Herridge Papers, Herridge to Hanson, May 15, 1940; Hanson Papers, File P-450-C, Hanson to Clark, May 21, 1940.

[9]Bennett Papers, Notable Persons File, Hanson to Bennett, July 4, 1940; Hanson Papers, File W-110, Hanson to T. G. Norris, June 20, 1940; Bruce Papers, Mrs. Bruce's Diary, June 17, 1940; Pickersgill, *The Mackenzie King Record*, I, 94–5.

[10]Pickersgill, *Mackenzie King Record*, I, 95.

[11]Hanson Papers, File W-110, Hanson to T. G. Norris, June 20, 1940.

[12]Canada, *Statutes*, 4 Geo. VI, c. 13.

Hanson had less success with his demand for national government. The idea had already been broached in the House by Conservative members, but to King it seemed that this demand was always made in conjunction with appeals either for his resignation or for immediate and full conscription.[13] With these considerations in mind, the Prime Minister discussed the question of national government in the House of Commons, saying "that I think a party which represents in this parliament some 183 members out of a total membership of 245 may pretty well claim to be a 'national' government in the truest sense of the word." He was, King did say, quite agreeable to strengthening his government, but there were certain ground rules which would be followed in any future reorganization of the cabinet. First, he would not consider taking as colleagues "any of those in the front benches before me who have said that they thought I was quite unqualified to be the leader of a government at the present time." Furthermore, he continued, one of the first qualifications required of any man taken into the government would be "loyalty to myself, and not a disposition to stab the leader of the party in his breast when he is trying to serve his country to the best of his ability at a time of war."[14]

In Hanson's view, these were specious arguments, and they "made any Union Government, any Government including members of other Parties, any National Government, impossible under [King]." King's requirements, the Conservative leader added, "can only be interpreted as meaning that he places his own political safety above that of the State, and . . . that he assumed that men would join his Government to lead a palace revolution. . . ."[15] Mackenzie King doubtless would have objected publicly to Hanson's verdict, but he very likely agreed with it. The Prime Minister believed that he, and only he, could preserve national unity during the war, and, ever suspicious of the motives of his opponents, he did view the cry for national government as a transparent attempt to remove him from office.

The need to strengthen the government by inviting some prominent public men to join it still existed, however. But, of the first six men approached by the Prime Minister, five declined to "run the risk of spoiling their own reputations by taking responsibilities," King recorded in his diary: "yet those of us who have assumed this job and are carrying it out are being criticized for not taking these 'best brains' . . . into

[13]House of Commons, *Debates*, May 23, 1940, pp. 151, 164; Pickersgill, *Mackenzie King Record*, I, 79–83; House of Commons, *Debates*, June 20, 1940, p. 966 (Mr. W. L. M. King).
[14]House of Commons, *Debates*, June 20, 1940, p. 966.
[15]Bennett Papers, Notable Persons File, Hanson to Bennett, July 4, 1940.

the Cabinet."[16] Following the almost total failure of this first attempt to make his cabinet more representative, King conceived the idea of inviting leading members of the Opposition to become members of the War Committee of the cabinet. He broached the idea to Hanson on June 28, "making it clear," as he said in his diary, "that in the war effort we were not trying in any way to monopolize or conceal."[17] "My first reaction," Hanson wrote to Sir Edward Beatty, "was against Mr. King's . . . proposal. As I understand it, he offered only that I and Stirling should advise and consult."[18] Nonetheless, Hanson spoke with his advisers about the offer, but they also were against the idea, feeling that responsibility without power, which was indeed what they were offered, could only place the party and the leader in an untenable position dependent on King's whims.[19] When, therefore, King told the House of Commons of his suggestion to Hanson, the Conservative leader's reaction was to dismiss the offer as "impossible."[20] The Prime Minister was frankly relieved at this turn of events. "I would never have felt secure," he said, "with any of them in the Ministry. . . ." The Tories "can say nothing more from now on about every effort not having been made to meet their wishes for inside knowledge. . . ."[21]

The rest of the session was anticlimactic. By August 7, when parliament adjourned for three months, Hanson had established a reputation for quiet competence, the caucus had asked him to continue as Leader of the Opposition, and even Mackenzie King was not displeased with the Conservative leader's performance. "The Opposition," he noted in his diary on July 31, "has been helpful in causing the Government to perhaps determine more quickly and definitely what was to be done in some matters than might otherwise have been the case. On the whole, their attitude has been constructively helpful although there has been more party politics than one would have liked to see at a time like this."[22] Coming from the Prime Minister this was high praise indeed,

[16]Pickersgill, *Mackenzie King Record*, I, 100. Those asked to join the cabinet were Angus Macdonald, the Liberal premier of Nova Scotia, who accepted; J. W. McConnell of the *Montreal Star*; J. S. Duncan of Massey-Harris Company; Tom Moore, President of the Trades and Labor Congress; G. W. Spinney of the Bank of Montreal; and J. M. Macdonnell of the National Trust Company.
[17]*Ibid.*
[18]Hanson Papers, File P-100, Hanson to Beatty, July 11, 1940.
[19]*Ibid.*, File P-100-N, Memoranda, n.d. (probably by R. A. Bell, then Hanson's private secretary, and Grote Stirling.)
[20]House of Commons, *Debates*, July 8, 1940, p. 1401; July 11, 1940, p. 1515.
[21]Pickersgill, *Mackenzie King Record*, I, 102.
[22]*Ibid.*, p. 103.

but even more surprising was that Meighen agreed with this assessment. "Hanson is doing very well," he wrote to a friend in Saskatchewan. "One thing you may be sure of, he never over-estimates himself, and is true as steel."[23] The former Prime Minister well knew how difficult it was to push Mackenzie King into action, and he could not fail to be impressed with Hanson's success in getting action on the issue of conscription for home defence. As long as Hanson's course agreed with his, Meighen would support him, but if Hanson should ever "over-estimate himself," Meighen's position could change. This was as yet no problem, however, for on the next issue to arise the two Conservative leaders were in complete agreement.

Through the dreadful summer of 1940, Winston Churchill's splendid, stirring oratory notwithstanding, there was an understandable fear in Canada and the United States that Great Britain might not hold out against German power. In these circumstances, American intervention in some form was necessary. The great hope was that the republic would enter the war as a belligerent, but despite some ill-advised efforts to draw the United States into the war,[24] there was little chance of this with presidential elections only three or four months away. More likely, but still difficult to arrange in view of American neutrality legislation, was some dramatic gesture to indicate clearly that American sentiment and American power were behind the hard-pressed Allied cause. It was to the realization of this hope that Mackenzie King bent his efforts during the early summer of 1940.

Certainly the Canadian Prime Minister was the best man for the job. He had always been friendly to the United States—too friendly, said his Conservative critics[25]—and he was on particularly warm terms with President Roosevelt. More important still, King cherished the hope that one day he could play the role of intermediary, of interpreter, between the United States and the United Kingdom. In his first conversation with the American Minister in Ottawa after his election in 1935, he

[23]Meighen Papers, Meighen to F. R. McMillan, Aug. 2, 1940.
[24]Bennett Papers, Notable Persons File, Meighen to Bennett, July 23, 1940, asking Bennett to arrange for Churchill's assistance in launching a campaign by Canadians and others to press the United States to enter the war. This was, of course, precisely the method not to use. For comments on this point, see Eayrs, *In Defence of Canada*, II, 189–91. But King did add a long postscript to a letter to Roosevelt suggesting how the United States could best operate its neutrality legislation for the benefit of the Allies. Roosevelt Papers, P.S.F. Canada, King to Roosevelt, May 1, 1940.
[25]E.g., Bennett Papers, Notable Persons File, Meighen to Bennett, July 23, 1940; Meighen Papers, Meighen to Lord Beaverbrook, July 31, 1940.

pointed out that he had twice before acted as an intermediary, once for President Theodore Roosevelt and once for Secretary of State Hughes. "Mr. King," the Minister reported, "said that he merely cited these instances to show that he was not only a believer in Canada's role as a possible intermediary between the United States and Great Britain, but that he had actually put it into practice and was prepared to do so again."[26] Although there was no opportunity for the Canadian leader to practise his art for several years, Canadian-American relations had developed warmly, if quietly. Secret staff talks on Pacific defences had taken place in Washington in January 1938,[27] and later that same year Roosevelt had pledged in a speech at Queen's University, Kingston, "that the people of the United States will not stand idly by if domination of Canadian soil is threatened by any other Empire." Within a few days of this unexpected promise, Mackenzie King had returned the favour, vowing that Canada would always act in such a way that unfriendly forces could not "pursue their way, either by land, sea or air, to the United States across Canadian territory."[28] The outbreak of the war made relations between the two North American states more important, and the Nazi victories of May and June 1940 had given King his opportunity to play the interpreter for Churchill and Roosevelt. The "destroyer deal" was in part a product of King's intervention,[29] and his role in this instance was perhaps significant enough that at last the after-dinner oratory about Canada's role as the linch-pin, as the bridge between the old world and the new, had real meaning.

Mackenzie King's services were valuable in the negotiations leading to the destroyer deal, but he had also to consider Canada's defences in the light of the changed war situation. In one of his first interviews with the new American Minister to Canada, the perceptive J. Pierrepont Moffat, the Prime Minister gave his opinion:

[26]Roosevelt Papers, P.S.F. Canada, William Phillips to Roosevelt, enclosing memorandum by Norman Armour, Minister in Canada, Oct. 25, 1935. The previous occasions were when King was asked to interpret American policy on Japan to the United Kingdom at the time of the "Great White Fleet," and when he was asked to secure British support for American action against rum-runners beyond the three-mile limit in 1923.

[27]Eayrs, *In Defence of Canada*, II, 179–82. Roosevelt Papers, P.S.F. State Dept., Sumner Welles to Roosevelt, Dec. 20, 1937; Memorandum, F.D.R. to Welles, Dec. 22, 1937; P.S.F. Welles, Welles to Roosevelt, Jan. 10 and 14, 1938. Richard Kottman, "The Diplomatic Relations of the United States and Canada, 1927–1941," unpublished Ph.D. dissertation, Vanderbilt University, 1958, pp. 463–4.

[28]Eayrs, *In Defence of Canada*, II, 183.

[29]King's role is detailed in Pickersgill, *The Mackenzie King Record*, I, chap. VI; Eayrs, *In Defence of Canada*, II, 197–202; and less usefully in Philip Goodhart, *Fifty Ships That Saved the World* (Toronto, 1965).

Has not the time come for staff talks to begin between the two countries [Moffat recorded after the interview]? There had been informal talks . . . three years ago about the Pacific. Then both countries were at peace; now Canada was at war. Perhaps such a suggestion might embarrass the President; this was the last thing he wanted. On the other hand as no interests were involved, the President might welcome the suggestion. In the circumstances he asked me to feel out the situation and let him know.[30]

Moffat's initial soundings were unproductive, and he noted on June 27 that the "matter did not seem opportune" as yet.[31] Early in July, however, the American domestic scene was more settled, and arrangements were made for Canadian staff officers to meet secretly with American officers. On August 14 Moffat suggested a new approach when he sent a significant cable to Washington assessing the growing Canadian demand for a defence arrangement with the United States:

Even elements which in the past have been least well disposed to us such as the Toronto public and the English-speaking sections of Montreal are now outspoken in its favor. . . .
To Canadians such a joint defence understanding,—whether it took the form of a treaty or merely of publicly announced staff talks,—seems a reasonable reinsurance policy. The old fear that cooperation with the United States would tend to weaken Canada's ties with Great Britain has almost entirely disappeared. Instead, Canada believes that such cooperation would tend to bring Britain and the United States closer together, rather than to force Britain and Canada apart.[32]

Some of Moffat's assumptions were questionable, but his representations had the desired effect. On August 16 Roosevelt conceived the idea of meeting Mackenzie King at Ogdensburg, New York, the next day,[33] and there the two statesmen proceeded to draft the Ogdensburg Agreement.

The Agreement called for the establishment of the Permanent Joint Board on Defence which would at once commence studies relating to sea, land, and air problems. "It will consider in the broad sense," King later told the House of Commons, "the defence of the north half of the western hemisphere."[34] The establishment of the Board had both immediate and future significance. "The most important thing in 1940

[30]Moffat Papers, Vol. 46, Memorandum of conversation with Prime Minister King, June 14, 1940.
[31]*Ibid.*, June 27, 1940; Pickersgill, *Mackenzie King Record*, I, 126–7; William L. Langer and S. Everett Gleason, *The Challenge to Isolation, 1937–1940* (New York, 1952), p. 703.
[32]Roosevelt Papers, P.S.F. Canada, Moffat to Sumner Welles, Aug. 14, enclosed with Welles to Roosevelt, Aug. 16, 1940.
[33]John M. Blum, *From the Morgenthau Diaries. II. Years of Urgency, 1938–1941* (Boston, 1965), p. 180.
[34]House of Commons, *Debates*, Nov. 12, 1940, p. 57.

about the Ogdensburg Agreement," Professor Mansergh has aptly pointed out, "was that it associated the United States with a belligerent Commonwealth; the most important thing about it on the longer view was that the Joint Board it established was permanent."[35] Unfortunately, the first of these considerations was forgotten by some Conservatives who were troubled by the second.

Hanson heard the announcement of the signing of the Agreement on the radio at his home in Fredericton on August 17. He "got quite worked up about the whole thing" and decided to go to Ottawa. "Stirling was there," he wrote to Meighen a few days later, "and we met together and asked King for an interview which he granted to us."

We found out that the whole thing was Roosevelt's idea to help him out with Congress and give him a quid pro quo for anything he might do with Great Britain, but that there are no commitments whatsoever and the only agreement is that of a joint Study Board. . . . At any event King told me . . . that Roosevelt had asked for the interview and asked for the joint board as window dressing which he can take to the Congressional leaders . . . for their allowing him to send the fifty obsolete destroyers to Churchill without any Congressional authority.

My other anxiety was that King was not doing the thing behind Churchill's back and I put the question to him point blank and was assured by him that Churchill knew all about it. . . .

King left the impression with me that Churchill was exceedingly anxious over the whole situation and anxious to get in as much support from the U.S.A. as possible.[36]

After this meeting with the Prime Minister, Hanson issued a brief statement to the press. The Agreement, he said in one of the Conservatives' last public comments of approval for the King-Roosevelt pact, "is an exploratory and consultative arrangement that may have the highest value, and I am frank in saying that, on the facts presented to me, I approve it." [37]

Meighen's immediate reaction to "this world-shaking achievement that King and Roosevelt have staged in Ogdensburg" was quite different:

[35]Nicholas Mansergh, *Survey of British Commonwealth Affairs: Problems of Wartime Co-operation and Post-War Change, 1939–1952* (London, 1958), p. 52.

[36]Hanson Papers, File S-175-M-1, Hanson to Meighen, Aug. 23, 1940. Professor Stacey has pointed out that Churchill's reaction to Ogdensburg was cool but that King did not yet know this when he met Hanson (C. P. Stacey, "Twenty-One Years of Canadian-American Military Co-operation," *Canada-United States Treaty Relations*, ed. David R. Deener (Durham, 1963), pp. 105–6). King's notes of the meeting generally confirm Hanson's record, with the one exception that King does not mention "window dressing" (Pickersgill, *Mackenzie King Record*, I, 138).

[37]*Toronto Daily Star*, Aug. 21, 1940, p. 1.

Really I lost my breakfast [he wrote to Hanson] when I read the account this morning . . . and gazed on the disgusting picture of these potentates posing . . . in the very middle of the blackest crisis of this Empire.

There is no objection at all to staff conversations between Canadian and United States war officials but the less said about it the better. . . . We don't want Canadians to get the idea that we don't need to exert ourselves and this is just the idea they will get from this disgusting publicity. . . .

King refused to have Canada sit on the Committee of Imperial Defence for fear it might entangle us in war. He has no objection, though to such an arrangement with the United States. Neither have I for that matter. There is no danger of it entangling us in war because there is no Spain left that the United States could lick. . . .[38]

Meighen's visceral reaction was a revealing one, reflecting his hatred of King, his dislike for the United States,[39] and his complete unawareness of the value to the British of having a Commonwealth country's defences linked with those of the United States.[40]

The former leader's views seem to have altered Hanson's initial reaction to the agreement. "I personally do not accept the statement which has been made to you," Meighen wrote his former subordinate, "that this Conference business is entirely the idea of Mr. Roosevelt. It is too much in line with Mr. King's life long inclinations. That the thing is window dressing insofar as practical effect on the war is concerned, I quite agree. In its general tendency, though," he added, "it is not window dressing but something the people of Canada do not want."[41] In a speech at Toronto on Labour Day, 1940, Hanson revealed the effect of Meighen's representation. The conference, he told the guests of the Board of Directors of the Canadian National Exhibition, "was designed in part . . . to assist Mr. Roosevelt in his present position," and its "practical effect on the fortunes of the war is merely that of window dressing. . . . I am glad to know," he continued, "that the Government of the United Kingdom is aware of these discussions—otherwise, to me, it would have the appearance of casting off old and now embattled ties and taking on new and untried vows. I am not," he added darkly, "unaware of the inclinations of Mr. King in days gone by."[42]

[38]Hanson Papers, File S-175-M-1, Meighen to Hanson, Aug. 19, 1940.
[39]"Arthur Meighen struck a sour note. His anti-Americanism is growing by leaps and bounds. . . ." Moffat Papers, Vol. 46, Notes on a visit to Toronto, n.d.
[40]Meighen's unawareness in 1940 demonstrates the increasing rigidity of his views as he grew older. In 1921 he had secured the abrogation of the Anglo-Japanese Treaty on the grounds that it threatened American relations with the empire. The best published source on this is now Graham's *Arthur Meighen*. II. *And Fortune Fled* (Toronto, 1963), chapters III–IV.
[41]Meighen Papers, Meighen to Hanson, Aug. 27, 1940.
[42]Text of the speech is in Hanson Papers, File S-802.

Hanson's speech, parroting Meighen's prejudices and even his phraseology, roused a storm of protest, and Hanson was forced to spend much of his time explaining his words.[43] "Your difficulty," the editor of Toronto *Saturday Night* wrote him, "lies in the fact that while there is an immense amount of feeling in the Conservative party which corresponds exactly to what you said . . . there is also a widespread fear of expressing that feeling at the moment on account of possible international repercussions."[44] Certainly, the speech was ill advised. It illustrated all too clearly, as T. A. Crerar, King's Minister of Mines and Resources, said on another not dissimilar occasion, that the Conservatives "honestly think it a sort of sacrilege, that when Canada is at war, the disloyal Liberals should be in charge."[45] In accepting Meighen's opinion, Hanson had made a mistake that Manion would have avoided, and the results were costly. The Toronto speech, a political commentator noted, showing as it did that Hanson lacked an appreciation of the fundamentals of the war, was possibly the death blow to the Conservative party.[46]

Certainly very little effort would have been necessary to kill the party. The disastrous election of 1940 had left its federal organization in a state of collapse, and the provincial parties were scarcely better off. No Conservative government was in office in any of the nine provinces, and there were party leaders in only five. In Alberta, Saskatchewan, and Quebec, as Hanson noted, the party had virtually "ceased to exist."[47] Without strong provincial parties upon which to build, reorganizing the federal party would be slow and exceedingly difficult.

If the party were to live at all, money was immediately necessary. It was not forthcoming. Had Meighen returned to the leadership in the House in May of 1940, the problem would have been solved. Sir Edward Beatty, Hanson had been informed, had guaranteed relief from financial worries, but "when Mr. Meighen decided not to come, this undertaking no longer obtained."[48] Possibilities for fund-raising existed in Montreal now that Manion was gone, but the sudden collapse of the European front took the heart out of attempts to approach contributors.[49] As a

[43]E.g., *Toronto Daily Star*, Sept. 3, 4, 1940, pp. 6, 5; Montreal *Le Devoir*, 18 oct. 1940, p. 1; Saint John *Telegraph-Journal*, Oct. 9, 1940, p. 6; House of Commons, *Debates*, Nov. 12, 1940, p. 26.

[44]Hanson Papers, File S-802-1, B. K. Sandwell to Hanson, Oct. 7, 1940.

[45]Dafoe Papers, Microfilm roll M-79, T. A. Crerar to Dafoe, June 10, 1940.

[46]Politicus, "Can the Conservative Party be Revived?" *Saturday Night*, LVI (Oct. 5, 1940), 8.

[47]Hanson Papers, File P-450-HB, Hanson to Bell, Sept. 9, 1940.

[48]*Ibid.*, File O-100-F-1, Hanson to G. B. Foster, June 19, 1940; File O-150, Hanson to D. C. Coleman, June 11, 1940.

[49]*Ibid.*, File O-100-F-1, Hanson to G. B. Foster, June 19, 1940.

result, while Hanson was estimating that $5,000 monthly was necessary to carry on a proper party organization, the party on July 1 had a bank balance of $222.94.[50] So serious was the party's plight that the salaries of the regular headquarters office staff were placed in jeopardy, and Hanson was reduced to pleading that "I need $1,000 before the end of the week. I could put this up myself and impoverish my family, but I do not see any use in doing that."[51] In desperation Hanson appealed to the members and senators for contributions to keep the headquarters operating.[52] Each gave $50, and in this way $3,350 was raised. Apparently this was all the money available in the last six months of 1940.[53]

Hanson's despairing search for money was made more urgent by his belief that if the Conservative party died the only alternative to the Liberals would be the socialist C.C.F. In a letter to Meighen, Hanson detailed his conversations with a newspaper publisher who had promised support "on the theory that they should build up the Conservative Party between now and the next election with the hope that we might be able to form an alternative Government when the Government falls, as fall it will, rather than that the country should have a Red Government."[54] Hanson's fears were based on information given him by a C.C.F. Member of Parliament, Clarence Gillis, that organized labour, "controlled, I am told, directly by the C.I.O. in Indianapolis," had come to an arrangement with the C.C.F. to make a bid for power at the next election. This was based on the theory, Hanson said, "first that the present government would be defeated at the next election, second that the Conservative Party was too weak to form an alternative government." The policy of such a labour-C.C.F. link, he added, "is to be National Socialism."[55] Other Conservatives were reaching the same conclusions. "I am trying to put together some thoughts on the desirability of a resurgence of the Conservative Party," J. M. Macdonnell, president of the National Trust Company, wrote from Toronto to his friend, John Dafoe. "The lower we fall, the more I feel we are needed. The opposition should not be allowed to get into the hands of the CCF. Only a handful of people in this country want Socialism."[56]

James MacKerras Macdonnell was an extraordinary man. Born in

[50]*Ibid.*, File O-160-F, Miss J. E. Denison to Gordon Graydon, Feb. 25, 1941.
[51]*Ibid.*, File O-160-F, Hanson to G. H. Ferguson, June 24, 1940.
[52]Meighen Papers, Sen. G. V. White to Meighen, June 26, 1940.
[53]Hanson Papers, File O-160-F, Denison to Graydon, Feb. 25, 1941.
[54]Meighen Papers, Hanson to Meighen, Aug. 27, 1940.
[55]Hanson Papers, File O-160-F, Hanson to J. M. Macdonnell, Dec. 9, 1940.
Cf. File O-160, Hanson to H. A. Newman, Oct. 8, 1940.
[56]Dafoe Papers, Microfilm roll M-79, Macdonnell to Dafoe, Oct. 14, 1940.

1884, he had been a Rhodes Scholar and had served with great distinction in the Great War. Although a Conservative by inheritance and conviction, he was not bound by the dogmas that inhibited so many Tories, and perhaps because of this, he had been one of the national figures asked to enter the King government in June 1940. Deeply patriotic though he was, Macdonnell believed that the proffered post, Minister of National War Services, was a trivial one, and he had refused the offer, feeling that it was a serious matter to leave one's party.[57] Troubled about the state of Conservatism, Macdonnell was searching for some way to assist in restoring his party's fortunes when, by chance, he met Hanson on the train to Montreal on December 7, 1940.

The two men talked of the party's condition, and Macdonnell suggested that a confidential and informal meeting to discuss organization and finances might be useful. "To know that you and other responsible friends of the Conservative Party outside the House of Commons were concerned not only with the future of the Party but with the future of Canada," the surprised and pleased leader wrote Macdonnell, "was indeed most welcome."[58] Within a week plans were in hand for the meeting and discussions in progress concerning the guest list.[59] With Hanson's complete agreement, Macdonnell decided that with the exception of one or two senators long prominent in party financing no members of the parliamentary party would be invited other than the Leader of the Opposition himself. If some were asked, the two believed, others would be jealous.[60] For similar reasons, it was decided to allow no press publicity.[61]

The meeting—"a meeting of friends in no way intended to be representative in any technical sense"—convened at the Mount Royal Hotel in Montreal on January 11 and 12, 1941, "for the purpose of considering what they could do to assist the Party to resume the important part it has played in the maintenance of constitutional government in Canada."[62] Representatives from every province except Prince Edward Island, numbering some thirty in all, were present. The delegates included George Drew, Hugh Mackay, and John Diefenbaker (then the provincial party leaders in Ontario, New Brunswick, and Saskatchewan), seven members of Manion's defunct financial organization,

[57]The Hon. J. M. Macdonnell Interview, July 10, 1963.
[58]Hanson Papers, File O-160-F, Hanson to Macdonnell, Dec. 9, 1940.
[59]*Ibid.*, Hanson to Sen. G. B. Jones, Dec. 11, 1940.
[60]*Ibid.*, File P-450-HB-1, Bell to Hanson, Dec. 18, and 24, 1940; File O-160-F, Macdonnell to Hanson, Dec. 31, 1940.
[61]*Ibid.*, File O-160-F, Macdonnell to meeting guests, Dec. 30, 1940.
[62]*Ibid.*, Macdonnell to guests, Jan. 13, 1941.

and a number of prominent industrialists and financiers.[63] Discussion was wide-ranging but centred on the need to rebuild the party's organization and leadership and on the necessity for new policies.

The meeting did more than talk. Under Macdonnell's lead, it decided that a strong Dominion organization, with an efficient organizer, was needed to co-ordinate provincial efforts in the federal field, and that the organizer should be appointed immediately; that the Dominion organization should assist provincial organizations with money if they were unable to support themselves; and that constituency organization should be encouraged with a view to the early selection of candidates for the next general election.[64] Most important for the party's immediate needs, the guests agreed to use their collective influence to raise funds for the establishment of a central federal organization. On Hanson's advice that $60,000 annually would be necessary—$20,000 for salaries and expenses and the balance for publicity—financial committees were created in Toronto and Montreal, each responsible for half the required amount.[65] The Montreal committee was formed of George B. Foster, Senator C. C. Ballantyne, and W. P. O'Brien, all of whom had previously raised funds for the party. The Toronto committee was led by Macdonnell and had Robert Bryce, a mining engineer, and R. A. Laidlaw, a financier and company director, as members. None of the Toronto group was an experienced "bagman", and perhaps for this reason it was more inventive than the Montreal group which relied on the traditional method of collecting from large corporations. Macdonnell arranged a dinner for thirty guests and asked each for $1000. Senator A. D. McRae, Bennett's organizer for the 1930 election, was one of those invited. He "nearly queered the pitch," Hanson, the principal speaker at the dinner, wrote, "by telling the meeting . . . that $5000 a month was a bagatelle, and that when he started out with Bennett, previous to the 1930 election, they had a budget of from $25,000 to $30,000 a month, which I understand Bennett paid out of his own pocket. We are," Hanson added, "a little more modest."[66]

The reorganization of the Conservative party was given considerable impetus by the Montreal gathering. Difficulties still remained, however,

[63]A list of delegates is in Hanson Papers, File O-160-F. Those who had been "collectors" for Manion were H. R. Milner of Alberta; A. C. Des Brisay of British Columbia; G. B. Jones of New Brunswick; G. B. Foster, W. P. O'Brien, and J. C. H. Dussault of Quebec; and Frank Stanfield of Nova Scotia. Diefenbaker was also a Saskatchewan M.P. Because of his dual role, he was the only M.P. other than Hanson at the meeting. Hanson to M. MacPherson, Jan. 23, 1941.

[64]*Ibid.*, File O-160-F, Macdonnell to guests, Jan. 13, 1941.

[65]*Ibid.*

[66]*Ibid.*, File O-160, Hanson to Bell, Feb. 4, 1941.

as pledges proved difficult to convert into cash, and the hope of $60,000 soon faded. In all, only $36,000 was collected, and of this sum Toronto contributed almost twice as much as did Montreal.[67] Strenuous efforts to collect the outstanding donations failed,[68] but the money raised was a far cry from the $3350 squeezed from the members and senators, and some organizational work was begun. The caucus made plans for a party conference in the fall of 1941 and selected Gordon Graydon, the member for Peel (Ontario), as national chairman. Graydon set to work immediately and spent $6500 on a prolonged organizing trip across the country.[69] The provincial party in Nova Scotia received a grant of $2500, and $9000 was sent to Saskatchewan in a vain effort to revive faltering Conservatism on the prairies. A further $9600 was spent by the party offices in Ottawa.[70] "With regard to organization," Hanson could soon write, "let me say that we are now well on our way."[71]

The question of leadership was not solved so easily. Many names had been canvassed at Montreal, and the consensus there was that none of the Members of Parliament was of leadership calibre.[72] There were also difficulties in finding someone from outside the House of Commons. "Could any outsider," Hanson challenged one critic, "be put into the saddle without Parliamentary experience? I think that would be impossible."[73] The only solution in his view was to persuade new men to enter the House, and there demonstrate their quality to party and country. Among those considered by Hanson were Murdoch MacPherson, runner-up to Manion in 1938, and Sidney Smith, one of those fleetingly considered as possible "stop-Manion" candidates at the last convention. On a trip to the West late in January, Hanson spoke with Smith in Winnipeg and urged him to enter the Commons. The Montreal meeting believed that he might be the "Moses", Hanson told the political novice, if he could get some practical experience. Smith was interested in the offer,[74] but nothing conclusive was decided, and the matter lapsed.

[67]*Ibid.*, File O-160-T, "Statement of Trust Account #1," Feb. 3, 1942.

[68]Meighen Papers, Macdonnell to Meighen, Sept. 25, and Meighen to Macdonnell, Oct. 6, 1941.

[69]A description of Graydon's work is in Bell Papers, Vol. 1, Minutes of the Meeting of Conservative Representatives in Ottawa, November 7–8, 1941, pp. 28–31. (Cited hereafter as Minutes, 1941.) See also Hanson Papers, File O-160-G, press release, May 22, 1941.

[70]Hanson Papers, File O-160-T, Statement, Feb. 3, 1942.

[71]*Ibid.*, File D-320, Hanson to H. P. Duchemin, Feb. 5, 1941.

[72]*Ibid.*, File O-100, Memorandum of conversation between RBH[anson] and SES[mith] in Winnipeg, Jan. 25, 1941. When word of this attitude filtered back to the caucus, there was some bitterness (The Hon. Howard C. Green Interview, Aug. 23, 1966).

[73]Hanson Papers, File P-100, Hanson to C. O. Knowles, Feb. 17, 1941.

[74]*Ibid.*, File O-100, Memorandum RBH-SES, Jan. 25, 1941.

Similarly, all questions of party policy were held in abeyance. Hanson told the Montreal delegates that policy must be studied, certainly, but that it was still too soon to determine the party's course.[75] The proper way to prepare a programme in lieu of a convention, he believed, was by a series of resolutions in the House of Commons. But he was only a temporary leader and thus not prepared to commit the party to any policies. Hanson's position, quite properly, was based on his realization that the permanent leader, whenever he might be selected, "should have a great deal to say about what the policy should be as he is to be its chief exponent. . . ."[76] The Leader of the Opposition's views were undeniably correct, but the mood of the nation demanded something more.

Canadians were in a condition of frustration in 1941. Taxes were rising, both government demands and exhortations were increasing, and still there was nothing to show for the national efforts. The military situation in North Africa and southeastern Europe continued to deteriorate, and there was a natural feeling of guilt, shamefacedly mingled with relief, that the 100,000 Canadian troops overseas by the fall[77] had not yet suffered any major casualties. What did exist, the Chief of the General Staff wrote in March 1941 to a friend in London, was

a widespread feeling that the Government is not getting on quickly enough with the war—which in general is not justified—and an equally widely held conviction that Mr. King's great abilities are not suited to the conditions of the world today—which may indeed be true. The man on the Canadian street is clamoring for leadership of the Churchill or Roosevelt variety and this technique is, I believe, foreign to the Prime Minister's makeup.[78]

Mackenzie King's orotund platitudes neither inspired nor satisfied weary Canadians. Still, national unity was being maintained. The explicit bargain with Quebec—a pledge of no conscription for overseas service in return for full co-operation in the war effort—was being honoured,[79]

[75]*Ibid.*, File O-160-F-1, Hanson's notes on the Montreal meeting, Jan. 11, 1941.
[76]*Ibid.*, File D-320, Hanson to C. O. Knowles, Jan. 23, 1941; File O-150, Hanson to Bell, June 27, 1941.
[77]Strength overseas on November 7, 1941, was 6,232 officers and 99,405 men. Directorate of History, Canadian Forces Headquarters, File 133.065 (D207).
[78]Directorate of History, Canadian Forces Headquarters, General H. D. G. Crerar Papers, 958.C.009 (D338), Crerar to L. B. Pearson, March 18, 1941.
[79]Moffat Papers, Vol. 46, Moffat to Sumner Welles, May 6, 1941. Attempts to create division in the country were not limited to enemy propaganda. In what can only be described as "Luce talk," *Life* examined the Canadian scene in the spring of 1941: ". . . the timid, unimaginative Mackenzie King Government continues to be blackmailed by the crudely pro-Axis French Canadian minority (an ideal Nazi Fifth Column). . . . Ottawa's job is to declare independence from the Axis transmission belt in French Quebec." Extract from *Life*, May 5, 1941, 108, in Lapointe Papers, Vol. 78.

but criticism was concentrated increasingly on the government's manpower policies.

The National Resources Mobilization Act of June 1940 was still the basis of government policy. A national registration had been carried out in August 1940 virtually without incident, and in September a formal announcement had been made that single men between the ages of 21 and 24 would be subject to compulsory military training beginning the next month.[80] The initial term of service was thirty days. It was, of course, completely impossible to train recruits in one month, but as General H. D. G. Crerar, the Chief of the General Staff, later recalled, "Thirty days' training was all I wanted, initially, because all we had to train with were U.S. rifles of last war vintage—and no ammunition!"[81] The thirty-day scheme was clearly an interim move, and the army chiefs had impressed this upon the government,[82] but nevertheless it served a useful purpose in convincing citizens "after twenty years of pacifist debauchery" that the military was not so bad after all, or so at least thought some officers.[83] Early in 1941 the period of training was extended to four months, and in April the Minister of National Defence announced that the N.R.M.A. soldiers would be retained in the service and posted to coast defence units, "thereby enabling the men in coastal defence units in Canada to go overseas."[84] Two armies—one of conscripts for home defence and one of men enlisted for service anywhere—resulted from the government policy, and to some Canadians this was criminal.

The demand for an end to the imposed dualism of the Canadian army gathered momentum throughout the spring of 1941. In the House of Commons Hanson was confronted with a difficult problem. "From the very beginning," he wrote a Calgary Conservative who was urging action upon him,

we have endeavoured to manœuvre the position so that the Liberals will have to adopt conscription. Our view is that those who are anxious for conscription underestimate the sentiment in the country against it and that

[80]See Raymond Ranger, *Report on the Operations of the National Registration and Military Mobilization World War II* (mimeographed, Ottawa, 1949). Copy in Directorate of History, File 951.013 (D5).

[81]Crerar Papers, 958.C.009 (D129), Crerar to Lt.-Gen. Price Montague, Dec. 11, 1944; 958.C.009 (D13), Memorandum, Col. E. L. M. Burns to Crerar, Oct. 29, 1940.

[82]*Ibid.*, Crerar to Montague, Dec. 11, 1944; 958.C.009 (D12), Crerar to Gen. A. G. L. McNaughton, Aug. 8, 1940.

[83]Lapointe Papers, Vol. 16, "Survey of Conditions Prevailing in Military District #5, 9–22 Feb. 41."

[84]Quoted in Stacey, *History of Second World War*, I, 121.

it is not opportune for us to come out at this time flatfooted for conscription. The time will arrive and that time will be when the voluntary system has demonstrated its failure. Meanwhile our rural Members are absolutely opposed to it, and without unanimity in the Party here I could not take this step. My own view is in favour of conscription but I cannot carry the rank and file of the Party in the House with me and it is useless to take this step without that unanimity, which is so essential. You just have to balance things, one against the other.[85]

The effects of 1917 on the fortunes of the Conservative party were fresh in Hanson's memory, and he hoped to attach the blame for the inevitable enforcement of conscription in this war to the Liberals.

As Hanson had indicated in his comments, however, the caucus was not united in its view of the problem. The rural members opposed conscription, but those from the metropolitan areas did not share their fears. One of the most vociferous conscriptionists was Dr. Herbert Bruce, the Toronto M.P. In a speech on May 12, 1941, Bruce stated his position:

I am not a politician and I am speaking only for myself when I call upon the government to take immediate steps to meet the present urgent situation and make available by a national selective process the men necessary to bring our armed forces up to the strength that represents the fighting might of Canada. We should have the compulsory selective service which was visualized by the sweeping powers of the National Resources Mobilization Act . . . without the hamstringing clause that prevents men who train under that act from being used wherever the need is urgent.

Bruce's speech went as far as any Conservative member was prepared to go in the spring and summer of 1941, and, despite his careful avoidance of the shibboleth "conscription," his speech was not well received by the caucus. But, as Bruce wrote a friend, he "didn't care a d—— about the fortunes of the Conservative Party," nor did he care what the other members thought "because they are only thinking of the political effect."[86]

Impatient spirits outside the House of Commons shared Bruce's views. The press, led by the Toronto *Evening Telegram*, the Toronto *Globe and Mail*, and the Montreal *Gazette*, was becoming increasingly virulent in its attacks on government policy,[87] and some prominent Conservatives

[85]Hanson Papers, File O-160, Hanson to H. C. Farthing, May 27, 1941. Cf. Herridge Papers, Hanson to Herridge, May 25, 1941.

[86]House of Commons, *Debates*, May 12, 1941, p. 2729; Bruce Papers, Bruce to C. G. McCullagh, May 15, 1941.

[87]E.g., Toronto *Evening Telegram*, April 22, 1941, p. 6. Cf. Dafoe Papers, Microfilm roll M-79, T. A. Crerar to Dafoe, April 25 and 30, 1941.

were coming out for conscription. Murdoch MacPherson was the first bluntly to advocate conscription for overseas service in a Regina speech on May 9. Warned of MacPherson's intentions, Hanson telegraphed him that "there is no objection but you must make it plain that you are speaking for yourself and not officially. Our rural members emphatically object to coming out four square at this time desiring to fasten the odium on the government if possible." MacPherson agreed to speak on his own responsibility, but his wired reply added that "to avoid any complication am today resigning from provincial executive."[88] The speech received good coverage in the press, but its timing raised doubts in the minds of some Conservatives. "To many people," said R. K. Finlayson, once Bennett's private secretary, "it doesn't seem to be playing the game to make a demand for conscription just as the government is launching its recruiting drive. . . ." (The first major recruiting campaign of the war had opened on May 11.) "I meet men here," Finlayson continued from Winnipeg, "who say they will not help in the drive. Briefly put, they want the drive to fail so that conscription will then become absolutely necessary."[89]

There was no longer any argument from Liberals that it was becoming more difficult to find the men needed for both the rapidly expanding armed forces and the war industries. Before the war, there had been some 600,000 unemployed; by mid-1941, most of these men had been absorbed either into the labour force or into the armed services.[90] The navy was growing quickly and was ten times its prewar strength of approximately 2000 men; the strength of the Royal Canadian Air Force was approaching 90,000 by the fall of 1941; and the army consisted of 218,000 volunteers for service anywhere and some 13,000 N.R.M.A. soldiers on July 1, 1941. For a country with a population of only 11,500,000 which was simultaneously devoting every effort to increasing its manufacturing and agricultural production, more than 300,000 volunteers in two years was a highly creditable achievement. As the Canadian correspondent for the English quarterly, *Round Table*, remarked, the figures made the position of those advocating conscription "a curious one." "The number of men in the fighting services who have been embodied as volunteers available for duty anywhere already exceeds the figure at the end of the second year of the last war. Recruits for the

[88]Hanson Papers, File W-110, Hanson to MacPherson, and reply, May 9, 1941.
[89]*Ibid.*, File P-450-F; Finlayson to Hanson, May 14, 1941. For details on the recruiting campaign, see Stacey, *History of Second World War*, I, 115.
[90]A. F. W. Plumptre, *Mobilizing Canada's Resources for War* (Toronto, 1941), pp. 13, 44–5. This fact, of course, made the conscription cries in 1940 and early 1941 even less realistic.

navy and air force have continued to offer themselves faster than it has been possible to absorb them. Recruitment for the army has been slower. . . ."[91] But, despite a slow start, even the army's mid-1941 recruiting drive achieved its objective of 32,000 men with something to spare.[92] The position of the conscriptionists was a curious one indeed, even more so because the army overseas had not been committed to action as yet and so had incurred no serious casualties. Moreover, as the Canadian Corps in the United Kingdom was fulfilling a mobile counter-attack role designed to meet a German invasion, it seemed unlikely that heavy casualties would be expected in the immediate future.

In these circumstances, why would anyone favour conscription? The reasons, being based on an amalgam of emotion, prejudice, wisdom, and experience, are complex and difficult to discover. Conscription had had to be imposed in the Great War, and those, like Arthur Meighen, who had been instrumental in securing it in 1917 believed that only similar legislation could produce results in the new world war, that without conscription the war effort was bound to be a poor one. "How many Germans," Meighen asked in July 1941, "have been killed by Canadian Forces?"[93] Meighen's query, coming from one of the most lucid, if blinkered, men in Canadian political history, illustrates the emotional nature of the issue, the feeling that conscription was necessary to fight the war—regardless of the large air force and the growing navy both of which had scarcely existed in the Great War, regardless of the differences between the two world wars, regardless of the greatly increased war production of 1941 compared with 1916, and regardless of the steady flow of volunteer enlistments.

Certainly conscription was probably the fairest method of raising men, and if its implementation would not have produced drastic effects on national unity, few would have opposed it. Conservatives generally tended to discount perennial Liberal claims of preserving the unity of the two Canadian races, but many were not averse to calculating just how far Quebec lagged behind the "loyal" provinces. One memorandum in Meighen's papers compared the contribution of Ontario with that of Quebec:

[91]"Transformations since 1939," *Round Table*, XXXII (Dec., 1941), 144–5.
[92]Stacey, *History of Second World War*, I, 116. On the other hand, at least one experienced observer felt recruiting "is dead." Lieutenant-General E. C. Ashton wrote that a recruiting sergeant "told me recently that in two weeks he had had one man approach him and he was 56 years old. . . . The people generally are quite apathetic—simply not interested" (Crerar Papers, 958.C.009 (D10), Ashton to Gen. Crerar, Nov. 21, 1941).
[93]Meighen Papers, Meighen to Bennett, July 24, 1941.

Quebec population (1939 est.)	3,210,000	(Quebec is
Ontario	3,752,000	85.5% of
		Ontario)
As of October 31, 1941		
Ontario voluntary enlistments	147,114	
Quebec share (85.5%)	125,783	
Quebec actual	61,247	(48.7% share)
Ontario overseas troops	89,618	
Quebec share (85.5%)	76,624	
Quebec actual	34,293	(44% share)[94]

Superficially, Meighen's figures bolstered his implicit conclusion that Quebec was uninterested in the war. But as a perceptive army report on "The Recruiting Problem in the Province of Quebec" noted in June 1941, such an attitude could only be held by those "who fail to appreciate either the tactless blunders of a past generation, or the difficult and complex technical obstacles to proportional mobilization of French-speaking Army units."[95] There were two fundamental problems. The civil education system in Quebec, one senior staff officer observed, was based on metaphysics rather than physics and did not produce men fitted for the technical services.[96] The second problem, of course, was language. Virtually all technical military pamphlets were produced only in English. The language of instruction in the technical corps and in most officer training units was similarly unilingual, and this seemed to close the door in the face of French Canadians. "Even when joining the Army," the editor of Montreal's *Le Canada* told an English-speaking audience,

French Canadians know that their chances for advancement are slight unless they are English-speaking. There is no French counterpart for Kingston Royal Military College. Partly owing to that fact, almost all the Canadian high command and superior staff officers are English-speaking. . . .

No doubt there are some very good reasons for this. . . . But the fact nevertheless remains that in war as well as in peace, the French Canadian cannot escape the feeling that he is a second class citizen in his own country. . . .[97]

[94]*Ibid.*, Memorandum, n.d. Cf. Bruce Papers, Bruce to Lord Beaverbrook, June 25, 1941: "The real ruler in Canada today is not Mr. King, but Mr. Lapointe and his French Canadian compatriots . . . dominated by the Roman Catholic Church. . . . Before any legislation is introduced it must be submitted to Mr. Lapointe and have his approval. King is an isolationist and anti-British, and so are his friends and supporters in the Cabinet from Quebec. . . ."

[95]Directorate of History, File 112.3S2009 (D36), June 9, 1941. A draft of this paper, dated June 2, 1941, is in the Lapointe Papers, Vol. 45.

[96]Directorate of History, File 112.3S2009 (D36), Memorandum, Director of Military Training to Chief of the General Staff, June 25, 1941.

[97]Edmond Turcotte, "What Canada's War Effort Might Be," in A. R. M. Lower and J. F. Parkinson, eds., *War and Reconstruction* (Toronto, 1942), p. 35.

The only branch of the army that welcomed the French Canadian was the infantry, but here, too, errors had been perpetuated. Throughout the Great War French Canadians had called for the formation of a French-Canadian brigade. Nothing had been done then, and still in 1941 no action had been taken.[98] Despite this, an army report noted, total army enlistments in Canada were 18 per cent lower on March 31, 1941, than on March 31, 1916, but Quebec enlistments were 15,000 higher—58 per cent—in 1941.[99] Meighen and his conscriptionist friends also neglected the consideration that, like it or not, popular opinion in Quebec viewed the proper aim of the war to be the defence of Canada, not "overseas adventures."[100] All these factors notwithstanding, conscription was still necessary, and there could be no argument about this, or so thought the conscriptionists, if one was to be considered a true Conservative.

There was no truer Conservative than Arthur Meighen. He had favoured conscription from the opening shot of the war, but he had said nothing, fearing that an immediate campaign would do more harm than good.[101] In the general election of 1940 he had continued silent on the subject, although he disagreed violently with Manion's taking the pledge,[102] and even after the collapse of May and June 1940, his voice had remained muted. By May 1941, however, he was ready at last. "I have not taken the field as an aggressive conscriptionist," he wrote to a friend who urged the necessity for action upon him, "being somewhat reluctant to appear as usurping leadership. That the time has come I have no question," he continued, "and the Party cannot too soon take up its true position to suit me."[103] As Meighen saw it, the problem of getting conscription was complicated by the praise lavished on Canada's war effort by British leaders. In a letter to Bennett, a month after the one-time prime minister had been elevated to the peerage in his adopted country, he urged that something be done to damn the flow of compliments. "In driving against an apathetic, deliberately non-aggressive and dishonest Administration," he charged, "one cannot get far when met

---

[98]Directorate of History, File 112.3S2009 (D36), District Officer Commanding, Military District #5, to Secretary, Department of National Defence, July 15, 1941.

[99]*Ibid.*, "The Recruiting Problem. . . ."; Elizabeth Armstrong, *The Crisis of Quebec, 1914–18* (New York, 1937), p. 249, estimates that some 32,000–35,000 French Canadians served in the Great War. No exact figures exist for either the Great War or the Second World War (Information from Directorate of History), but in July 1943 one army estimate was that 82,917 soldiers were French-speaking or bilingual. This was approximately 19 per cent of army strength. Ralston Papers, Vol. 29, File 429–43, Memorandum, July 5, 1943.

[100]Mason Wade, *The French Canadians, 1760–1945* (Toronto, 1956), p. 935.

[101]Graham, *Meighen*, III, 89.

[102]*Toronto Daily Star*, Feb. 4, 1942, p. 9.

[103]Meighen Papers, Meighen to H. R. Milner, May 14, 1941.

continuously with a torrent of insincere approbation coming from overseas. . . ."[104]

Meighen's disgust mounted throughout the summer of 1941; Hanson continued to equivocate. Personally, Hanson favoured conscription, but he remained reluctant to test the limited powers of his temporary position by attempting to foist it on his balky colleagues.[105] As a result, Meighen and some of his followers began to mull over the question of the leadership. In May the caucus had decided that a party conference should be held in the fall to consider the date and site for a leadership convention in 1942. But, as Meighen wrote to Murdoch MacPherson, "I am steadily moving to the conviction that we ought to move faster than that and that the Conservative Party has to take this thing in hand as its own mission, that it must choose its leader and choose him soon and get into action on strong British total war lines without delay. . . . I believe that whatever is done should be done this Fall."[106] The party conference was scheduled for November 7 and 8, but before it could be held, the growing resentment over Hanson's course burst into the press.

The Leader of the Opposition had flown to England with several parliamentary colleagues in September. For twenty-three days he toured military camps, interviewed commanding officers, and held meetings with British leaders, including Prime Minister Churchill.[107] The subject of conscription naturally arose in the discussion and, as the British High Commissioner in Ottawa told his American colleague, "Mr. Churchill had made it exceedingly plain to Mr. Hanson and the Conservative leaders that he was *not* pressing Canada on this issue at the moment."[108] A few weeks after his return to Canada, Hanson came to Toronto to address the Board of Trade. On the afternoon of October 29 he spoke to a gathering at the Albany Club, the citadel of Toronto toryism, and sorely disappointed his hosts. "I have been urged to declare for conscription of manpower," Hanson said.

[104]*Ibid.*, Meighen to Bennett, July 24, 1941. Cf. Herridge Papers, Herridge to Bennett, May 24, 1941. Hanson told Churchill much the same thing when he was in Ottawa in December 1941 (Hanson Papers, Personal Correspondence, Hanson to R. K. Finlayson, Jan. 3, 1942). Cf. W. S. Churchill, *The Second World War.* III. *The Grand Alliance* (London, 1950), p. 601.

[105]Bruce Papers, Hanson to Bruce, June 28, 1941; Hanson Papers, File W-110, Hanson to E. G. Phipps Baker, June 30, 1941, and File P-450-HB-2, Bell to Hanson, June 13, 1941.

[106]Meighen Papers, Meighen to MacPherson, Aug. 7, 1941.

[107]Mr. Hanson's account of his trip is in House of Commons, *Debates*, Nov. 4, 1941, pp. 4061–4.

[108]Moffat Papers, Vol. 47, Memorandum of conversation with Malcolm MacDonald, Oct. 18, 1941; Ralston Papers, "Diary—English Trip, Fall, 1941." Cf. Dafoe Papers, Microfilm roll M-79, Grant Dexter to Dafoe, Nov. 18, 1941; Pickersgill, *Mackenzie King Record*, I, 272–3.

What would happen if I did? Immediately the Conservative party in Parliament nailed conscription to its masthead, we'd consolidate all those forces that have been opposed to us since 1917 and they would be marshaled against us. Conscription is bound to come to the front more and more insistently—but it must come from the people themselves. To make it a political move would defeat the very purpose of those who have it in view.[109]

The speech was eminently sensible, but it was not the speech the audience had come to hear. The Conservative press unanimously condemned the unfortunate Hanson.[110] Meighen was shocked:

. . . . I have to admit with the sincerest regret that I could not follow him in what he said on the conscription issue. He takes the stand, and in this says he is supported by the majority of our Party in the House, that conscription must wait until public opinion is educated on the subject and becomes so strong that such public opinion compels its adoption by the King Government. Meantime, he said, we cannot take a stand in favour of it because that would consolidate those opposed. . . . If the people have to be enlightened on the subject, have we not a duty to enlighten them?

"Frankly," he added in a second letter, "his speech was a failure and has made a most unfortunate impression."[111] Hanson's address, coming only a few days before a major party conference, gave the conscriptionists the opportunity for which they had been searching. They would not fail to make the most of it.

[109]Toronto *Evening Telegram*, Oct. 30, 1941, p. 18.
[110]See the survey of press opinion in the Montreal *Gazette*, Nov. 3, 1941, p. 8.
[111]Meighen Papers, Meighen to A. C. Casselman, M.P., Oct. 29 and 31, 1941.

5.   The Conscriptionist Interlude

The opposition to the King government reached its most virulent stage in the months from November 1941 to February 1942. Grievances, real and imagined, were aggravated by frustrated and impotent rage at the seemingly endless series of Allied defeats. The government's refusal to implement conscription, its unwillingness to form a national government, and its increasingly heavy hand on the economy created forces that led to startling and far-reaching changes on the Canadian political scene. The Conservative party was captured by its conscriptionist wing, a new leader was installed, and the old party became the vehicle for an attempt to unseat Mackenzie King. The scheme was faulty in planning, in execution, and in its leaders' assessment of the national mood; in the *dénouement* the fortunes of the Conservative party, already tattered by defeat and the war, fell even lower.

Hanson's forthright speech at the Albany Club crystallized the feelings of those Conservatives who believed that a change in the leadership and policies of the party was essential. Coincidentally, the means to effect these changes were at hand. At the adjournment of parliament in June 1941 Hanson had agreed to continue as Leader of the Opposition until the end of the 1942 session "unless other arrangements are made . . . but," he added, "beyond this I will not go."[1] Because of Hanson's wish to relinquish his onerous job, a meeting of the general executive of the Dominion Conservative Association had been summoned to meet in the Railway Committee room of the Parliament Buildings on November 7, 1941. The conference's purpose, as emphasized in the invitations, was to decide "*when* and *where* the Dominion Conservative Convention to select the permanent Leader of the Party should be held. . . ."[2]

Despite its grandiose title, the General Executive of the Dominion Conservative Association was "a bastardized organization, bearing some

[1]Bell Papers, Vol. 1, Minutes, 1941, pp. 9–10.
[2]Meighen Papers, J. R. MacNicol, M.P. to Meighen, Oct. 20, 1941 (mimeographed form letter). (Italics in original.)

resemblance to the Dominion Conservative Association, some to the National Conservative Council [a stillborn body organized in the closing moments of the 1938 convention], and some to God knows what," that had been created by caucus on May 30, 1941, at the insistence of its chairman, John R. MacNicol, M.P.[3] MacNicol had been the president of the D.C.A., a virtually defunct organization of vague status within the party, since its formation in 1924. Anxious to restore his moribund organization—no list existed, for example, of the provincial presidents of the D.C.A.—MacNicol somehow persuaded the reluctant caucus that he should call the conference to decide on the date and site of a leadership convention through the D.C.A.[4] In agreeing to MacNicol's request, the members constructed the General Executive, a body with a paper strength of at least 360 persons.[5]

In the invitation sent to the delegates to the conference and in the agenda prepared for the meeting, "it was clearly and *deliberately* specified that the *only* purpose was to determine the *'time and place'* to hold a national convention." This provision, wrote R. A. Bell, Hanson's private secretary, "had been deliberately framed. By that I mean that the possibility of an attempt being made to convert the Conference into a Convention was foreseen and the restriction was designed to forestall such an attempt."[6] Despite these efforts, the purpose of the meeting was to be subverted.

The view that the General Executive should select a new leader was vigorously propounded by the Toronto *Globe and Mail*, published by George McCullagh. Once a Liberal, McCullagh had been drifting toward Conservatism since he became disillusioned with Mackenzie King in the late 1930's. The Liberal leader's conduct of the war had confirmed the publisher in his new allegiance, and he showed a convert's zeal in his attacks on the administration. Beginning on November 1 his extremely influential newspaper began a series of editorials calling for the immediate strengthening of the Opposition in the House of Commons. The

[3]Bell Papers, Vol. 1, Bell to John A. Lederle, April 2, 1942; Progressive Conservative Party Files, File M-M-3a, Miss J. Denison to R. K. Finlayson, Oct. 25, 1941; Bruce Papers, Bruce to his son, Max, May 30, 1941.

[4]Hanson Papers, File O-160, MacNicol to Hanson, May 20, 1941. On the D.C.A. generally, see Bell Papers, Vol. 1, Bell to Meighen, Sept. 26, 1942; Meighen Papers, J. R. MacNicol, "The Evolution of Procedure Followed in Summoning Conservative Conventions and Conferences," n.d. The national membership of the D.C.A. in November 1941 was probably under 1,500, for as late as May 1942 MacNicol was writing that a "strong effort" had raised membership to 3,000 (Meighen Papers, MacNicol to Meighen, May 12, 1942).

[5]Hanson Papers, File O-160-2, "Invitation Summary," Nov. 6, 1941. For the organization of the General Executive, see Appendix 1.

[6]Bell Papers, Vol. 1, Bell to Lederle, Jan. 6, 1942 (letter not sent).

government, this first editorial charged, had committed a series of dictatorial acts, including the incarceration of persons without trial and an
economic revolution by Order in Council. Without a "devoted band of
strong men in Opposition to keep the faint spark of democracy from
being stamped out," Canada could only become a dictatorship, the
newspaper claimed (November 1, 1941).

To prevent the imminent destruction of liberty, Mr. Hanson had to go.
He "is not in robust health," the next editorial on November 3 declared,
"and his willingness to accept an unwelcome responsibility . . . will
always be remembered to his credit. But, when he was asked to assume
the task, it was made clear to him that it would only be for a while. . . ."
What the Conservative party now required was "a man of ability with an
established record and ample Parliamentary experience to serve as the
spearhead of the Opposition forces in the House." Difficult as such
qualifications were to find in the Conservative party in 1941, the *Globe
and Mail* was equal to the task, and on November 4 the newspaper
revealed its choice for the leadership: "a leader of experience in war
administration who is at the same time skilled in Parliamentary debate,
equipped with a keen intellect and fortified by moral courage . . . Arthur
Meighen."

These laudatory phrases used to describe Senator Meighen were by no
means exaggerated. Even his bitter opponents—and they were legion—
conceded that Meighen possessed a formidable, incisive mind, superb
oratorical powers, and high principles. "All that has ever been said
against him," the *Globe and Mail*'s editorial continued ingenuously, "is
that his political judgment is faulty."[7] Here was the rub. *Canadian
Forum*, a left-wing monthly, expressed the views of many Canadians
when it caustically wondered

how any group of saviours-of-the-country, even with the *Globe and Mail*
helping to pull the strings, could be so insane as to imagine that they have
any chance of getting into power under the lead of the man whose record in
the last war includes the alienation of the French by conscription, of the west
by the War Times [*sic*] Election act, and of labor by his activities in the
Winnipeg strike. . . .[8]

First elected to the House of Commons in 1908 for a Manitoba seat,
the slender, handsome Meighen had quickly attracted attention with a
number of brilliant speeches.[9] He was taken into the cabinet at the age of

[7]November 4, 1941, p. 6.
[8]"Meighen," *Canadian Forum*, XXI (Dec., 1941), 260.
[9]One observer wrote "deliberately" that Meighen "at his highest and best" was
a better orator than Roosevelt, Churchill, Laurier, or Viviani. M. G. O'Leary in
the foreword to Arthur Meighen, *Unrevised and Unrepented: Debating Speeches
and Others* (Toronto, 1949), p. x.

41 in 1915 as Solicitor General, and when the Union government was formed in 1917 he was made Minister of the Interior. In this portfolio, Meighen was given the task of carrying out every "dirty, political chore"[10] the government required, and there were many. The abilities of the man could not be denied, and Meighen succeeded to the office of prime minister when Borden retired in 1920. As "the father of railway nationalization,"[11] he was at that time the "rising hope of the progressive young Conservatives" and, as Eugene Forsey later wrote, in financial circles in Montreal "it was possible to acquire . . . a reputation as a 'Bolshevik' simply by praising or defending Meighen."[12] The Conservative leader's career in the 1920's was dogged by similar labels. To French Canada, Meighen was the bloody-handed monster who had filled the cemeteries of Flanders with the conscripted youth of Canada; to the West and to the political left, he was a high-tariff reactionary and a strike-breaker; and at the same time to certain segments of industry and finance, Meighen was a potentially dangerous radical.[13]

Because of the opposition to him and also because of his own rigidity, his unshakable confidence in the correctness of his views, his uncompromising bitterness towards political enemies, and his political naïveté,[14] the otherwise immensely able Meighen was never able to lead the Conservative party to a clear victory in a general election, although he twice held the premiership for short periods. Retiring as leader after defeat by his hated rival, Mackenzie King, in the general election of 1926, Meighen entered the business world in Toronto and stayed out of active politics until he was appointed to the Senate and selected as Conservative leader in the upper chamber in 1932. After the outbreak of war Meighen delivered a series of oratorically brilliant speeches in the Senate excoriating the King government for its handling of the war effort. With this as proof of his undiminished vigour, and rightly confident that his years in business and the Senate had modified his earlier "radicalism," the *Globe and Mail* now urged that Meighen should leave the politically impotent upper chamber, take the party leadership, and carry the fight against King and his limited war effort into the House of Commons.

[10]G. Gerald Harrop, "On Ruling Canada," *Queen's Quarterly*, LXXX (spring, 1964), 14–15.

[11]Graham, *Meighen*, II, 44.

[12]Eugene Forsey, "Arthur Meighen," *Canadian Forum*, XL (Sept., 1960), 121–2.

[13]"Meighen," *Canadian Forum*, XXI, 251; Harrop, "On Ruling Canada," pp. 8, 14; Forsey, "Meighen," pp. 121–2; Graham, *Meighen*, II, chap. XII.

[14]Meighen's contemporaries are virtually unanimous in this assessment, and especially so with regard to his naïveté. Coldwell Interview, July 6, 1963; Macdonnell Interview, July 10, 1963; Eugene Forsey Interview, Aug. 25, 1964; Stevens Papers, Vol. 163, Transcript of tape recording, p. 83. See especially, the most revealing incident cited in Graham, *Meighen*, III, 82.

Though the *Globe and Mail* was only the publicity agent in the drive
to have Meighen selected as leader, the evidence would indicate that
McCullagh was a key figure in the movement. According to Clifford
Sifton, one of the owners of the *Winnipeg Free Press* and a man with
excellent contacts, McCullagh's reasoning generally followed the line
taken by the editorials that had initiated the publicity campaign. He had
become convinced that King had developed irresponsible fascist prac-
tices that could only be checked by a greatly strengthened opposition
and a strong new leadership.[15] In addition, McCullagh believed that
Meighen was the one man strong enough to force the enactment of
conscription.[16] Aside from a genuinely patriotic belief that conscription
was a necessary war measure, McCullagh's associations and past activities indicated that he believed conscription would be a useful device in
controlling the growing obstreperousness of the C.I.O. in the mining
areas of northern Ontario. W. H. Wright, the owner of the *Globe and
Mail*, was also vice-president of Wright-Hargreaves Mines, McCullagh
himself had extensive mining interests, and in November 1941 a strike
was imminent in the Ontario gold fields on the question of union recognition. In all likelihood, this factor accounted for some of the support given
Meighen, a man who reputedly had little sympathy for labour, by
McCullagh and his mining friends.[17]

The strong campaign to change the purpose of the Ottawa conference
had additional supporters. According to a third-hand report in the
Mackenzie King Record, George McCullagh told one of the Prime
Minister's secretaries that while he had come down to support Meighen
"in order to force the conscription issue," he had discovered after his
arrival in Ottawa,

that the men who were backing Meighen were doing so because of the
Government's Price Control policy; that up to the time of my broadcast
[King had announced the policy on October 18, 1941] they had been
indifferent about war matters, but after the broadcast felt there was a danger
of their way of life being changed and some of their profits limited. . . . Now
they were afraid that if they did not get control of government, or of

---

[15]Dafoe Papers, Microfilm roll M-79, Clifford Sifton to Dafoe, 1941 (confidential); Macdonnell Interview, July 10, 1963; Bell Interview, Aug. 24, 1964.

[16]John A. Stevenson Interview, July 15, 1964.

[17]For McCullagh's past history in dealing with the C.I.O., see Young, "C.
George McCullagh and the Leadership League," unpublished M.A. thesis, Queen's
University, 1964, *passim*, and Brian Young, "C. George McCullagh and the
Leadership League," *Canadian Historical Review*, XLVII (Sept., 1966), 205–7.
On McCullagh's role in the 1941 strike, see Toronto *Globe and Mail*, November–
December 1941; Arnold Brown, "A Newspaper Fights a Miner's Strike," *Canadian
Forum*, XXI (Jan., 1942), 301–2; Coldwell Interview, July 6, 1963.

government policy, power would pass out of their hands. McCullagh said he felt rather ashamed of himself trying to support Meighen on grounds of the kind.[18]

The evidence is inconclusive on this point, but it is not unlikely that the imposition of price controls had some effect on the motivations of those opposing the government.

The third component of the forces within the party pressing for Meighen's selection was the parliamentary group. The senators, numbering forty-eight, were almost all older men who had served in the cabinet, in the House, or in the party with Meighen. Indeed, five of them owed their appointments to Meighen. In the House of Commons, eleven of the forty M.P.s had served under Meighen as prime minister. Eleven represented constituencies in and around "Tory Toronto," the centre of conscription agitation, and the remainder, including those who were not yet in favour of conscription, were more than a little awed by Meighen's reputation. Here, they must have believed, was the leader who could put fear into Mackenzie King and life into the Opposition.

The parliamentarians, industrialists, and anti-labour forces forming the "Meighen for Leader" group have been characterized by one observer of the conference as "all the undesirable machine politicians" of the party.[19] This may be unfair. They wanted Meighen for a variety of reasons, some of which were patriotic in the highest degree, but essentially they wanted him because they believed he was an able leader who hated Mackenzie King and all his works as they did. Meighen, they hoped, would be the bully boy able to put the French in their place and handle labour by forcing the resignation of King, the formation of a national government, and the introduction of conscription for overseas service.[20]

Almost without exception, the delegates travelling to Ottawa for the conference were unaware of the motives behind the sudden campaign

---

[18]Pickersgill, *Mackenzie King Record*, I, 277. Cf. Dunning Papers, Dunning to G. W. Spinney, Dec. 6, 1941; Moffat Papers, Vol. 47, Memorandum of conversation with J. W. Pickersgill, Nov. 26, 1941; *Ottawa Journal*, Nov. 3, 1941, p. 1.

By almost any standard the price control policies were a brilliant success. The cost of living in April 1945 was up only 18 per cent above the August 1939 figure, compared with a 74 per cent increase in the period from 1914 to 1919. A Wartime Prices and Trade Board, controlling selected items only, had been set up on Sept. 3, 1939. King's October speech, announcing an over-all price ceiling, made Canada the first democratic country in the world to do this. Canada, Wartime Information Board, *Canada at War* (Ottawa, 1945), pp. 142–5.

[19]Bell Papers, Vol. 1, Bell to Lederle, Jan. 6, 1942 (not sent).

[20]Graham, *Meighen*, III, 106; Meighen Papers, Hon. C. P. Beaubien to Meighen, Nov. 22, 1941; Stevenson Interview, July 15, 1963. The phrase "bully boy" was used by J. M. Macdonnell in an interview, July 10, 1963.

for Meighen. The leadership had been a subject of speculation for several months, but the guessing had centred on George Drew and Murdoch MacPherson, and on their chances at the leadership convention.[21] After November 1, however, few delegates could have escaped the widespread comment on the meeting. The newspapers were full of stories about Meighen's position, the motives of the *Globe and Mail*, the suddenly assumed authority of the conference, and assessments of delegates likely to be friendly to Meighen. On November 8, *Saturday Night* commented that the Meighen campaign "has been one of the most rapidly developed in the whole history of Canadian politics and one of the most efficient. The move shows a considerably greater degree of political astuteness than most of the recent performances of the Conservative party."

In Ottawa, meanwhile, with final preparations under way for the meeting, the Conservative party's sole French-Canadian Member of Parliament, J. S. Roy of Gaspé, announced that he was leaving the party and would henceforth sit as an Independent. Alarmed by the rising tide of conscriptionist sentiment, Roy attacked the "imperialist" attitude of his erstwhile colleagues and noted that a French Canadian had to realize certain things if he wished to be a Conservative. He is not a member of their political family, he said. "He is at best a tolerated stranger, accepted from necessity and looked at with a certain degree of curiosity. . . . he is and always will be a poor relation." The Conservatives, he concluded, "are firm in the opinion that we French Canadians are a source of trouble in their endeavours to make Canada an American England."[22] Roy's defection, leaving Conservatism without French-speaking representation other than a few Senators, was reported to have divided the few French-Canadian delegates to the Ottawa conference, with the younger men generally agreeing with him.[23]

The campaign for Meighen was not affected by the actions of the Gaspé M.P., however, nor was it affected by Meighen's own wishes. On October 30, even before the *Globe and Mail* launched its campaign, the Senator knew that he would be asked to return to the House of Commons as leader:

[21]Adamson Papers, Diary, May 12, 15, Sept. 26, 1941; Bruce Papers, Bruce to son, Max, Sept. 15, 1941; Bennett Papers, Notable Persons File, Bruce to Bennett, Oct. 15, 1941; Hanson Papers, Personal Correspondence, Vol. 32, Hanson to Dana Porter, Sept. 4, 1941; Bell Papers, Vol. 1, Bell to Lederle, Jan. 6, 1942 (not sent); Hanson Papers, File O-100-M, Bell to Hanson, Oct. 20, 1941.
[22]House of Commons, *Debates*, Nov. 4, 1941, p. 4058.
[23]Montreal *Le Devoir*, 7 nov. 1941, p. 3.

They are determined to name me leader and to come out for a total war, national Gov't and conscription [he wrote to his son]. I have worried over this—feeling for months that just such a situation would arise. Hanson I am sorry to say has failed. The job is too big. I really thought he would do better. Cannot go into a long review but I am in a terrible position. If I refuse under the desperate circumstances of this time I will unquestionably lose the regard of the party and in large degree of Canadians. . . . If I agree— well the consequences are so many and so awful I simply shrink from reciting them. Not unlikely at my age and taking things as hard as I do the turmoil and strain will—well, shorten my life.[24]

While there is no doubt that Meighen did not want the job for himself, he did hope to see the leadership settled at the Ottawa conference. In consequence, he had travelled to Winnipeg a few days before the meeting opened to meet with John Bracken, the Liberal-Progressive premier of Manitoba, and to offer him his support for the leadership.[25] Bracken had traces of Conservatism in his past (his father was said to have attended Sir John A. Macdonald's funeral), he had run his province efficiently for almost twenty years, and Meighen had hit upon him as a likely choice. No definite conclusions were reached in the Winnipeg conversations, and upon his return to Ontario, Meighen leaked the story to the press. This trial balloon did not get off the ground,[26] however, and Meighen realized that only his own selection would satisfy the old guard at the conference.

The Ottawa meeting began on Friday morning, November 7, 1941, with addresses to approximately 150 delegates from John R. MacNicol, the chairman of the meeting, and Hanson, the House leader. At last, as party leader in the Senate, Meighen was called upon to speak. While he did not actively seek the leadership or aid those planning to offer it to him, Meighen's speech was not calculated to give an impression of indifference. Despite his sixty-seven years, he was in good health and of undiminished mental vigour, his attack on the government providing ample proof of his unweakened powers. He charged the Liberal party with the abuse of parliament through rule by Order in Council, with turning the Canadian Broadcasting Commission into a party propaganda outlet, and chiefly with waging a feeble war effort. The only ambition of the Conservative party, he said, should be to increase the "striking power of Canada." To do this the party had to educate the people "on the

[24]Meighen to his son, Ted, Oct. 30, 1941, quoted in Graham, *Meighen*, III, 97.
[25]Graham, *Meighen*, III, 97–9.
[26]Finlayson Interview, June 1, 1963; Pickersgill, *Mackenzie King Record*, I, 276; *Winnipeg Free Press*, Nov. 6, 1941, p. 1.

subject that dominates the nation."[27] This subject, it was clear, was conscription.

Meighen's fighting speech was enthusiastically received by the delegates, and at the earliest opportunity his supporters were on their feet. The effort to alter the purpose of the meeting was led by C. H. Cahan, the octogenarian Montrealer who had been a member of Bennett's cabinet and a Member of Parliament from 1925 until his defeat in 1940. In a remarkable, passionate address, Cahan called for "action now," urging the delegates to reject the delay involved in a convention and to select the leader then and there. This leader could only be Arthur Meighen, he said, "a man who has experience in the procedure of the House, who knows something of the traditions of the House. . . ." But would Meighen accept? This was no obstacle for Cahan was unable to see how Meighen "after the speech which he has made . . . could refuse the unanimous request of this Council or Convention . . . to make the largest possible sacrifices in order to lead this Party again. . . ."[28]

Cahan's eloquent speech and the support it attracted from other delegates led to the formation of a 54-member committee to consider the course that the conference should follow. Twenty M.P.'s, six senators, three Young Conservatives, and twenty-five provincial representatives were chosen to make up the committee.[29] The mandate of this large body was unclear. MacNicol's understanding of the situation—never too clear at the best of times—was that the "Committee will have full power to make recommendations, so far as I am aware of their powers," but that these recommendations would be in no way binding upon the conference as a whole.[30] Three resolutions were considered in committee. The first concerned the advisability of summoning a full national convention; another recommended that caucus select the leader on its own responsibility; and the third simply stated "that it is the opinion of this meeting that the Right Honourable Arthur Meighen be asked to be our leader."[31] The deliberations in committee, of which no minutes were kept, were apparently spirited, and it took some seven hours to reach decisions on the three resolutions.

The committee's votes at once settled and created problems. The idea

[27]Minutes, 1941, pp. 17–27.
[28]*Ibid.*, pp. 37–40.
[29]How the committee members were chosen is unclear. Minutes, 1941, p. 45, simply state that "the several delegations gathered together in groups and chose their representatives for appointment to the committee." Ontario had eighteen members on the committee, Quebec seven, and no other province had more than six (*ibid.*, pp. 43–4).
[30]*Ibid.*, p. 44.
[31]*Ibid.*, p. 53.

of a convention was rejected by thirty-four votes to seventeen, and the committee also turned down by a margin of forty-two to eight the resolution that would have empowered caucus to select the leader. Only the last motion, to ask Meighen to become leader, carried. The vote on this question was thirty-seven to thirteen, but significantly a request for unanimity had been refused. When the results of the committee's deliberations were presented to the conference at 11 P.M. by Grote Stirling, M.P., the committee chairman, a new problem faced the weary delegates. None knew whether Meighen would accept even a unanimous call, but none doubted that he would refuse the mandate of a split conference.[32] With the question of the leadership still very much in doubt, the conference adjourned until 10 A.M. on Saturday. It seemed clear, however, that discussion would continue late into the night in the delegates' hotel rooms and that it would centre on the motives of the thirteen men who had opposed the return of the former prime minister.

The leader of this group was J. M. Macdonnell of Toronto, the organizer of the financial meeting that had saved the party eleven months before. Macdonnell personally favoured conscription for overseas service,[33] but he based his opposition to Meighen's return on his reasoning that "Meighen would be a source of dissension" in the country and that his return would create such hostility in Quebec that the war effort might be jeopardized.[34] This would be tragic for the nation, he believed, and it might so cripple the party's postwar prospects that the field would be left to the C.C.F. In the committee, Macdonnell had been joined by a small group, largely from western Canada, which included Howard Green of Vancouver, the only M.P. actively to oppose Meighen's return; E. G. Phipps Baker, a Winnipeg investment broker; R. K. Finlayson, the Winnipeg lawyer and former private secretary to Bennett; and Murdoch MacPherson and H. Ray Milner, both close friends of Meighen and both zealous conscriptionists.[35] Certainly not all these men believed that Meighen would be a disruptive force in the country; they did, however, agree without exception that the Ottawa meeting had been called only to select the date and site for a full-fledged leadership convention. They

[32]*Ibid.*, p. 92.

[33]Dafoe Papers, Microfilm roll M-79, Macdonnell to Dafoe, Sept. 15, 1941.

[34]Macdonnell Interview, July 10, 1963; Dafoe Papers, Microfilm roll M-79, Clifford Sifton to Dafoe, "Memorandum of a Conversation at Toronto Club" [evidently with Macdonnell], Nov. 24, 1941.

[35]Dafoe Papers, Microfilm roll M-79, Grant Dexter to G. V. Ferguson, Nov. 11, 1941; Bell Papers, Vol. 1, handwritten addendum to Minutes, 1941; Macdonnell Interview, July 10, 1963; Finlayson Interview, June 1, 1963. According to Howard Green, Dr. George MacKinnon, M.P. for Kootenay East, also opposed Meighen (Interview, Aug. 23, 1966).

objected strenuously to the plan to subvert the purpose of the meeting, claiming quite accurately that many delegates entitled to attend the conference had stayed home, planning to save their money in order to attend the anticipated leadership convention.[36] The Ottawa meeting, they maintained, was not representative of the party as a whole, and because of distance, it was attended by a disproportionate number of Ontario delegates.[37]

One other factor that played a part in arousing the outraged delegates was their dislike of the organized efforts to manipulate the conference so that Meighen would be chosen. They resented the high-pressure tactics of McCullagh's *Globe and Mail*: the editorial build-up for Meighen; the slanted editorializing that masqueraded as news; and the delivery of special copies to the delegates.[38] One of the dissenting delegates, R. C. Smith of Calgary, later wrote an angry letter to the *Financial Post* about the Ottawa conference:

It was the most brazenly organized effort to put the delegates . . . in a false and embarrassing position I have ever seen. . . .

Western delegates . . . voted against the hole-in-corner organized movement. There was nothing personal in this opposition. The disgust and contempt was for the manner in which the movement was organized, which turned an executive meeting into a convention. . . .[39]

Whatever their reasons for rejecting Meighen, the thirteen members of the committee—and their supporters in the conference itself—were standing firm that Friday night.

For Meighen the effects of the hectic day could only have been distressing. Long accused by his critics of lacking political sense, Meighen's judgment for once was correct. His common sense must have told him that he could not get wide support in the country, and yet his combative spirit and personal pride must have made him almost hopeful that he would be given the task. Meighen was convinced that King's heart was not in the war, and he was sure that he could run the country

[36]Bell Papers, Vol. 1, Bell to Lederle, Jan. 6, 1942 (not sent). The President of the Saskatchewan Conservative Association wrote to MacNicol on Oct. 21, 1941, as follows: ". . . it has been suggested that if the Executive merely intends to meet, discuss the advisability of holding a convention . . . and fix the time and place . . . then, in view of the expenses . . . Saskatchewan views might be recorded by resolution [and] forwarded. . ." (Progressive Conservative Party Files, File S-S-3a, H. J. Burrows to MacNicol, Oct. 21, 1941).

[37]See Appendix 1. Ontario delegates made up almost half those attending.

[38]Toronto *Globe and Mail*, Nov. 1–8, 1941. The effect of the *Globe and Mail* campaign was noted by R. A. Bell (Interview, July 15, 1964).

[39]"The Mailbox," *Financial Post*, Dec. 20, 1941. Cf. Meighen Papers, MacPherson to Meighen, Nov. 25, 1941.

better than his despised opponent. For the moment, however, Meighen's reason was still governing his emotions.

The conference resumed Saturday morning, and the struggle was immediately joined between the group around Macdonnell and those who wanted to select the leader. A motion to confirm the report of the committee in favour of Meighen's selection was instantly countered by a motion demanding that the committee's recommendations be rejected on the ground that the meeting had not been called to select a leader.[40] Hanson, who was not enthusiastic about the prospect of Meighen's return, but who had played a moderating role throughout,[41] then suggested that Meighen be permitted to state his position. This the Senator proceeded to do.

Meighen said that he knew many in the party wanted him to return, "and among them practically all those whose opinion I [value] very highly in this country and in this Party." But he was sixty-seven and dreaded the task; yet, if he refused, it would mean that he was evading an urgent war duty. He had attempted, he continued, to ascertain what had occurred in committee, and what he had learned had shaped his course. While he agreed that he had no right to expect unanimity, thirteen negative votes was a considerable number. "I know it wouldn't have taken them long to scale the hurdle in front if they in their hearts really felt that I should take the helm. . . ." These thirteen, he concluded, doubtless represented many in the country, and "without any reservation in the world in their hearts and their minds, I wouldn't dream of accepting this terrible responsibility. I therefore shall not."[42] Meighen's speech seemed to imply that the opposition to him was the rankling point that prevented him from acceding to the wish of the majority. When, therefore, a delegate asked him "if these gentlemen and ladies make it unanimous, will you accept this office?" his reply seemingly squelched all possibility of his taking the post: "I don't want to be short or brief if I ask that I do not be pressed further. I gave my decision and the reasons I gave still apply for all time."[43] Meighen then retired from the meeting, leaving bickering and confusion behind him.

Delegates hurled recriminations at the "noble thirteen" who had seemingly blocked the return of the man wanted by the majority. Others reiterated their demand for a convention, and the meeting seemed on

[40]Minutes, 1941, pp. 56–8.
[41]Hanson Papers, File O-100, Macdonnell to Hanson, Nov. 10, and reply, Nov. 12, 1941.
[42]Minutes, 1941, pp. 59–64.
[43]*Ibid.*, p. 68.

the verge of dissolution in a welter of accusations and counter-accusations. A meeting *in camera* of those opposing the selection of a leader was then held, but after three hours the approximately forty delegates returned with a new demand for a convention in January 1942.[44] This resolution provoked new assaults on the "thirteen"; one delegate accused them of acting "too much on principle and not enough on the practical," while another stated that he respected them but could only doubt their judgment.[45] After further dispute the question of whether a convention should be held, the question for which the delegates had assembled, was put to the vote and defeated. A second vote was then taken on the motion that "it is the opinion of this meeting that the Right Honourable Arthur Meighen be asked to be our leader." Apparently believing that it was either Meighen or chaos, the solid front of opposition cracked, and the resolution carried by 129 votes to four. A motion to make the selection unanimous was declared carried,[46] and a committee of three was selected to present the results of the conference to Meighen.

The onus of decision passed once again to Meighen. The leader-designate described his feelings in a letter to an old friend, Colonel Hugh Clark:

. . . when I got to the [railway] station at four o'clock, a bunch [of delegates met me] and told me the whole thing was over; that the Resolution was unanimous, and that was what I had to meet. I still told them the same thing [i.e., that the answer was no], and indeed, when I got home . . . I had decided not to take the job. Reflections over Sunday and Monday compelled me to change my mind. I became convinced, and certainly my wife became convinced, that I would lose what respect and regard the people felt for me if in the full light of day and with an appeal which had by that time reached Coast-to-Coast dimensions, I refused to try to do the one thing I can do, if, indeed, there is anything I can do, entirely well. . . .

The decision was an agonizing one, for Meighen knew well the political difficulties he would face. Also, his investment business was at last beginning to prosper, and he hesitated to leave it in other hands. "It will really be weeks yet before I get straightened away," he wrote. "You quite realize that whatever I have it is here. It is the product of a life's work and I have to make the best possible arrangements."[47] Characteristically, however, once the decision was reached, Meighen entered into the struggle wholeheartedly and released a long manifesto.

[44]*Ibid.*, p. 121.
[45]Senators McRae and Black in *ibid.*, pp. 132, 133.
[46]No count was taken on the first vote (*ibid.*, p. 135). The second vote is in *ibid.*, p. 136, and the vote on the motion for unanimity is in *ibid.*, p. 144.
[47]Meighen Papers, Meighen to Clark, Nov. 14, 1941; Meighen to Sen. A. D. McRae, Nov. 24, 1941.

After first explaining how the task of leadership had fallen to him once more, the new leader flatly threw down the challenge to the King government:

A Government on a strictly party basis is in office and exercising despotic powers. This state of affairs in a war of life and death is anomalous. Such a Government . . . cannot bring the whole nation to its maximum endeavour. . . .

. . . This nation is in the throes of a crisis. . . . That Britain is doing its mightiest few will dispute. . . . Who will dare to say that Canada is even in sight of a total war?

. . . I shall, therefore, urge with all the power I can bring to bear compulsory selective service over the whole field of war. . . .[48]

Meighen's statement left no room for doubt as to his policy. The battle would be fought for conscription and national government. Mackenzie King would have to be excluded from any coalition, and this could only be accomplished if an alliance, strong enough to form a government, could be forged from Conservatives and conscriptionist Liberals. The policy was to be 1917 all over again.[49]

Mackenzie King did not relish the return of his old antagonist to active politics. "Meighen will be for railway amalgamation, have the C.P.R. and other big interests back of him and Imperialistic jingoes in Canada and Britain alike. . . . life day by day will be made intolerable by his attacks, misrepresentations and the like." At a cabinet meeting on November 13, the day Meighen released his manifesto, King discussed the issue with his colleagues. He pointed out "that my position now is the same as Sir Wilfrid's was in 1917: that Meighen was no longer for co-operation with Government policy, but opposition to Government policy—opposition first for conscription, National Government, and against our policies generally. It meant the financial forces and the press would rise against us." The Prime Minister also indicated something of his own plans. Following a suggestion that the conscription issue be fought on the grounds that it was unnecessary, King agreed but stated that he wanted to keep alive the possibility of an election. "It was necessary to put the fear of the Lord into the Tories, who did not want to face the people and who knew that the people generally were against conscription for overseas. . . ."[50] At the same time, however, King told the cabinet that he would do nothing to impede Meighen's entry into the House. "While I saw Meighen's entry significant of strife," he

---

[48]"I Shall Answer the Call," Toronto *Globe and Mail,* Nov. 13, 1941, p. 1.
[49]Graham, *Meighen,* III, 106.
[50]Pickersgill, *Mackenzie King Record,* I, 278, 281–2.

said, "it was not for me to begin the strife by taking any step which could be construed as a desire to maintain government by party lines to the point of keeping out of the Commons the leader of another party. . . ."[51]

The lines were clearly drawn for one of the most significant struggles in Canadian history. Before the main engagement could be joined, however, Meighen would have to leave the security of the Senate, find a seat in the House of Commons, and contest a by-election. Only the most pessimistic of Conservatives could have doubted that these steps would be anything but formalities.

Barring the possibility of a member's death or an unexpected general election, Meighen could only secure a seat if one of the sitting Conservatives resigned, forcing a by-election. The problem, of course, was to pick a "safe" seat certain to return the leader. At the same time, with the party desperately short of legislative talent, no one wanted to deprive one of the more capable members of his place. Not surprisingly, perhaps, it proved rather difficult to induce a suitable M.P. to offer his place to Meighen.[52] Immediately Meighen had been selected as leader, two members had offered to resign: the Hon. Earl Rowe, M.P. for the rural Ontario constituency of Dufferin-Simcoe, and Major Alan Cockeram from the Toronto riding of York South.[53] Apparently, Meighen did not want either of these seats. Rural ridings might not be safe ground for a conscriptionist, and Cockeram was on active service with his regiment, a valuable asset to a party claiming to represent the serviceman's interest. The most obvious choice after these two was the Toronto constituency of High Park, held since 1925 by the lacklustre A. J. Anderson, a 78-year-old lawyer. In precarious health, Anderson at one point agreed to give up his seat for his leader, but he soon renegued. The sticking point apparently was the compensation Anderson required for his sacrifice. Estimates of the amount ranged from $12,000 to $20,000, a sum that Meighen and his party presumably were not prepared to pay.[54] Finally, on November 26, Major Cockeram was allowed to resign, opening the way for Meighen's entry into the House of Commons.

The constituency of York South appeared to be a safe seat for the

[51]*Ibid.*, p. 279.

[52]Meighen Papers, Meighen to MacPherson, Nov. 27, 1941.

[53]Rowe Interview, Sept. 9, 1964; House of Commons, *Debates*, Jan. 30, 1942, p. 177 (J. F. Pouliot, M.P., citing Judith Robinson, "Tory Patriot Offers Costly Seat," *News*, date unknown).

[54]Meighen Papers, J. R. MacNicol to Meighen, Dec. 5, 1941; Adamson Papers, Diary, Dec. 4, 1941: ". . . Anderson asked $12,000 for his seat. Shocking this just the curse of the Tory party again [*sic*]"; House of Commons, *Debates*, Jan. 30, 1942, p. 177.

Conservative leader. Since its formation in 1904, the constituency had never failed to vote Conservative, often with large majorities. In recent elections, however, the Conservative plurality had been decreasing, and the victory of 1940 was probably attributable mostly to the popularity of Cockeram, a decorated veteran of the Great War, a militia officer, and an outgoing individual. The electorate of approximately 33,500 had given Cockeram a comfortable 2,500-vote plurality over his Liberal oppenent, and a 10,000-vote lead over the C.C.F. candidate, Joseph W. Noseworthy. Within the boundaries of York South lay the wealthy and exclusive suburb of Forest Hill Village, the middle-class area of Weston, and the heavily populated working-class districts of York Township. The population was largely of British stock, although there were substantial numbers of Jews in the Village.[55] There was some party dispute about the selection of York South, and R. A. Bell, for one, tried to dissuade Meighen from running there. Bell believed that High Park would be more receptive to the party leader, but John R. MacNicol, M.P. for Toronto Davenport, wrote Meighen that he was relieved he would run in York South. The reason was that "there are many foreigners and railroad men" in High Park. Nonetheless, it is hard to see how Meighen could have done better at that time than to contest York South.[56]

With a seat now opened for him, the next problem facing Meighen was whether or not he would face opposition in York South. This question did not remain unanswered for long as the C.C.F. again nominated Joseph W. Noseworthy on December 1 to contest the vacancy. The nomination of the candidate was no mere whim of the local party organization but was the result of a deliberate policy decision taken by the C.C.F. National Executive on November 15–16, shortly after Meighen's designation as leader. As the archetypal representative of the "Old Gang" and of the "profit seeking wolves of Big Business,"

[55]The population of the constituency of York South, as reported by the 1941 census, was 78,167. Of this number, 5,740 lived in Weston, 11,757 in Forest Hill Village, and 60,670 in York Township (Canada, Dominion Bureau of Statistics, *Eighth Census of Canada, 1941*, 11 vols., Ottawa, 1944, II, 35). Well over three-quarters of the population was of British stock (*ibid.*, II, 442–3). Income distribution was sharply varied in the three districts making up the riding. The head of a household in Forest Hill earned an average of $3,504 yearly and lived in a house valued at $12,611. In Weston, the averages were $1,715 and $4,583 respectively, while in York Township the average income was $1,622 and the average house was valued at only $3,783. *Ibid.*, IX, 162–7. The York Township averages above are raised by the "better" districts bordering on Forest Hill Village.

[56]Bell Interview, July 15, 1964; Meighen Papers, MacNicol to Meighen, Dec. 5, 1941. Election results in High Park show a progressive decline in Conservative strength. In 1925, the plurality was 10,344; in 1930, 6,042; in 1935, 2,592; and in 1940, only 205 votes.

Meighen was to be opposed by the C.C.F. wherever he might run.[57]

The heir of the Progressive party, the C.C.F. had been formed in 1932–33 to provide the Canadian people with an alternative to the two "old parties." Despite the suffering of the 1930's and despite the leadership of the remarkable J. S. Woodsworth, the social democratic movement had not managed to impress itself on the voters and had elected only a handful of members. With the two exceptions of Grey-Bruce in Ontario (whose long-time M.P., Agnes Macphail, was not quite a C.C.F.er) and one Nova Scotia seat won in the 1940 election, the C.C.F. had never returned a Member of Parliament east of the prairie provinces. On the outbreak of war in 1939, the party, divided between its neutralists and its proponents of an all-out war effort, had taken a somewhat equivocal stand on the question of Canadian participation, and this had seemed to weaken it even more. The party's war policy, however, had kept pace with changing Canadian opinion, undergoing a metamorphosis from pacifism to conscription of wealth rather than men, to no conscription of men without conscription of wealth and, finally, by late 1941, to conscription of both men and wealth.[58] Coincident with this shift in policy, the C.C.F. found its extensive and well-developed programmes of social welfare were becoming increasingly more attractive to the public. The depression of the war years seemed to be encouraging people to look ahead to a brighter postwar world, to a prospect of prosperity and peace. When this hope was coupled with the present realities of full employment, stronger trade unions, and an admiration for the effective resistance of the "socialist" Soviet Union, the C.C.F. was the beneficiary. The party was ready to move into Ontario.[59]

Joseph Noseworthy, the nominee in York South, was a good choice to lead the attack. A long-time resident of the constituency, Noseworthy was the popular head of the English department at the neighbourhood high school, Vaughan Road Collegiate, and as such he had a ready-made group of youthful supporters, a large number of former students, and hundreds of parents ready to work for him. Despite his crushing defeat

[57]C.C.F. Records, Vol. 8, National Executive Minutes, Nov. 15–16, 1941; Toronto *Globe and Mail*, Dec. 2, 1941, p. 2; Descriptive phrases from a C.C.F. York South campaign pamphlet.

[58]Leo Zakuta, *A Protest Movement Becalmed: A Study of Change in the CCF* (Toronto, 1964), p. 60. For the C.C.F. dilemma in 1939, see Kenneth McNaught, *A Prophet in Politics: A Biography of J. S. Woodsworth* (Toronto, 1959), pp. 305–7.

[59]G. L. Caplan, "The Failure of Canadian Socialism: The Ontario Experience, 1932–1945," *Canadian Historical Review*, XLIV (June, 1963), 99; David Lewis and Frank Scott, *Make This Your Canada* (Toronto, 1943), pp. 3, 14, 25; M. J. Coldwell, *Left Turn, Canada* (New York, 1945), pp. 26–30.

at the hands of Major Cockeram in 1940, Noseworthy had a bare chance to win in the changed circumstances of 1942, but only if the vote was not split by the entry of a Liberal candidate.

What, indeed, would the Liberals do? Meighen would be very dangerous to the government in the House of Commons, and his cutting attacks might destroy Mackenzie King's grasp on his increasingly restive English-speaking supporters. The York South Liberal Association (or rather one of the two feuding groups in the riding claiming that title) provided the answer on December 5 when it declined to contest the seat, declaring that as Cockeram had resigned only to facilitate Meighen's entry into the House, his wishes should be respected.[60] These were praiseworthy sentiments, but they concealed definite attempts to stop any Liberal from running against Meighen.[61] The Conservative leader, certainly, had no doubts as to the reasons for this uncommon courtesy. The Prime Minister, he wrote long after the event, "would not put a candidate in the field knowing if he did so the vote opposing me would be divided, and he wanted it entirely concentrated, and did not care much under what auspices it was concentrated. . . ."[62]

Meighen's jaundiced view of Liberal motives was probably correct, although there were some extenuating factors. A "tradition" that the leader of a party seeking to enter the House in a by-election should not be opposed did exist, and the Liberals could claim that they were honouring this often violated custom.[63] Furthermore, it has been alleged that there was an agreement between the Liberals and Conservatives that Meighen would be unopposed in York South if the Conservatives did not oppose Humphrey Mitchell, the newly appointed Minister of Labour, who was seeking election to the House in a by-election in Welland, Ontario, also scheduled for February 9, 1942. There is no doubt that Meighen made at least one attempt to get a candidate to run in Welland, but there is also no doubt that after his first choice refused to consider seeking the nomination, he dissuaded the Welland Conservatives from

---

[60]Toronto *Globe and Mail*, Dec. 6, 1941, p. 4. Details of the split between the two riding associations may be found in *Toronto Daily Star*, Dec. 3, p. 8, and Dec. 5, p. 8.

[61]F. J. MacRae, the Liberal candidate in 1940, was visited by the Postmaster General, W. P. Mulock, and was politely advised not to seek the nomination (MacRae Interview, June 2, 1965). The Hon. M. J. Coldwell, C.C.F. leader at the time, said in an interview that he learned after the election that Mackenzie King had dissuaded the Rt. Hon. Sir William Mulock (then 98 years old!) from contesting the seat (Interview, July 6, 1963).

[62]Meighen Papers, Meighen to Theodore Ropp, July 9, 1957, and Meighen to H. E. Wilmot, Jan. 17, 1942.

[63]See *supra*, p. 18.

entering the contest.[64] Although Meighen later denied that there had been any pact with the Liberals, many contemporary politicians believed that some agreement had been reached.[65]

In the weeks after his selection as leader, Meighen was busy with the difficult tasks of arranging his personal affairs and with party organization. He was painfully aware of the inadequacy of the party's representation in the House of Commons, but he was unable to induce the men he wanted to stand for election when vacancies could be opened for them.[66] There was more success with finances. The system created by J. M. Macdonnell in Montreal in January 1941 ceased to function, and a new organization under Senator A. D. McRae, the organizer of the Conservative victory in 1930, was formed.[67] "The arrangement with Meighen," Hanson wrote some months later, "was that an entirely new financial set-up was made and he was guaranteed relief from any worry over finance." Meighen's biographer has indicated obliquely that some $200,000 was to have been provided for the party's initial needs, and that this sum was intended to finance a national movement for conscription. "We all realize that organization in the old Party line is not either wise or in our minds at all," Meighen wrote to H. R. Milner in Calgary. "It is a national new movement we want to generate to get national results."[68]

Without its leader in the House of Commons, however, the national movement for a total war effort would be stillborn, and thus the first task was to get Meighen elected. The job of running the by-election campaign was turned over to J. Earl Lawson, the former federal member for York South. Lawson's chief aide was Leopold Macaulay, York

[64]Meighen tried to persuade M. A. MacPherson to run (Meighen Papers, Meighen to MacPherson, Dec. 13, and reply, Dec. 16, 1941). For Meighen's efforts at dissuading the Welland Conservatives, see Meighen Papers, Meighen to T. F. Forestell, Dec. 16, 1941.

[65]This belief was shared by members of both parties. T. A. Crerar Interview, July 17, 1964; Finlayson Interview, June 1, 1963; Dafoe Papers, Microfilm roll M-80, T. A. Crerar to Dafoe, Jan. 31, 1942: "We did not nominate a Liberal against Meighen and there was some understanding—how complete it was I do not know—that the Conservatives would not nominate against Mitchell." Meighen's denial of an arrangement is in Meighen Papers, Meighen to John Bird, Feb. 17, 1942.

[66]Meighen tried to persuade MacPherson and Drew to enter the House (Meighen Papers, Meighen to H. R. Milner, Nov. 28, and Meighen to MacPherson, Nov. 27, 1941). Meighen apparently also wanted W. D. Herridge to enter the House, but there is no evidence for this in Meighen's papers (Herridge Papers, Herridge to A. P. Waldron, Nov. 24, 1941).

[67]Hanson Papers, File O-160-F, Hanson to Meighen, March 23, 1942.

[68]*Ibid.*, File O-167, Hanson to D. C. Coleman, May 30, 1942; Graham, *Meighen*, III, 162–3; Meighen Papers, Meighen to H. R. Milner, Nov. 28, 1941.

South's Conservative representative in the Ontario legislature since 1926. Under the leadership of these experienced local politicians, a full campaign organization detailing responsibility for everything from publicity to "citizen's committees" was created and staffed before Christmas 1941.[69] Ample funds were available for the campaign, although all but a small portion of the $7500 expended apparently came from Meighen's own pocket.[70]

While the campaign organization was wisely left to local politicians, Meighen himself determined the issue upon which he would base his fight for election. This issue—the only one as far as Meighen was concerned—was the winning of the war, and this meant conscription and national government. His decision to stand on this platform was probably intuitive and was grounded upon his belief that conscription was the foundation without which an effective war effort was an impossibility. It was obvious to Meighen that "no nation has any right to go into a war on any other than a compulsory selective service system."[71] Nonetheless, to get the statistics necessary to bolster his beliefs, Meighen commissioned research into the war efforts of the other British dominions (none of which had imposed conscription for overseas service), into the war policy of the C.C.F., and into Canada's military condition. The result of all this effort was minimal. R. A. Bell prepared an elaborate memorandum on recruiting in the dominions which proved inconclusive but upon which Meighen proceeded to base his attacks. The C.C.F. press of the 1930's was searched for anti-war sentiments without success, and efforts to discover weaknesses in the armed forces were hampered by the requirements of military security.[72]

[69]Meighen Papers, Lawson to Meighen, Dec. 22, 1941.
[70]Meighen put up $7300 himself, while $159.85 was received in contributions (*ibid.*, C. F. Moore to Meighen, March 10, 1942). The money was spent as follows: $1800 for radio advertising; $1000 for billboard advertising; and $2750 for printing, engraving, and distribution of leaflets (*ibid.*, Return of election expenses). If these figures are correct, Meighen's campaign was a reasonably inexpensive one. Official returns, however, have often been regarded as mere formalities—and the expenses are often scaled down drastically (Norman Ward, *The Canadian House of Commons: Representation*, Toronto, 1950, chap. xv). Graham, *Meighen*, III, 161, implies that part at least of the $7300 Meighen put up came from his financial backers who were supporting the conscription campaign.
[71]Toronto *Globe and Mail*, Jan. 30, 1942, p. 1; Forsey Interview, Aug. 25, 1964.
[72]Bell Interview, Aug. 24, 1964; Meighen Papers, Milner to Meighen, Jan. 12, 1942, and "CCF Attitudes Toward War," n.d. Meighen's principal correspondents on the military situation were Senator McRae and Murdoch MacPherson (e.g., Meighen Papers, MacPherson to Meighen, Dec. 23, 31, 1941). This last letter contains a report from A. H. Bence, M.P. for Saskatoon, dated Dec. 30, 1941, that is revealing as to the tenor of the reports: "I am afraid that there is nothing that I can point out of a critical nature as far as the local situation is concerned."

Meighen's advisers were not entirely pleased with the candidate's choice of campaign issues. As early as December 9, before Meighen's first meeting with the executive of the York South Conservative Association, Earl Lawson urged his leader not to oppose an excess profits tax and to support the conscription of wealth and industry as well as the conscription of manpower.[73] Remembering the unemployment and distress of the 1930's when parts of the constituency had been among the hardest hit in the nation, Lawson based his advice on a realistic assessment of political conditions in York South. F. G. Gardiner, the reeve of Forest Hill Village and a key figure in the campaign staff, took a similar tack, and his persistence became so tiresome that Meighen took to calling him "Social Security Gardiner" each time they met. These warnings fell on deaf ears, however, for Meighen was concerned solely with the war.[74]

Meighen's obsession was readily apparent in his first major address of the campaign, a local radio speech on January 9. After a brief attack on the C.C.F. for blocking his election by acclamation, the candidate turned directly to his joint themes of national government and conscription. His thesis was simple: "we are not organized politically as we should be. . . ." and "as a consequence of an unsuitable political set-up we are not organized militarily as we should be." In proof of this contention the Conservative leader cited the example of New Zealand, claiming that the small Pacific dominion had contributed a proportionately greater share to the empire war effort than had Canada.[75] How could this alleged disparity be made up? "We need more men for overseas service," Meighen claimed. "We cannot organize this nation without ample power to direct the energies of every man and woman to the place where those energies are needed. That power this government refuses to exercise. The cold hand of political expediency has held it in its grip. A trembling servitude to a sinister tradition has gone far to benumb the striking power of Canada." In Meighen's opinion there could be no excuse for refusing to conscript men in any war. Certainly Mackenzie King's reason—"that if we compel Canadians to serve where Canadians have to fight to save Canada, we will destroy the unity of the Nation," as Meighen put it— was foolish. "Can any normal mind accept such a preposterous con-

[73]Meighen Papers, Lawson to Meighen, Dec. 9, 1941.
[74]F. G. Gardiner Interview, Sept. 8, 1964; Leopold Macaulay Interview, Sept. 17, 1965.
[75]The example of New Zealand was not entirely appropriate for Meighen's needs. Not only did that country lack the manufacturing and mineral resources that absorbed much of Canada's manpower, but its government was formed by Labour.

tention?" he asked. But in spite of what he believed to be the government's cowardly course thus far in the war, the Conservative leader generously offered to share the burden of the direction of the war with the Liberals. "If wanted, we of the Conservative party will . . . help within [the government]; if not wanted, we will help from without; but we insist on action. We shall not be satisfied with substitutes or subterfuge. To the utmost of our strength we shall urge abandonment of things secondary and things that make for division and delay. . . ."[76]

Arthur Meighen's speech was forcefully, even brilliantly delivered, but in the context of wartime Canada its logic left much to be desired. The Hon. T. A. Crerar, King's Minister of Mines and Resources and a colleague of Meighen's in the Union government of the Great War, wrote to a friend about the opening salvo of the Conservative leader's campaign:

Meighen's speech the other night was a characteristic one. He offers to place himself on the altar of his country in a National Government—and then proceeds to make it impossible. I doubt if I have known anyone during my political life with less political instinct or sense than Meighen has. In this he is the victim of his limitations.[77]

Who could doubt Crerar's judgment? Meighen showed no glimmer of understanding for the objections of French Canada to overseas conscription. For attempting to abide by his pledge to Quebec, Mackenzie King was guilty of "trembling servitude to a sinister tradition." Anyone who agreed with King and his policy lacked a "normal mind." Meighen's views, with their emphasis on victory and sacrifice, were truly "patriotic," but they were hardly open to compromise. In Canada, as elsewhere, compromise was the stuff of politics—even in wartime—and without it eventual defeat was inescapable. Meighen, however, had made one further error of more immediate import.

The opening speech of the campaign was notable for Meighen's almost total neglect of his immediate opponents. Other than to level a perfunctory blast at the C.C.F. for daring to force a test at the polls, Meighen had scarcely glanced in Noseworthy's direction. All his heavy fire was directed at the Liberal government. There was no appeal to the voters of York South, no recognition of the C.C.F. campaign for social welfare measures, and no sign of an understanding of local issues. Meighen's faith in the broad interests of his electorate was evidently

[76]Meighen's speech is printed in full in *Toronto Daily Star*, Jan. 10, 1942, p. 31. This theme was repeated again and again (Toronto *Globe and Mail*, Jan. 17, p. 1, Jan. 21, p. 4, Jan. 30, 1942, p. 1).
[77]Dafoe Papers, Microfilm roll M-80, T. A. Crerar to Dafoe, Jan. 13, 1942.

real—but was it realistic? Might not the electors feel that Meighen was using them only as a springboard to a better platform? Might not the Liberals of the constituency resent Meighen's attacks on their party's policy and translate this resentment into votes—if not for Noseworthy, then against Meighen? More directly, might not Meighen's total reliance on war issues alienate an electorate that was being promised social reform by his opponent?

A new factor was interjected into the campaign on the day after Meighen's opening address. By a "spontaneous and enthusiastic expression of the people's will"[78] and apparently without Meighen's knowledge,[79] the Committee for Total War was organized at a meeting on the roof garden of Toronto's plush Royal York Hotel. The Committee's avowed purpose was to mobilize public opinion behind a policy of conscription and to exert pressure on Ontario's Members of Parliament, in the hope of forcing this predominantly Liberal group to desert Mackenzie King and demand conscription.[80] The Committee for Total War, more popularly known as the "Toronto 200," had met at the call of three prominent businessmen, J. Y. Murdoch of Noranda Mines, C. L. Burton of the Robert Simpson Company, and F. K. Morrow, a Toronto financier and corporation director. In the background was George McCullagh, who was hoping to organize all Ontario into a grass roots movement that could propel Meighen into power.[81]

The formation of the Toronto 200 marked the shift of the conscription campaign into high gear. Meighen's election campaign was merged into a province-wide effort, featuring a lavish use of the mass media, all paid for "by a small group of patriotic citizens."[82] Full-page advertisements calling for "Total War Now" were placed in every daily and weekly newspaper in Ontario.[83] In Toronto, of course, the *Globe and Mail*

[78]Toronto *Globe and Mail*, Jan. 12, 1942, p. 1.

[79]Meighen said he knew nothing of the Committee "until the call for the meeting was being complied with." Hanson Papers, File S-175-M, Meighen to Hanson, Feb. 13, 1942.

[80]Toronto *Globe and Mail*, Jan. 12, 1942, p. 1, address by the Committee's chairman, J. Y. Murdoch.

[81]Adamson Papers, Diary, Jan. 10, 1942: "Today is the day of the 'All Out War' meeting at the Royal York. Murdoch and Burton and George McCullagh. Will it prove another Globe stunt [*sic*]." Dafoe Papers, Microfilm roll M-80, T. A. Crerar to Dafoe, Jan. 13, 1942; Meighen Papers, C. O. Knowles to Meighen, Feb. 18, 1942; House of Commons, *Debates*, Jan. 29, 1942, pp. 145–7 (Mr. Turner).

[82]Toronto *Globe and Mail*, Jan. 12, 1942, p. 8.

[83]The *Toronto Daily Star*, Jan. 12, 1942, p. 10, published a memorandum distributed at the meeting detailing publicity plans. See the file of editorials in P.A.O., Prime Minister's Department, G. A. Drew Papers, Leader of the Opposition, Box 7, "War Effort" File.

spearheaded the campaign, turning over its news columns to the Committee's activities. On one typical day at the beginning of the drive, the morning newspaper had five articles about conscription on the front page, two on page 2, one on page 4, one on page 6, two on page 8, all of page 9, and even an article demanding compulsory service on the social page.[84] In other communities similar efforts were in progress. As the *Globe and Mail* put it on January 13, "The heather is on fire in Ontario."[85] Indeed it was, and if the fire was not quite as spontaneous as McCullagh's newspaper claimed, it was nonetheless dangerous. The threat of a revolt of Ontario backbenchers, coupled with the imminent return of Meighen to the Opposition ranks, posed one of the gravest threats of the war years for the Liberal government.

The demand for conscription in January 1942 was entirely "political and psychological," Mackenzie King believed, for no practical difficulty had yet been experienced in finding volunteers for Canada's overseas armies. The government's opponents were trying to make "conscription for overseas service the symbol, in English-speaking Canada, of a total war effort,"[86] and although he believed this view to be wrong, King could see that his pledge not to conscript men for overseas service would be a potentially embarrassing commitment when casualties began to mount. As early as mid-December 1941, therefore, he had begun to feel that the government would have to be released from its pledges by a plebiscite.[87] "We might get into Parliament," King told his cabinet, itself restive on the issue of conscription, "and find the party divided; already, there were some for and some against. . . . The situation might become such that to settle the matter there might have to be a change of Government. One thing I did not want was to see any Government managing Canada's affairs of which Arthur Meighen would be the head, or a member. . . ."[88]

Characteristically, King saw that the idea of a plebiscite would also serve to cut the ground out from under the Conservatives.[89] With Meighen, McCullagh, and the Toronto 200 all demanding conscription, the plebiscite concept offered a way around the Conservative leader's attempt to win his by-election simply on a show of hands between those

---

[84]Jan. 13, 1942.

[85]*Ibid.*, p. 1. The fire apparently spread to the prairies, and a Total War advertisement was placed in a Regina newspaper (Gardiner Papers, T. H. Wood to Gardiner, Jan. 20, 23, 1942).

[86]Pickersgill, *Mackenzie King Record*, I, 333 [Editor's comments].

[87]*Ibid.*, p. 314; Dafoe Papers, Microfilm roll M-79, Grant Dexter to Dafoe, Nov. 18 and Dec. 22, 1941.

[88]Pickersgill, *Mackenzie King Record*, I, 314.

[89]*Ibid.*, p. 313.

for and against conscription. With the prospect of a plebiscite before them, only those who wanted conscription immediately, regardless of the situation in the country, would be compelled to vote for Meighen.[90] Accordingly, the Speech from the Throne that opened the 1942 session of parliament on January 22 included the following statement of policy: "My ministers . . . will seek, from the people, by means of a plebiscite, release from any obligation arising out of any past commitments restricting the methods of raising men for military service."[91] The announcement of the plebiscite produced the predictable charges of political cowardice from the Opposition.[92] Meighen was "shamed and humiliated by our Government's despicable evasion. . . . It is a base and cowardly insult. . . ." Major Cockeram, on leave from his regiment to participate in Meighen's attempt to win his old constituency, called the plebiscite the "rankest insult to men on active service." Mitchell Hepburn, the Liberal premier of Ontario, announced that because of the plebiscite he would support Meighen in his bid for election. As George Drew, the Ontario Conservative leader, was already in the fight, Hepburn's entry seemingly united all right-of-centre shades of the Ontario political spectrum directly behind the Conservative leader.

Mesmerized by the conscription issue, Meighen believed that the plebiscite would increase his chances for success in his attempts to destroy the King government. Who would not be outraged by this shameful attempt to evade the responsibility for settling the conscription question? "A fair, decent breakaway from King in the House on this plebiscite would be a magnificent achievement," he wrote. "It would probably lead to the only move that would save the situation. . . ." This move, he continued, "is for the Government members assisted by us if they want us, to unitedly tell the country what has to be done. . . ." What had to be done, it was evident, was the launching of total war— conscription and national government.[93]

Other observers were not misled by the effect of King's call for the plebiscite, for the new dilemma facing the Conservatives was becoming clear. The announcement of the forthcoming vote on conscription seemingly solidified the Liberal party behind the Prime Minister,[94] and

[90]Ralph Allen, *Ordeal by Fire* (New York, 1961), p. 416; Graham, *Meighen*, III, 108.

[91]House of Commons, *Debates*, Jan. 22, 1942, p. 2. The bill to permit the plebiscite was not introduced until late February.

[92]Meighen Papers, Meighen to John Bracken, Jan. 23, 1942; Toronto *Globe and Mail*, Jan. 30, 1942, p. 1; Hepburn Papers, Supplementary Correspondence (private), 1942, Hepburn to Meighen, Jan. 27, and reply, Jan. 28, 1942.

[93]Meighen Papers, Meighen to A. B. Watt, Feb. 2, 1942.

[94]Moffat Papers, Vol. 47, Memorandum of conversation with Mr. J. W. McConnell, Jan. 24, 1942, and Notes on political situation, Feb. 7, 1942.

the chances for the breakaway foreseen by the Conservatives were now decreasing despite the best efforts of Meighen and the Toronto 200. In the light of this changed situation, attacks on the idea of the plebiscite inevitably became attacks on the question posed by King—conscription or not? Whatever their contempt for King's political expediency, the Conservatives could hardly afford to see the idea of conscription defeated. As Senator McRae wrote to Meighen, "like it or not," the party had to work to bring out the largest possible affirmative vote in the plebiscite. The Prime Minister, he added, "has once more proven himself the most astute politician Canada has ever had."[95] Indeed he had. King's plebiscite had destroyed Meighen's chief issue; more important yet was the Conservative leader's failure to realize this. The C.C.F. organization in York South, however, was not about to make this mistake.

The strategy and organization of the C.C.F. in the Toronto constituency were superb. By deliberate plan the policy of Noseworthy's headquarters was to stir up interest in the campaign and to force Meighen to defend his past record. This strategy was working better than expected, E. B. Jolliffe, a vice-president of the Ontario party, wrote to national headquarters on January 18. The *Globe and Mail*, he reported, was beginning to attack the C.C.F. each day, and Meighen was being forced to devote more and more of his time to defending himself and to setting out his "real" views on social security.[96] At the same time the C.C.F. message of social reform and total war was being delivered to each home in the riding by an army of dedicated volunteers, gathered together from the entire metropolitan area.[97] In sharp contrast to the usual C.C.F. penury, money was available for the by-election fight. A nation-wide appeal for funds produced more than $5000,[98] and as the party relied on volunteer workers, this money could be used for radio and press publicity.

The plebiscite, which had effectively forced Meighen into an untenable

[95]Meighen Papers, McRae to Meighen, n.d. Meighen's reaction to the comments on King can be imagined. Cf. *Winnipeg Free Press*, Feb. 3, 1942, p. 1.

[96]C.C.F. Records, Vol. 54, E. J[olliffe] to David Lewis, Jan. 18, 1942. For the tenor of Meighen's defence: Toronto *Globe and Mail*, Jan. 17, p. 1, Jan. 21, p. 4, Feb. 4, p. 4.

[97]Noseworthy reported that "several hundred" canvassers were organized (C.C.F. Records, Vol. 54, Noseworthy to David Lewis, Jan. 9, 1942). For the reactions of a "typical" canvasser, see Hester James, "I Canvassed for Noseworthy," *Canadian Forum*, XXII (April, 1942), 16–18. The methods used in York South are still in use by the party today; *The Riverdale Story: A By-Election Campaign* (Toronto, 1964) details the winning of a by-election with similar techniques.

[98]The budget was figured on a range of between $3600 and $5000 (C.C.F. Records, Vol. 54, F. A. Brewin to D. Lewis, Jan. 9, 1942). E. B. Jolliffe states that this maximum figure was exceeded (Interview, June 2, 1965).

position, hardly bothered Noseworthy's campaign. The C.C.F. candidate readily fell back on his already well-worn themes of social security and "conscription of wealth" and redoubled his attacks on Meighen's past. "Tories of his type," Noseworthy said of his opponent's attempts to defend himself, "always become interested in the poor at election time." "The Tory clique who drafted Mr. Meighen," he charged on another occasion, "want to give us the old 1914–18 leadership for the war, and they want the same type of leadership for the reconstruction period that follows the war." This clique, he claimed, was using conscription to divert attention from "other phases, such as the mobilization of all our material resources. They hope, moreover, to give to the Conservative party . . . a momentary flicker of life. They hope to get through the election of my opponent some control of our war policy."[99]

Faced with this barrage of C.C.F. charges, Meighen began to modify his stand on social welfare as the campaign drew to a close. First, however, the Conservative leader found himself embroiled in a dispute with the *Toronto Daily Star*, the one local newspaper that was unfriendly to him. The *Star* had reported Meighen as saying in a speech on January 29 that "if we have to conscript wealth to win the war, we will, but people of common sense don't advocate that until the last gasp." Six days later, Meighen belatedly claimed that he had been misquoted and announced that he now favoured the conscription of wealth.[100] This last-minute conversion was scarcely believable.

After the entry of Premier Hepburn into the campaign at Meighen's side, Noseworthy's efforts received an evidently unsolicited boost when Arthur Roebuck, a Liberal Member of Parliament from Toronto and Hepburn's Attorney General from 1934 to 1937, attacked both his old leader and Arthur Meighen in two hard-hitting radio speeches. Roebuck claimed that he was acting on his own responsibility, but it would appear that he asked for and received Mackenzie King's permission to join in the fray.[101] His entry roused other Liberals. Brooke Claxton, the M.P.

[99]*Toronto Daily Star*, Jan. 22, p. 9, Feb. 3, p. 5, Feb. 4, p. 8. Meighen's biographer discusses the C.C.F. campaign at great length (Graham, *Meighen*, III, 109–24).

[100]In an extraordinary front-page statement on Feb. 5, 1942, the *Star* denied having misquoted Meighen. The reporter who covered the meeting in question, the paper stated, had specifically asked Meighen if his words were intended, and had been informed that they were. Meighen's charges against the *Star* are in the issue of Feb. 4, 1942, p. 9. See Roy Greenaway, *The News Game* (Toronto, 1966), pp. 67–8.

[101]At a party caucus on Jan. 29, King asked his M.P.s to support government candidates in the by-elections of Feb. 9 (Pickersgill, *Mackenzie King Record*, I, 343–4; the Hon. Arthur Roebuck Interview, July 15, 1964). After this caucus, Roebuck apparently persuaded the unbelieving King that there was a chance to

for Montreal St. Lawrence-St. George, approached Norman Lambert, the controller of Liberal party finances, and asked for $1000 for the C.C.F. in York South. Apparently acting on his own responsibility, Lambert made arrangements on January 30 with David Lewis, the National Secretary of the C.C.F., for the transfer of the funds. It would seem that this $1000 was the extent of direct financial assistance.[102] The C.C.F. received additional aid, however, when T. Wilbur Best, a prominent businessman in the constituency who with others of the "Liberal Citizens' Committee of South York" had earlier supported Meighen's campaign,[103] withdrew his endorsement of the Conservative leader. Because Meighen was unfairly attacking the government, he wrote in an open letter to the *Toronto Daily Star*, "I am . . . withdrawing my support from Mr. Meighen like most other Liberals in the riding."[104]

Whether most other Liberals shared Best's views was questionable, but the election results of February 9 were not. Noseworthy, who had won exactly one poll in his first try for parliament in 1940, carried 159 of 212 in the by-election and won easily with a 4,456-vote majority. What had happened? Meighen had run well in Forest Hill Village, winning twenty-three of thirty polls and a majority of 1,537 votes. In middle-class Weston, the Conservative leader held his own, even picking up the

---

beat Meighen in York South and convinced him that he should be allowed to enter the campaign on his own responsibility. Roebuck was likely motivated by his extreme distaste for both Hepburn and Meighen; his feeling was strong enough that he was willing to pay for his own radio time—or so it appears (Roebuck Interview; Jolliffe Interview, June 2, 1965). Roebuck's speeches are printed in the *Toronto Daily Star*, Feb. 2, p. 3, and Feb. 4, 1942, p. 9.

[102]Norman Lambert Diaries, Jan. 29–31, 1942. According to the diary, the money was picked up by Andrew Brewin of the Noseworthy campaign staff. In a letter to the writer, Nov. 23, 1966, Mr. Brewin stated that his recollection was that there was no direct cash contribution from the Liberals.

[103]Under the signature of twelve prominent Liberals, including the Mayor of Weston and a local M.P.P., the committee had urged Meighen's election, believing that this was "no time for a discussion of a change in our form of government." Letter, Jan. 29, 1942, copy in Hepburn Papers, Supplementary Files (private), 1942.

[104]*Toronto Daily Star*, Feb. 7, 1942, p. 21. Meighen alleged that the King government had forced those Liberals who had endorsed him to withdraw support on pain of losing their war contracts (Meighen Papers, Meighen to John Bird, Feb. 17, 1942, and to Dr. T. Ropp, July 9, 1957). Best, the only Liberal to publicly withdraw support, flatly denies that any pressure was put upon him (Letter to writer, Oct. 19, 1964).

No evidence at all has been discovered, other than Meighen's own letters, that Liberal "wardheelers" campaigned for the C.C.F. (Graham, *Meighen*, III, 126–7). Mr. Jolliffe stated that on election day some Liberals appeared with cars to drive voters to the polls, but he denied that there was any other assistance (Interview, June 2, 1965).

only three polls that had voted Liberal in 1940. Only in York Township had he done badly—so badly in fact that he lost the election. The working-class districts of York South had cast 11,720 votes for the Conservative candidate in 1940, but only 7,683 for Meighen, a loss of 4,037 votes. In the general election, Noseworthy had won only one poll in York Township; two years later he captured 141, most of which had been Conservative in 1940.[105] Only in the areas of the township bordering on Forest Hill Village and in the "better" districts had the electorate voted for Meighen. What had happened, it is clear, is that Meighen had done well in the wealthier sections of the constituency but had lost in the working-class districts.[106]

Other factors than the defection of the working-class vote had undoubtedly contributed to the C.C.F. victory. The weather, first, had been uncommonly bad, the *Toronto Daily Star* noting that Toronto had been struck by "the worst blizzard . . . in recent years" barely 48 hours before the polls opened,[107] and this may have kept the number of voters below that in the 1940 election. If the C.C.F. organization was as efficient in getting out the vote as in canvassing, this could have been an important factor in determining the outcome. And what of conscription? In the plebiscite held ten weeks after the by-election, York South voted 93.7 per cent in favour of releasing the government from its pledges

[105]In 1940, the Conservative won 104 polls in York Township, the Liberal 48, Noseworthy 1, and 4 were tied. The numbering of polls in the by-election did not follow precisely the same pattern as for the general election two years earlier.

[106]The following table, derived from Canada, Chief Electoral Officer, *Report on the General Election of 1940* (Ottawa, 1941), and *Report on By-Elections Held in 1942* (Ottawa, 1943), shows the distribution of the vote in 1940 and 1942:

		Forest Hill	York Twp.	Weston	Total
1940	Lib.	2,138	9,586	1,140	12,864
	Con.	2,454	11,720	1,172	15,346
	C.C.F.	350	4,742	280	5,372
	TOTAL	4,942	26,048	2,592	33,582
1942	Lib.	—	—	—	—
	Con.	3,218	7,683	1,051	11,952
	C.C.F.	1,681	13,565	1,162	16,408
	TOTAL	4,899	21,248	2,213	28,360

Details of polls won and lost are derived from the *Reports* cited above. Professor Graham's assessment—"the bulk of the normally Liberal vote had gone to Noseworthy"—seems highly suspect in the light of the examination above (Graham, *Meighen*, III, 130).

[107]*Toronto Daily Star*, Feb. 9, 1942, p. 10.

against conscription.[108] Presumably, then, the announcement of the plebiscite had some effect in destroying part of the Conservative leader's support. The one certainty in all this, however, is that more than 4000 Conservative voters in York Township had either stayed home on election day or else had switched their allegiance to Noseworthy. As a result, Meighen was decisively defeated "and defeated in the strongest riding in Toronto, which means the strongest Tory riding in all of Canada." "Defeated," exulted the jubilant Mackenzie King, "while supported by financial interests and the press—everything in the way of organization and campaign power that could be assembled for any man. . . ."[109]

The loss was a bitter blow to Meighen. "While I was the most doubtful of any of our organization as to the outcome in South York," he wrote indignantly,

the result, I must admit, was much worse than I thought possible. Truly it is discouraging that the foul and despicable methods which were initiated right at the beginning there and carried on without the slightest regard for truth, and on a wholesale scale, could be successful in a constituency almost wholly of Anglo-Saxons. Undoubtedly the average level is not what it was, and just as undoubtedly we are in for real trouble as a result.

Politics in Canada, the defeated leader concluded bitterly, were even more rotten than in the France of 1940.[110] Later, Meighen would attribute his defeat to the "common resolve of not one, not two, but three party leaders—the Liberal, the CCF, and the Communist. . . ." and to the absence from the riding of 4000 men on active service.[111]

Meighen's reaction to his defeat was understandable, but his analysis of the causes was as wrong as his choice of issues. Certainly the C.C.F. campaign with its focus on Meighen's personality and past record was

[108]Canada, *Canada Gazette*, LXXV (June 23, 1942), "Statement of the Result of the Plebiscite. . . ." The results in York South were 29,860 in favour of releasing the government and 1,778 against.

[109]Pickersgill, *Mackenzie King Record*, I, 348. King was so pleased by the defeat of Meighen that he told C.C.F. leader M. J. Coldwell that "if titles were in order, I'd make you a K.C.B." (Coldwell Interview, July 6, 1963).

[110]Meighen Papers, Meighen to M. G. O'Leary, Feb. 12, 1942. This paragraph was repeated in at least two other letters by Meighen: Hanson Papers, File P-450-M, Meighen to Hanson, Feb. 11, 1942; Bennett Papers, Notable Persons File, Meighen to Bennett, Feb. 12, 1942. See Adamson Papers, Diary, Feb. 6, 7, 9, 1942.

[111]Meighen, *Unrevised and Unrepented*, p. 420 (speech of Dec. 9, 1942); Toronto *Globe and Mail*, Feb. 10, 1942, p. 1. No voting arrangements were made for military voters outside their home constituencies in by-elections. Canada, Chief Electoral Officer, *Active Service Voting Regulations* (Ottawa, 1940).

not a gentle one, and it seems clear that some Liberal aid was given directly to the C.C.F. But it is difficult to escape the conclusion that the major cause of the defeat was Meighen's inept campaign. His political blindness, aggravated by unreasoning patriotism, had led Meighen to fight his battle solely on the issues of the war and to neglect all positive mention of social welfare until the closing days of the campaign. This obsession with conscription and national government had left him in an exceedingly vulnerable position when the government announced the plebiscite. By his attacks on the King government and by his reliance on the support of the Toronto 200 and of renegade Liberals, Meighen undoubtedly weakened his position with the Liberals of York South. At the same time, and most decisively, the Conservative leader had alienated the working-class voters of the constituency by his attitude on social reform. The C.C.F. campaign, painting Meighen a profiteer, a strike-breaker, and a tool of the "interests," undoubtedly assisted in this process. As one of Meighen's key workers mournfully noted, "I think the CCF are starting to make inroads in the working vote of both parties."[112] With its well-organized, well-run campaign, the C.C.F. had capitalized on Meighen's errors and scored a stunning upset. Moreover, the attractiveness of social welfare as an election issue had been effectively demonstrated.

The primary effect of Meighen's defeat was to destroy the hopes and plans of those who had arranged his selection as leader in November 1941. With the rebuff in York South, the Conservative drive for conscription and national government fizzled out. At the same time, the C.C.F. victory gave tremendous impetus to the fledgling social democratic movement. "From that moment," wrote C.C.F. leader M. J. Coldwell, "the CCF ceased to be an interesting minority movement"[113] and rapidly expanded to the point where it threatened the major parties. The danger was, naturally enough, most extreme for the weakest of the old parties, and Meighen's defeat brought the Conservative party as close as it had yet been to extinction. The delegates at the Ottawa conference had had the choice of Meighen or chaos put before them; they chose one, but after York South they had both.

[112]*Toronto Daily Star*, Feb. 10, 1942, p. 5.

[113]Coldwell, *Left Turn, Canada*, p. 26; Dana Porter, "The Future of a Conservative Party," *University of Toronto Quarterly*, XII (Jan., 1943), 196; Caplan, "Failure of Canadian Socialism," 99–100; "Tumult and Shouting," *Canadian Forum*, XXI (March, 1942), 357; George Hogan, *The Conservative in Canada* (Toronto, 1963), p. 15.

6.   Dynamiting the Wreckage

Arthur Meighen was still leader of the Conservative party despite his crushing defeat in York South, but now he had to exercise his control over the parliamentary party *in absentia*. Inevitably, problems arose with the members of the House of Commons, caused by differing conceptions of the party's role and attitude to the war. The situation quickly became intolerable, and it was soon evident that the leadership could not remain in suspended animation if the party was to last out the war. Simultaneously, a group of "laymen," troubled by the party's leadership dilemma and particularly concerned with the lack of clear policies, seized the initiative. They held a conference and produced a platform upon which a new and progressive Conservatism could stand to counter the appeal of the C.C.F. The culmination of their work came at a leadership convention at Winnipeg in December 1942. With a new leader, a new policy, and a renewed lease on life, the Conservative party moved to the left, leap-frogging the Liberals, into a fresh position from which to fight the advance of socialism.

Meighen's defeat occasioned no rejoicing within the Conservative party. Even those who had bitterly opposed his selection in November 1941 were shocked by the results of the by-election. "I feel terribly sorry for Meighen," wrote J. M. Macdonnell. "Our poor party is in a sad plight. . . ."[1] The members of Parliament were equally disturbed but hastened to express their loyalty to the defeated leader:

The Members of the Conservative Party in the House of Commons unanimously express their confidence in the leadership of the Right Honourable Arthur Meighen and their appreciation of his great abilities. They look forward to the early day when elected in one of the several seats offered him, he will be enabled to use those abilities to assist in our war effort and in the solving of the problems which lie ahead.[2]

---
[1]Dafoe Papers, Microfilm roll M-80, Macdonnell to Dafoe, Feb. 10, 1942.
[2]Meighen Papers, MacNicol to Meighen, Feb. 12, 1942. A seat was offered by Herbert Bruce immediately (Bruce Papers, Bruce to Hogarth, Feb. 12, 1942; Meighen to Bruce, Feb. 11, 1942).

Arrangements would have to be made about the leadership of the party in the House of Commons, however, and Meighen came to caucus on February 19 to discuss the situation.

He was not optimistic about his chances of getting to parliament. "I made very plain that in my judgment the tactics adopted by the Government in South York would at this time succeed anywhere," he recalled.[3] "King would see to it that the Meighen bogey was raised. The C.C.F. would see to it that the man who dared to say that the incentive of profit, however small, must be retained if free institutions are to survive, was pilloried as a cold and burnt-out reactionary."[4] He had not yet made up his mind on retaining the leadership, Meighen indicated, but he promised a further statement of his views in one week. His decision was given in a letter read at caucus on February 26:

For reasons outlined to you at some length on 19th instant, it does not seem wise at this time that the generous offer of several Conservative Members of the House to resign their seats in my favour should be accepted. . . .

This means that my re-entry into Parliament is subject to more or less indefinite postponement. The onerous and responsible duties of Party Leader cannot be efficiently or conscientiously discharged unless one is able to take up his post as Leader in the House of Commons. Direction given to Party moves and Party policy must necessarily many times be given or affected as a result of occurrences on the floor of Parliament. . . . Indeed, a House Leader within his sphere cannot well be circumscribed in the discharge of his responsibilities by the fact that there stands outside a Party Leader with general, and perhaps overriding powers. The man who directs in Parliament must direct and cannot merely be the spokesman for another. . . .

You have expressed your unanimous wish . . . that I should not now retire from Leadership. I am prepared to accede to this desire and await for a reasonable time the development of events. Inevitably I must be the judge of what constitutes a reasonable time. . . .

In the circumstances reviewed above, it seems to me the clear duty of the Members of the House that they should so adjust their organization as to be in the best possible position to meet the contingency of my retirement. Choice of a House Leader is entirely the prerogative of the Members, but whoever such Leader may be, whether the present one or another, he should be such as will prepare himself and shape himself to qualify for definite and permanent leadership of the entire Party. . . .[5]

This letter clearly seemed to rule out Hanson as House leader, for he had already indicated that he was not prepared to continue indefinitely in that post. Nonetheless, whether wilfully or accidentally, the caucus

[3]Meighen Papers, Meighen to A. D. McRae, March 3, 1942; Adamson Papers, Diary, Feb. 19, 1942.
[4]Herridge Papers, Meighen to Herridge, May 14, 1942.
[5]Bell Papers, Vol. 1, Meighen to Hanson, Feb. 24, 1942.

misinterpreted Meighen's views and determined that a new House leader would not be selected until just before the summer adjournment of parliament.[6] Hanson was to continue for at least six months more.

Meighen's letter provides a succinct analysis of the proper relationship between a House leader and a permanent leader outside parliament, but over the course of the 1942 session, this sharp delineation of spheres of activity became blurred. Three major issues arose to disturb the already strained partnership of Hanson and Meighen, and before the session adjourned for the summer, the relationship between the two had cooled perceptibly. These issues were the debate on the amendment of the National Resources Mobilization Act, the Hong Kong Inquiry, and the subject of the leadership itself.

The announcement of the conscription plebiscite, which had stolen the wind from Meighen's sails in York South, posed a delicate problem for the Conservatives in the House of Commons. The members could denounce the government for the "greatest exhibition of lack of national leadership this country has ever witnessed,"[7] but the dilemma confronting them was all too clear. "I have been giving some thought as to how I should vote personally," a perplexed Hanson wrote to his nephew. "If I vote 'No,' I am in effect telling King that he has been right all along and that he should adhere to his policy of 'no conscription for overseas service'. . . . if I vote 'Yes' and to relieve him of his obligations, I have not the slightest assurance in the world that he will do anything. . . ."[8] Yet, as all Conservatives were aware, they could not allow conscription to be defeated, and even Arthur Meighen eventually had to indicate his support for the government's campaign to be freed from its pledges.[9] Mackenzie King had manoeuvred his political

[6]Adamson Papers, Diary, Feb. 26, 1942; Bruce Papers, Bruce to caucus, July 30, 1942.

[7]House of Commons, *Debates*, Jan. 26, 1942, p. 26 (Mr. Hanson). The plebiscite was discussed during the debate in reply to the Address and again when the plebiscite bill itself was brought forward for approval late in February.

[8]Hanson Papers, File P-951, Hanson to H. A. Hanson, Feb. 2, 1942. The Conservatives were not alone in their puzzlement, and even the cabinet did not know King's plans. Col. Ralston and Angus Macdonald, the Minister of National Defence and the Minister of National Defence for Naval Services, saw King on Jan. 31, 1942, in an attempt to pin the Prime Minister down as to what would happen after the plebiscite. "P.M. said the question had to be viewed as a whole," they were told. "It was a mistake to urge conscription just for conscription's sake. We must be sure we would get more men. . . . If you had to use the machine guns, what would be the use of conscription?" Ralston Papers, Vol. 34, File 554–25, "Conversation Ralston and I [Macdonald] had with P.M., Saturday, January 31."

[9]Meighen Papers, Statement by Mr. Meighen, March 31, 1942.

enemies into the unenviable position of having no choice other than to work for his policy.[10]

The results of the national balloting on April 27 made clear the division in the country on conscription. Every province except Quebec voted heavily in favour of releasing the government from its pledges; in the French-Canadian province only 27.1 per cent of those voting so indicated.[11] In fact, "l'artifice d'un plébiscite"[12] had produced a violent response in Quebec although some French-speaking Liberal M.P.s and the Liberal press supported the government.[13] La Ligue pour la Défense du Canada had been formed by *nationaliste* elements and a skilfully organized propaganda campaign launched. Why should you vote "No?" asked the Ligue manifesto. "Parce que," it told the voters, "nul ne demande d'être relevé d'un engagement s'il n'a déjà la tentation de le violer, et parce que, de toutes les promesses qu'il a faites au peuple du Canada, il n'en reste qu'une que King voudrait n'être plus obligé de tenir: la promesse de ne pas conscrire les hommes pour outre-mer."[14] There was more than a little justice in this attitude and in the singing by Ligue audiences of a parodied version of "God Save the King":

> A bas la cons-cription
> A bas la cons-cription
>   La conscription
> A bas la cons-cription
> A bas la cons-cription
> La-a-a-a-a (cafouillage) a-a-a-la-a cons-crip-tion.[15]

The pledge against conscription had been made to Quebec; now Mackenzie King had asked all Canada to release him from his promises. Worse, the government's "Yes" campaign was a feeble one. "We have been permitted only to spend public money to urge people to get out to vote," the Hon. T. C. Davis, Deputy Minister of National War Services,

---

[10]Moffat Papers, Vol. 47, Memorandum of conversation with F. C. Mears, April 20, 1942.

[11]The question on the ballot was obliquely phrased: "Are you in favour of releasing the Government from any obligations arising out of any past commitments restricting the methods of raising men for military service?" Results are found in Canada, *Canada Gazette*, LXXV (June 23, 1942). Ontario voted 82.3 per cent yes; Nova Scotia 77.9; New Brunswick 69.1; Manitoba 79.0; Saskatchewan 71.1; Alberta 70.4; British Columbia 79.4; and Prince Edward Island 82.4 per cent.

[12]So called by Rumilly in *Henri Bourassa*, p. 770.

[13]E.g., *La Presse*, 23 jan. 1942, and J. F. Pouliot, M.P., "Le Plébiscite," *La Presse*, 31 jan. 1942.

[14]Laurendeau, *La Crise de la conscription 1942*, p. 84.

[15]*Ibid.*, p. 90.

wrote. "The stand was taken that to urge them to get out and vote affirmatively . . . would be improper, and that if it were done a fair appropriation should be made to those who would want to advertise a 'No' vote, and that this would not be in the national interest." Nevertheless the question had been put, and Quebec had given its answer. Whether the response would have been different had Meighen and the Toronto 200 not forced the issue so blatantly is impossible to say, but the problem now could be solved only by Mackenzie King.[16]

The Prime Minister's response was to introduce, on May 15, House of Commons Bill No. 80 to amend the N.R.M.A. and repeal its limiting clause prohibiting the employment of conscripts overseas. Despite King's explanation that the amendment did "not denote any change in government policy," but was intended only "to obtain for the government the freedom of decision and action" approved by the plebiscite, P. J. A. Cardin, the senior French-Canadian cabinet minister since Lapointe's death, resigned.[17] As the departing minister knew, Mackenzie King had no intention of instituting conscription as yet, and Cardin's resignation merely strengthened the conscriptionists' hand in the cabinet. For the next two months, the Prime Minister was in a delicate position, daily facing his increasingly rebellious English-speaking ministers and a restive bloc of Quebec members.[18] His solution to the problem, revealed in the House of Commons on June 10, was a masterpiece of political balancing. To satisfy Quebec, he emphasized that conscription for overseas service was not yet necessary, might never be necessary, and would not be resorted to unless overriding circumstances made it necessary. The policy, in his now famous phrase, was "not necessarily conscription, but conscription if necessary."[19] At the same time, to placate Ontario and the conscriptionists, King agreed that the merits of conscription would not be debated again in parliament, and that should it be necessary to impose conscription, it would be done by Order in Council. If the government acted by Order in Council, however, he would come to parliament for a brief debate and a vote of confidence, not on conscription but on whether the Liberal government should remain in office.

Initially, the Conservative party was divided in its attitude to King's manœuvring. From Toronto, Meighen constantly urged the harassed

[16]Directorate of History, File 951.059 (D2), Davis to T. W. L. MacDermot, April 24, 1942. A good explanation of the Quebec vote is in F. R. Scott, "What Did 'No' Mean?" *Canadian Forum*, XXII (June, 1942), 71–2.
[17]House of Commons, *Debates*, May 11, 1942, pp. 2280–1. Lapointe had died on November 26, 1941, making Cardin senior minister.
[18]Pickersgill, *Mackenzie King Record*, I, chap. xiv.
[19]House of Commons, *Debates*, June 10, 1942, p. 3236.

Hanson to pound away at King's temporizing policies, but the House leader felt bound by the wishes of caucus. "My position is extremely difficult," he wrote his leader with understated irony on May 9:

Our people here are absolutely averse to our demanding immediate conscription, on the theory that now that the limitation is removed the responsibility is [King's], and [the government] have the information and the knowledge of the whole position, and that they should go forward. If we come out and declare now further for immediate conscription, it will give him the opportunity of saying when the time comes that the Opposition demanded it and that he was being driven into it. I am not merely reflecting my own view at the moment but the view of Caucus. . . .[20]

But at a long caucus on May 12, the day following King's introduction of Bill 80 with the advice that the bill meant no change in policy, the members overwhelmingly rejected Hanson's counsel and decided to press immediately for conscription.[21] Hanson loyally accepted the situation and said, as he wrote to one correspondent, that "I intend, with all the force at my command, to demand the immediate and full institution of compulsory selective service over the whole field of the war."[22]

He was as good as his word. "To everyone's surprise," Pierrepont Moffat remarked of Hanson's assault on the Prime Minister on June 10, "Mr. Hanson instead of mumbling his reply, let go with both fists and poured vitriol on Mr. King. It is the first and only time in the two years I have been here that he made an effective speech."[23] The criticism was unfair but the praise deserved. Hanson captured the nation's frustration at Mackenzie King and his tactics in eight lines of drollery from Gilbert and Sullivan:

> A complicated gentleman allow me to present,
> Of all the arts and faculties the terse embodiment,
> He's a great arithmetician who can demonstrate with ease
> That two and two are three, or five, or anything you please;
> An eminent Logician who can make it clear to you
> That black is white—when looked at from the proper point of
>   view;
> A marvellous philologist who'll undertake to show
> That "yes" is but another and a neater form of "no."[24]

---

[20]Hanson Papers, File S-175-M, Meighen to Hanson, May 8, 1942; Hanson to Meighen, May 9, 1942 and, File P-450-C, Hanson to J. A. Clark, May 6, 1942.
[21]*Ibid.*, File S–815–2, "Memo for Caucus," May 12, 1942, and attached notes. From Hanson's notes, it appears that he could only muster three definite supporters in caucus: Karl Homuth, Waterloo South (Ontario); J. G. Diefenbaker, Lake Centre (Saskatchewan); and Russell Boucher, Carleton (Ontario). Cf. Bruce Papers, Bruce to Meighen, May 12, 1942; Adamson Papers, Diary, May 12, 1942.
[22]Herridge Papers, Hanson to Herridge, May 25, 1942.
[23]Moffat Papers, Vol. 47, Memorandum of conversations . . ., June 11, 1942.
[24]House of Commons, *Debates*, June 10, 1942, p. 3244. The quote is from

Again, on July 22, the House leader attacked King for his "tortuous," "illogical" course and his "policy of procrastination and appeasement."[25] But, boxed in by King's tactics, the Conservatives had no alternative but to vote for the government's bill. "If we were to vote against the Government," Hanson earlier had written, "the thing would be very close—I have an idea that the Government might possibly be defeated. . . . If I wanted to play politics and were disregardful of results afterwards, we might defeat him. . . ." But he could not do this, Hanson concluded, as this "would bring down upon my head the execration of this generation and all future generations."[26] Hanson's difficulties with Bill 80 were largely caused by the Prime Minister, and after he agreed to accept the advice of caucus on the course to be followed, there was no serious disagreement with Meighen. The Leader of the Opposition, however, had no intention of being so tractable on the issue of the Hong Kong Inquiry.

The outbreak of war in the Pacific on December 7, 1941, had found two Canadian infantry battalions—almost 2000 men—among the defenders of Hong Kong. Canadian help had been requested by the British on September 19, because of "signs of a certain weakening in attitude of Japan towards United States and ourselves. . . . Under these conditions," the Dominions Office telegram continued, "our view is that a small reinforcement (e.g. one or two more battalions) of Hong Kong garrison would be very fully justified. . . . This action would greatly strengthen garrison out of all proportion to actual numbers involved. . . ."[27]

---

the comic opera, *Utopia Limited*. A political poet also captured King's philosophy of government in several biting phrases:

> He skillfully avoided what was wrong
> Without saying what was right,
> And never let his on the one hand
> Know what his on the other hand was doing.
> The height of his ambition
> Was to pile a Parliamentary Committee on a
>   Royal Commission.
> To have 'conscription if necessary
> But not necessarily conscription',
> To let Parliament decide—
> Later.
>
> Postpone, postpone, abstain.

F. R. Scott, "W.L.M.K.," *The Blasted Pine*, ed. F. R. Scott and A. J. M. Smith (Toronto: Macmillan of Canada, 1957), p. 28.

[25]House of Commons, *Debates*, July 22, 1942, pp. 4545–8.

[26]Hanson Papers, File S-175-J, Hanson to Senator G. B. Jones, July 16, 1942. Cf. the comment in "Conscription for Overseas," *Canadian Forum*, XXII (July, 1942), 100.

[27]Quoted in Stacey, *History of the Second World War*, I, 440; H. D. G. Crerar Papers, 958.C.009 (D26), War Diary, Oct. 21, 1941.

The British assessment was, of course, completely wrong, and the Canadian troops were lost to a man when the Crown Colony surrendered on Christmas Day.

The tragedy of Hong Kong was interjected into the political arena in January 1942 by George Drew. In a radio address in support of Meighen's by-election campaign, he urged the voters of York South to "face the shameful truth." "Let us consider the most terrible example of this shortage of trained men. At the very last moment, a large number of untrained men were attached to the forces leaving for Hong Kong in order that those units might be brought up to strength. . . . Let that simple and terrible fact . . . answer those who suggest that our need for men is being met by the present [voluntary] system."[28] Hanson's reaction to the disaster was rather different. After hearing an explanation in the House of Commons by the Minister of National Defence, the Hon. J. L. Ralston, the House leader said that he would "offer no criticism. If we are to be in a total war . . . we must expect to share . . . the fortunes of war. . . . Before this war is over," he said, "perhaps there will be more Hong Kongs."[29] After a telephone call from Meighen, however, Hanson changed his mind, and the next day he declared that "a very serious situation" regarding the "lack of trained man-power in Canada" had been revealed by Ralston's statement.[30] As a result of the Conservatives' pressing the point in the House, a one-man Royal Commission of Inquiry under the Chief Justice, Sir Lyman P. Duff, was established on February 13, 1942, "to enquire into the circumstances surrounding the dispatch of a Canadian Expeditionary Force to the Crown Colony of Hong Kong."[31] At Meighen's insistence, Drew was appointed counsel for Hanson on the Royal Commission.

The Chief Justice's report, tabled in the House on June 4, concluded that the expedition was neither ill-conceived nor mismanaged, although the Quartermaster General's branch of the Department of National Defence was censured for a lack of energy and initiative in moving the battalions' vehicles too late for loading with the expedition.[32] In addition, the Commissioner decided that the addition of 120 men who had

[28]Clipping from *Toronto Daily Star*, Jan. 13, 1942, in Directorate of History, File 111.13 (D72).
[29]House of Commons, *Debates*, Jan. 21, 1942, pp. 4473–4.
[30]Bell Interview, Aug. 24, 1964; Pickersgill, *Mackenzie King Record*, I, 352–3; House of Commons, *Debates*, Jan. 22, 1942, p. 3.
[31]Canada, *Report on the Canadian Expeditionary Force to the Crown Colony of Hong Kong by Right Hon. Sir Lyman P. Duff, G.C.M.G., Royal Commissioner* (Ottawa, 1942), p. 2.
[32]*Ibid.*, pp. 3–8. Ralston was aware of this shortcoming from the middle of December 1941. In early January 1942, in fact, he had held his own inquiry into

not completed their infantry training before their departure was not unfair to the battalions or the expedition as a whole.[33] The *Duff Report* was immediately attacked by Drew who charged that the government had refused the Commissioner "very serious information" and had withheld "blood-curdling facts" from the public.[34]

The furore occasioned by the *Report* embittered relations between Meighen and Hanson for the next six weeks. Meighen and Drew travelled to Ottawa on June 7 to urge vigorous action on the House leader and were told that, while he was prepared to agree that there were some inaccurate statements in the *Report,* he did not believe in attacking the Chief Justice. After consulting caucus on the question his feelings were strengthened, and Hanson now believed that the party should not touch Hong Kong. "Unless," he added bluntly in a letter to Meighen, "I get the support of the Caucus I cannot and will not do it, no matter how distressing this may be to you or to George Drew."[35] At another caucus on June 17, Hanson told the members that the whole affair was Drew's and that everything the parliamentary party might do on the issue was directed at preserving the Ontario leader's position. This speech provoked a fierce squabble in caucus, and Herbert A. Bruce, the member for Toronto Parkdale and a friend of both Meighen and Drew, led the attack on Hanson. Bruce stated flatly that Meighen was the leader, that Hanson was only the House leader, and that Meighen had studied the *Report* and reached his conclusion. If the caucus rejected his advice on this question, Bruce stated, it amounted to a repudiation of his leadership, and the next step was to ask for his resignation. The Toronto M.P. pointed out "our absurd position." Meighen had selected Drew as the best qualified man in Canada on military affairs to represent the Conservative party before the Commission, and the counsel had done a splendid job. In spite of this, he said, pointing at Hanson, the caucus was listening to the criticism of uninformed people.[36]

Hanson's position, despite Bruce's perfervid oratory and Meighen's scorn, was probably sound. He admitted that he was no military expert, but he would, perhaps, have been on solid ground if he had doubted

---

the transportation difficulties. Ralston Papers, Vol. 52, "Hong Kong Enquiry, Mr. Ralston's Notes on personal preliminary enquiry . . ."; Untitled folder with transcripts of Ralston's personal inquiry, Jan. 1, 2, 4, 1942.

[33]*Hong Kong Report,* pp. 42–3.

[34]C. C. Lingard and R. G. Trotter, *Canada in World Affairs, 1941–1944* (Toronto, 1950), p. 54.

[35]Hanson Papers, File W–150, Hanson to Meighen, June 11, 1942.

[36]Bruce Papers, Bruce to Meighen, June 17, 1942; Hanson Papers, File W-150, Hanson to Meighen, June 17, 1942.

Drew's supposed qualifications. Drew was a veteran of the Great War and a militia officer of some repute, but he had access only to material open to the public and could be considered as no more than a well-informed citizen. In addition, George A. Campbell, the government counsel on the Duff Commission and president of a Montreal Conservative association, had told Hanson that Drew "did not make a case!"[37] In these circumstances, with much of the evidence concealed by military security and with no more than Drew's word to go on, to press the charges as Meighen desired seemed to Hanson to be trading on human misery, to be using the deaths of Canadian soldiers for political purposes.[38] For these reasons, Hanson refused to direct the attack in the House,[39] and the party's efforts were led by Howard Green of Vancouver and John Diefenbaker, M.P. for Lake Centre, Saskatchewan. The debate, coming at a time when the great battles were all being fought off-stage and under an extraordinary degree of censorship, made little public impact. The Opposition's motion of censure was easily turned back, 130 votes to 34.[40]

The Hong Kong affair, however, did have a shattering impact on the Conservative caucus. Forgetting his February letter on the proper role of the House leader, Meighen was furious with his recalcitrant subordinate,[41] and his influence within caucus was strong. Hanson was accused by one member of "shirking a responsibility . . . owed to the parents of young men now serving in the forces,"[42] and the *Globe and Mail* magisterially noted (August 6, 1942) that "the Conservative group as a whole in the House of Commons has sunk low." The problem of the party leadership had come to a head.

Hanson had been concerned about the question of a successor since February. Meighen, he believed, had no intention of attempting to enter

[37]Hanson Papers, File MP-120, Hanson to H. R. Jackman, Nov. 10, 1942. "Someday," Campbell wrote later, "I hope to have an opportunity of telling my Conservative friends what a disservice they have done our cause in their attitude and utterances throughout this whole episode . . ." (Campbell to the Hon. J. L. Ralston, July 30, 1942, Directorate of History, File 111.13 (D73).
[38]Bell Interview, Aug. 24, 1964.
[39]Bruce Papers, Bruce to Meighen, June 30 and July 1, 1942; Pickersgill, *Mackenzie King Record*, I, 405. Because of Hanson's attitude, Drew wrote, he had no choice but to ensure that the facts reached the public. Accordingly, he released copies to the press of a long letter to the Prime Minister. The letter which detailed his charges, however, was blocked by the censors and was not made public in full until after the war. Hanson Papers, File W-560, Drew to Hanson, July 15, 1942, and File W-560-S, Drew to Mackenzie King, July 11, 1942.
[40]House of Commons, *Debates*, July 28, 1942, p. 4895.
[41]Meighen Papers, Meighen to H. R. Milner, Aug. 11, 1942.
[42]Bell Papers, Vol. 1, A. H. Bence, M.P., to Hanson, Aug. 22, 1942.

the Commons, and with the possible exceptions of Green and Diefenbaker, he was not impressed with the capabilities of his M.P.s.[43] The
situation became acute when Meighen showed no interest in refurbishing
the party's financial organization, although the York South *débâcle* had
caused the collapse of the financial arrangements made when Meighen
had been selected. Despite Hanson's best efforts, no new organization
was formed.[44] Once again the party was adrift, and its rehabilitation
seemed impossible as long as its leadership remained divided.

If Meighen could be brought to indicate his intention of retaining the
leadership, an unsigned memorandum in the Hanson Papers pointed out,
"then the responsibility for rebuilding the Party is largely his; and he
must be impressed with the urgent necessity of assuming immediate
responsibility in full." He should attend caucus regularly, perhaps undertake a national tour, and certainly seek entry into the House of Commons
as soon as possible. If Meighen planned to step aside, on the other hand,
either Hanson should remain as leader until a convention could be held
to select a permanent leader, or the caucus should choose one of its
number to fill the post. The latter course was not suitable, the memorandum continued, because of the "lack of satisfactory leadership material
available" in the caucus, and also because of the outcry that would be
raised by the rank and file to the effect that "the Party was being ruled
by a small clique of Members." In addition, the party desperately needed
a statement of policy and a creed, but nothing could be done until
Meighen decided either to act as leader or to withdraw.[45]

Meighen's position was a curious one. He had, he wrote a friend,
"given certainly over three-quarters of my time since last November to
the task then placed upon me, and in major matters have indicated very
clearly, and supported as forcefully as I could, the stand which I thought
should be taken. A Leader from the outside has a very delicate task
indeed, and I do not think he should interfere, except in matters of real
consequence. . . ." Whenever he had tried to urge a course upon caucus,
Meighen said, thinking no doubt of the Hong Kong affair, "I am afraid
I must say that I have not had great success in having my wishes carried
out. . . ."[46] Because of this feeling, when he was pressed by Herbert
Bruce and Howard Green, the two M.P.s most dissatisfied with Hanson's

[43]Hanson Papers, File P-450-C, Hanson to C. H. Cahan, March 14, 1942,
and File O-150, Memorandum, May 4, 1942 (no author indicated); Adamson
Papers, Diary, May 13, 1942.

[44]Hanson Papers, File P-450-M, Hanson to Meighen, March 23, 1942.

[45]*Ibid.*, File O-150, Memorandum, May 4, 1942, and Memorandum, May, 1942
(no authors indicated).

[46]Meighen Papers, Meighen to Gratton O'Leary, July 20, 1942.

course on Hong Kong,[47] to make clear his views upon Hanson's leadership, he refused. It was unfair to place him in this position, Meighen said
with some reason, and he did not see why he should have to beg caucus
to do what it had already agreed to do—select a new leader at the end
of the session. The members had a part to play too, he concluded, and
they could not evade their responsibility.[48]

At this point, however, in what could only be an attempt to forestall
Hanson's continuing as House leader, Meighen decided to remain as
permanent leader of the party. As a result, Hanson later wrote,

a number of members of Caucus reviewed the position and it was the considered opinion of many, including some of those who aspired to the
leadership, that no change should be made. In particular, I was told that
Mr. Diefenbaker would not consider taking over. I then called Caucus [on
the following day, July 16, 1942] and read a prepared statement, in which I
reviewed the whole position and left Caucus free to do as it chose. One thing
was clear—I did not ask to be returned. I then left Caucus and later was told
that it was the unanimous wish of Caucus that I remain until Mr. Meighen's
position was more clarified.[49]

"No one," Hanson later wrote in explanation to a friend in Montreal,
"wants to take over the House leadership with Meighen permanent
Leader and outside the House. . . ."[50] Meighen was furious at what he
considered a betrayal of caucus's word. "There certainly is no possibility
of my continuing the frightfully unsatisfactory and galling experience of
this past Session," he wrote to H. R. Milner. "In matters of consequence
where I indicated clearly the line which I thought should be taken, I
found no co-operation at all, just vacillation and, ultimately, resistance."[51] At a stormy caucus on July 29, Meighen put the question
squarely to the assembled members: the Conservative party's first duty,
he said, was to "hammer" at the "very definite commitments we have
made in the line of war policy and war organization," not as the caucus
seemed to think to try to discover a new formula of promises with which
to beat the C.C.F.[52]

---

[47]Bruce Papers, Bruce to Meighen, June 16 and July 6, 1942, and Meighen to
Howard Green, July 7, 1942 (copy).

[48]Bruce Papers, Meighen to Green, July 7, 1942 (copy).

[49]Hanson Papers, File P-450-Personal, Hanson to Bruce, July 31, 1942; Bruce
Papers, Bruce to Caucus, July 30, 1942. Hanson's address to caucus on July 16
is in Hanson Papers, File·P-450-M, "Statement for Caucus," July 16, 1942.

[50]Hanson Papers, Personal Correspondence, Vol. 35, Hanson to J. T. Hackett,
Aug. 3, 1942.

[51]Meighen Papers, Meighen to Milner, July 17, 1942.

[52]*Ibid.*, Meighen to Milner, July 30, 1942.

This was the crux of the matter. Meighen had learned nothing from his defeat at the hands of the C.C.F. in February, for he still believed that the party's only duty was to strive unremittingly for conscription and national government. That his attitude was patriotic few would deny, but that it failed to recognize reality was also undeniable. Hanson's policy was more attuned with the times. Stripped to essentials, it recognized that Mackenzie King would control the nation's government for the duration of the war. Hanson could deplore this situation and attempt to direct King into what he considered to be proper channels, but he was aware that he could not alter the realities of power. In these circumstances, what was the correct and patriotic course for the Conservative party? The answer was clear: the Conservative party had to be reorganized and provided with new policies so that it could take over the government at the end of the war when, Hanson believed, the Liberals would undoubtedly be turned out of office. If the Conservatives were not then in a position to form the administration, the C.C.F. would do so.[53] Socialism was a dreadful fate for the nation, Hanson believed, a conviction shared by many Conservatives outside the House of Commons. Meighen could control caucus and block or delay its attempts to draft new policies. (At the end of July, indeed, he had given a very cool reception to caucus's attempts to establish an executive committee to review "the position of our Party with respect particularly to policies and organization."[54]) But he could do little to curb the party's rank and file, and the nettle was grasped by a small group of progressive Conservatives.

A brief statement was released in Edmonton on August 4, 1942, by H. R. Milner, a friend of Meighen's but also one of those who had opposed the conversion of the Ottawa conference into a leadership convention. "A meeting of men and women from all parts of Canada," he said, "will be held at Port Hope [Ontario] in the first week of September to discuss Canada's war and postwar problems." The meeting would be known as the "round table on Canadian policy." It was "not intended that it should deal with leadership or with organization, and this is understood by the official leaders of the party." The decision to hold a conference, Milner continued,

[53]Hanson Papers, File O-167, Hanson to M. W. Wilson, May 30, 1942. Cf. Ramsay Cook, *The Politics of John W. Dafoe and the* Free Press (Toronto, 1963), p. 271.

[54]Hanson Papers, File O-160-W, Bell to J. H. Harris, M.P., Aug. 3, 1942; File S-175-M, Meighen to Bell, Aug. 5, 1942; File O-160-W-2, Meighen to Sen. J. T. Haig, Aug. 5, 1942 (copy). Subsequent events rendered the Executive Committee superfluous and the idea died.

resulted from a number of informal discussions first in Winnipeg and later in Montreal and elsewhere. The interest shown indicated that the Conservative Party holds the allegiance of a wide variety of people in all parts of the country who are thinking in terms of the problems of 1942.

Those responsible for calling the meeting believe that there is a new opportunity and responsibility facing the party, and it is their earnest hope that the present meeting may be the beginning of a broad movement which will help the party in the discharge of its duty to the country in these grave times.[55]

The Edmonton statement was correct as far as it went, but it revealed little of the men or the motives behind the call for the conference.

As with so many of the party's progressive ideas during the Second World War, the concept of a policy conference had originated with J. M. Macdonnell. After Meighen's defeat, Macdonnell had addressed a long and significant letter to Hanson. "Like many others," he began, "I have been thinking a great deal in the last month about the future of the Party." The two points that particularly concerned him were leadership and policy. "I understand that Mr. Meighen is not proposing to continue," he said, "but it would be quite improper to discuss the matter publicly in the meantime and until he reaches his own conclusion." The other question, he believed, urgently demanded discussion.

From all the enquiries I have made, the young people are supremely uninterested in both the old Parties, and—largely because of its novelty—much more inclined to be interested in the C.C.F.

As you know, I never did believe that a Party under the influence of those who managed the meeting of last November could get anywhere with the young, and that I should imagine is quite obvious to all concerned now. If we are going to attract the young we obviously have to have something young and vigorous and alive in our policy.

Notwithstanding our present low estate, I never felt more confident in my life of the overwhelming need for our Party. If we disappear . . . we then open the way to a lamentable situation. The C.C.F. will become the Opposition. They will attract the Leftist elements. All others, and particularly all reactionaries, will congregate in the other Party and we shall have a class war. . . . If one is an out and out socialist, the other an out and out individualist, a general election means in effect a revolution.

A meeting between Hanson and Macdonnell followed within a few days, and the idea of a conference apparently sprang from this.[56]

[55]Toronto *Globe and Mail*, Aug. 5, 1942, p. 2; Montreal *Gazette*, Aug. 5, 1942, p. 6. Cf. Douglas Library, Queen's University, J. M. Macdonnell Papers, Vol. 43, Draft of letter, July 7, 1942. The interest in Montreal referred to in the statement may not have been completely favourable to the enterprise. See Dafoe Papers, Microfilm roll M-80, Macdonnell to Dafoe, July 18, 1942.

[56]Hanson Papers, File O-150, Macdonnell to Hanson, March 24, 1942; File

Macdonnell immediately saw the possibilities inherent in the idea, and on a trip to the West in May he spoke with a number of like-minded Conservatives. The most important meeting took place at the Winnipeg home of E. G. Phipps Baker, a barrister who had been prominent in the Ottawa conference opposition. Among those in attendance were Milner and Sidney Smith. These men were agreed on the need for a new and progressive policy, and Macdonnell's suggestion of an unofficial, unauthorized conference of laymen—of non-practising politicians—was well received.[57] The site they chose for the meeting was Trinity College School, a private boys' school in Port Hope, a small town near enough to Toronto for convenience, but far enough away that the city's reputation as the centre of reaction would not frighten off delegates from Quebec and the West.[58] (An additional advantage was that the school was willing to provide room and board for $2.50 per day,[59] a bargain price that could not have been matched in Toronto or any other city.) The hard task of organizing the meeting was given to Rod Finlayson of Winnipeg, another of the dissenting "noble thirteen" at Ottawa. Finlayson, who had been secretary to Prime Minister Bennett, had achieved some notoriety among orthodox Tories for his part in drafting the 1935 New Deal speeches. There had been talk of bringing him to Ottawa again in 1941 as national secretary or national chairman of the party, but this attempt foundered on the opposition of the party caucus.[60] Enthusiastic about the possibility of rejuvenating the party, Finlayson temporarily abandoned his law practice and moved to Toronto in June 1942, prepared to devote the next three months to organization.[61]

O-150, Hanson to Macdonnell, March 26, 1942; Macdonnell Interview, July 10, 1963. A poll by the Canadian Institute of Public Opinion, released at the time of the Port Hope conference, provided graphic evidence of Macdonnell's contention with respect to youth and the Conservative party:

Age group	Percentage Voters Supporting			
	Lib.	Con.	C.C.F.	Others
21–29	41	18	21	20
30–39	36	18	25	21
40–49	39	24	22	15
50–59	33	28	23	16
60 and over	32	34	22	12

Toronto Daily Star, Sept. 5, 1942, p. 6.
[57]Finlayson Interviews, June 1 and July 7, 1963.
[58]Macdonnell Interview, July 10, 1963.
[59]Macdonnell Papers, Vol. 43, draft of letter, n.d.
[60]Hanson Papers, File O-160, Hanson to Macdonnell, May 16; Macdonnell to Hanson, May 19; Hanson to Finlayson, May 26, 1941.
[61]Finlayson Interview, June 1, 1963.

One of the earliest problems was the selection of the conference chairman. Macdonnell, the obvious choice, disqualified himself on the grounds that his position as president of the National Trust Company would surround the gathering with an unfavourable aura of high finance and big business. Milner was the second choice, and he agreed to take the job. The question of delegates, too, caused concern. The intention of holding a meeting limited to laymen had existed from the beginning, and Macdonnell and Finlayson now decided to exclude potential candidates for the leadership as well.[62] The professionals, they believed, could only inhibit the free-wheeling discussion they hoped to provoke, the prospective leadership candidates might turn the meeting into a popularity contest, and the real purpose of the meeting, in any case, was to infuse the party with new blood. Attendance would thus be by invitation only, and chairmen were appointed in each province to select the delegates.[63]

Macdonnell took on the delicate task of breaking the news of the conference to Meighen and of advising him that he would not be invited to attend. The time was unpropitious. "He asked me if I had any objection at all to this taking place," Meighen wrote to Milner, who had said nothing of his connection with the conference plans. "I told him I certainly had none," the leader continued, but added "that I might find it necessary myself to take some step somewhere around the close of the Session, the taking of which would necessitate re-consideration of at least the date of the meeting."[64] At the peak of his frustration with Hanson's leadership on the Hong Kong issue and evidently fearing that the House leader intended hanging on to the leadership, Meighen was inclining towards the idea of a leadership convention. A full convention would kill the Port Hope conference, and Milner was quick to urge delay:

I certainly hope that nothing of this character will be done. . . . It may be hoping for too much, but it does seem to me that the . . . meeting may accomplish a great deal in clarifying the situation of the Party, bringing in fresh blood, and perhaps formulating ideas which could be used as the

62Hanson Papers, File O-150-C, Meighen to Hanson, July 15, and Macdonnell to Hanson, July 15, 1942; J. M. Macdonnell, "Amateurs in Politics," *Queen's Quarterly*, XLIX (winter, 1942–1943), 385; Finlayson Interview, June 1, 1963.
    63The provincial chairmen were: British Columbia—R. H. Tupper, Saskatchewan—A. Moxon, Manitoba—L. D. M. Baxter, Ontario—J. M. Macdonnell, Quebec—J. C. H. Dussault, New Brunswick—Hugh Mackay, Nova Scotia—C. B. Smith, Prince Edward Island—W. C. S. McLure. Milner acted as Alberta chairman. Toronto *Globe and Mail*, Sept. 5, 1942, p. 7; *Public Opinion*, II (Aug., 1944), 11.
    64Meighen Papers, Meighen to Milner, July 9, and July 17, 1942.

foundation of a party platform. If the conference is a success, it may be logical and perhaps even essential to call a convention which could deal with such matters as platform.[65]

Meighen's immediate response was to accept no delay in calling for a convention, but he did agree that Port Hope might be helpful, and he eventually agreed to postpone any action until after the meeting.[66]

With this obstacle removed, the organization of the conference proceeded quickly under Finlayson's direction. Draft resolutions were prepared, largely by Finlayson himself, and individuals with special expertise were invited both to contribute their ideas and to attend at Port Hope as advisers.[67] Another of Finlayson's tasks was to ensure that the meeting received the fullest publicity. Without this, the conference would be pointless, for its purpose was to demonstrate to both the party and the public that Conservatives could think progressively. The organizer toured the country before the meeting, visiting publishers and editors and getting varying welcomes. The Winnipeg *Tribune*, for example, was not enthusiastic about the idea and refused to send a reporter to cover the proceedings. The Liberal *Winnipeg Free Press*, on the other hand, was enthusiastic at the prospect of Conservative revival, seeing in this the best hope of defeating the C.C.F., and promised complete co-operation.[68] In addition, Macdonnell prepared two articles for the Toronto weekly, *Saturday Night*, setting out his views on the proper course for the party. Harking back to Sir John A. Macdonald, he called for a "New National Policy" with social security as its goal. The state, Macdonnell wrote, had "to see that every citizen is provided with employment at a wage which will enable him to live in decency." Macdonnell was more explicit in a speech delivered to the Toronto Conservative Businessmen's Club in June: "I would say: 'Would you rather adopt a policy which will retain the largest amount possible of free enterprise or—hand over to the C.C.F.?' In plain words I would say—'Half a loaf is better than no bread.' "[69]

Others were also thinking in terms of specific policies. In a letter to Meighen, Milner agreed that the party's first responsibility was to press

[65]*Ibid.*, Milner to Meighen, July 11 and July 23, 1942.
[66]*Ibid.*, Meighen to Milner, July 24 and Aug. 11, 1942; *Winnipeg Free Press*, Sept. 15, 1942, p. 13.
[67]Finlayson Interview, July 6, 1963; Francis Flaherty, "A Conservative Philosophy," *Saturday Night*, LVIII (Sept. 19, 1942), 10–11.
[68]Finlayson Interview, June 1, 1963; *Winnipeg Free Press*, Aug. 8, 1942, p. 15.
[69]J. M. Macdonnell, "The Conservatives and a New National Policy," *Saturday Night*, LVIII (July 25, 1942), 6, and "A Conservative Party is Essential in Canada" (July 18, 1942), 6; Macdonnell Papers, Vol. 52, Address, June 12, 1942.

for a total war effort, but he insisted that other policies be subject to revision. The party had to modify its implied hostility to the United States, become "internationalistic," and abandon the high tariff as an article of faith. The "excrescences" of capitalism could not be allowed to continue, but if wartime controls had to go on, it must be within a capitalist framework. On that issue, he said, the party should face the C.C.F. "As I have said before," he concluded, "and as is now becoming obvious, the C.C.F. at the next election will be dangerous antagonists. It is almost incredible that the Liberal Party will out-live the war as an effective force which leaves the way open for a revival of the Party, but if the party is to be revived it must be founded on a broad and humanitarian policy."[70]

Meighen's reply set out his views. He could see no reason for altering the party's tradition of supporting the maintenance of the British connection, and while he said he favoured friendly relations with the United States, he stated that "we certainly have not reached the stage where we could make a commitment to this effect." He agreed that some controls would be necessary after the war, but he wanted a "determined march toward the restoration of free enterprise," for without this "no free political system can survive." In groping for humanitarian policies, Meighen concluded,

we must keep in mind that there will always be opposed to us radical, and, for a time, revolutionary elements. The Party which is loyal to sound principles can be at the same time progressive in every enlightened way, and if we insist on being that Party, those who believe with us will flock to our standard and we will survive. If we seek to compromise merely for the sake of votes, we will be the Party that will disappear.[71]

What the "Port Hopefuls," as they came to be called, would do, however, none could foresee.

The invited delegates gathered for their first meeting on Friday evening, September 4, 1942, in the spartan atmosphere of the Trinity College School gymnasium. Despite the difficulties of wartime travel, 159 were present, representing every province except Prince Edward Island. If only because of proximity, Ontario delegates were in the majority, but there were thirty-one representatives from the prairies and British Columbia, and sizable contingents from the Maritimes and Quebec, the latter including ten French Canadians.[72] In the main, the

[70]Meighen Papers, Milner to Meighen, Aug. 5, 1942.
[71]*Ibid.*, Meighen to Milner, Aug. 6, 1942.
[72]Delegates in attendance by province: Alberta—12; British Columbia—4; Manitoba—12, New Brunswick—9; Nova Scotia—9; Ontario—94; Quebec—16; Saskatchewan—3. Hanson Papers, "Conservatives in Attendance at Port Hope," mimeographed list.

delegates were veterans of the Great War and were of high intellectual calibre, one observer noting that there were "at least four" Rhodes Scholars in the group.[73] Grant Dexter, writing in the *Winnipeg Free Press* on September 14, quoted one Conservative newsman to the effect that "nobody can laugh this conference off for the good reason that the delegates happen to be the spinal column of the Conservative party in the country."

The meeting began with addresses from the organizers. Milner characterized the gathering as "unique" in Canadian political history[74] for its being held "without benefit of party leaders" and tacitly admitted that its purpose was to bring the pressure of progressive opinion to bear on the party leaders. "It is true," he said, "that we cannot speak of the party nor [*sic*] its leaders . . . [but] what we decide here will inevitably have an effect on their conduct and on the attitude of the Canadian people to the Conservative party."[75] Macdonnell expanded upon this theme by calling the participants the "Young Turks" of the party, but his assertion that there was no intention of creating a schism in Conservative ranks was greeted with applause. Continuing, he set the tone for the meeting by delivering a massive attack on socialism:

We have gathered here to support freedom—freedom of enterprise and all the other freedoms that go with it because I think that all are indivisible. . . . Regimentation must go the whole hog. You can't have regimentation in one sphere and not in others. None of us wish to believe that we are here for our own selfish advantage above the interests of the country. It is not for any selfish reason but because we believe in freedom, one and indivisible. . . .[76]

Milner had set out the purpose of the meeting and Macdonnell had provided it with a point of view. Both had anticipated the views of the conferees; when the floor was opened to the delegates, speaker after speaker voiced an insistence on free enterprise as the unalterable tenet of Conservatism. At the same time, however, the speakers condemned the doctrinaire beliefs of the party elders and advocated a shift in party policy to a "middle way" course between the left and right extremes of political thought.[77]

After the opening session, the delegates were assigned to one of four committees (war effort, labour relations, agriculture, and rehabilitation

[73]Armour Mackay, "The Men of 1914–18 Begin to Take Over," *Saturday Night*, LVIII (Jan. 2, 1943), 10; Flaherty, "A Conservative Philosophy," 11.

[74]The Conservative party had held a conference at Newmarket, Ont., in 1934, but this was "educational and inspirational" and "directed primarily toward young people in the Party" (Bell, "Conservative National Conventions," p. 4).

[75]*Winnipeg Free Press*, Sept. 5, 1942, p. 11.

[76]*Toronto Daily Star*, Sept. 5, 1942, p. 2.

[77]Toronto *Globe and Mail*, Sept. 5, 1942, p. 7.

and immigration). All the next day, they discussed and amended *in camera* the draft resolutions prepared by Finlayson and his experts. On Sunday, the committees' revised planks were consolidated and distributed to the delegates for private study. The floor was thrown open for free discussion on Labour Day.

Before the final discussions began, however, a letter of greeting from the leader was read. The party, Meighen said, was determined to restore "our British inheritance of free institutions" and to remain "in loyal association with Britain and the British Dominions." Conservatism, he admitted, must concern itself with "social reforms." "Its main duty now, however, is to throw the whole of its energies into this struggle to preserve the life of Canada, to become at whatever cost to itself the instrument of a great all-Canadian league for war. . . . a league whose mission is to forge into one irresistible force with the single thought of victory those who are really resolved to win this war, to live and not to die."[78] This was stirring stuff, but the barely muted cry for national government directly clashed with the purpose of the conference to which it was addressed. Meighen's call for an all-Canadian league was anathema to delegates who, while demanding a greater war effort, were adamant in their refusal to abandon the Conservative party. Fearing as they did that the only result of such a campaign would be to leave the field to the C.C.F. at war's end, the delegates deliberately opposed any move toward national government.[79]

Meighen's letter did not interrupt the proceedings, and the conference moved to consider the resolutions produced by the war effort committee. "We demand," the key resolution read, "the immediate and complete conscription of the manpower of the Dominion for the Armed Services for duty in any part of the world."[80] An attempt to replace "conscription," with its unhappy connotations, with "mobilization" was rebuffed. "I assure you," the committee chairman, C. B. Smith of Halifax, emphatically stated, "that the word 'conscription' is the one thing upon which the majority of our war committee absolutely insists. We don't want any pussy footing or evasion of that."[81] On this issue, if on few others, the delegates agreed with Arthur Meighen.

With conscription settled to their satisfaction, the delegates turned to

[78]*Ibid.*, Sept. 8, 1942, p. 2; *Toronto Daily Star*, Sept. 8, 1942, p. 16.

[79]*Winnipeg Free Press*, Oct. 19, 1942, p. 11. Cf. Macdonnell Papers, Vol. 52, Address to Toronto Conservative Businessmen's Club, June 12, 1942.

[80]Hanson Papers, *Report of the Round Table on Canadian Policy*, mimeographed copy, p. 1 (cited hereafter as *Report*). Portions of the *Report* will be found in Appendix 2.

[81]Montreal *Gazette*, Sept. 8, 1942, p. 7.

a "statement of aims and beliefs." They "recalled with pride and gratitude that our party rose to greatness through a fruitful partnership between two great races, French and English," and affirmed their belief that "the two cultures are part and parcel of our future development and that Canada's true greatness depends on sympathy and understanding between these two original races. . . ."[82] Another resolution called for a firm partnership between the Commonwealth and the United States and denounced isolationism as an acceptable postwar course for Canada. The spirit of internationalism extended to tariffs as well, and the delegates asked for the creation of machinery "designed to make for interdependence and co-operation across the whole field of economic policy."[83]

The harmony of the conference had been most impressive to this point, but when the agricultural committee's recommendations were presented, some delegates insisted on changes. Western Canada, they declared, demanded farm debt adjustment. "We'll lose thousands of votes if we ignore it," they said. Defending the committee's action in omitting such a resolution, G. S. Thorvaldson of Winnipeg stated that "we have held it to be a temporary, not a permanent problem. We have held also that there must be some sanctity of contract in any economic system, and therefore that debt adjustment and interest reduction can hardly be made part of a permanent long-term policy."[84] The requested alteration was made, nonetheless, and another amendment, pledging aid to the fishermen of both coasts, was also included on the insistence of some Maritime delegates.

The resolutions of the labour committee, perhaps similarly framed with the voters in mind, were far-reaching. The main provisions were dependent on the remote prospects of a federal-provincial agreement to vest industrial labour relations in the central government, but the spirit of the programme marked a significant change in attitude. Collective bargaining was accepted in principle, the formation of a national labour relations board on the American model was suggested, and labour's "full freedom of association, self-organization and designation of representatives of their own choosing" was recognized.[85] The labour proposals were doubly significant when it is considered that the committee included men like R. A. Bryce, the president of Macassa Mines, who had been involved in the long fight to keep the C.I.O. out of the mines of northern Ontario.[86]

[82]*Report*, p. 3.
[83]*Ibid.*, p. 3.
[84]Montreal *Gazette*, Sept. 8, 1942, p. 1.
[85]*Report*, p. 4.
[86]Montreal *Gazette*, Sept. 8, 1942, p. 8.

The spirit of change extended to other areas, and the delegates guaranteed every Canadian "a gainful occupation with sufficient income to enable him to maintain a home and a family."[87] They also asked for "a national long-range low-cost housing plan underwritten by the government," increased immigration, and social security. This last measure was to include unemployment insurance, adequate payments for the maintenance of unemployables, retirement insurance, increased old age pensions, pensions for the blind, adequate mothers' and widows' allowances, and a programme of medical services—a national contributory and equitably financed system of medicine. These were extraordinary resolutions for a Conservative conference to approve, and they certainly were, as Finlayson noted, "different from the old Tory stuff."[88] Only free enterprise could provide these benefits, the conference affirmed. Full employment was declared a national objective, but one which could only be achieved through

the strengthening of the basic Canadian tradition of individual initiative and individual enterprise and opportunity and the freeing of economic activities from bureaucratic controls. Government authority, however, should be maintained and exercised wherever necessary to protect primary producers, workers and consumers from exploitation through such abuses as price-fixing combines, monopolies and patent cartels. . . . if, in any field, private enterprise fails or is unable to serve these national interests, government should directly or indirectly develop in that field socially useful undertakings.[89]

Here was the Conservative answer to the socialism of the C.C.F. The "Port Hopefuls" believed in private enterprise, in individual initiative, and in a minimum of state control. At the same time, however, they recognized that another great depression could not be permitted, and that if state intervention was the only way of preventing such crises, they favoured such intervention.

The forward-looking results of the conference were greeted favourably by the press. The *Winnipeg Free Press* was highly flattering in its comments on the policy statement,[90] and *Saturday Night* saw the conference as having a decisive effect on Conservatism for the next ten years. "It will not, after Port Hope, be possible for the Conservative party to attempt to insinuate itself to the Right of the Liberals," the Toronto weekly said. Its only course henceforth "is to seek public approval as a party somewhat further Left than the Liberals but not so disturbingly Left as the C.C.F."[91] Of the English-speaking press, only the Montreal

[87]*Report*, p. 5.
[88]Finlayson Interview, June 1, 1963.
[89]*Report*, p. 5.
[90]*Winnipeg Free Press*, Sept. 14, 15, 16, 17, 1942.
[91]"The Front Page," *Saturday Night*, LVIII (Sept. 26, 1942), 1.

Gazette took exception to the work of Port Hope. "Are these Conservative principles?" the morning newspaper asked with its usual *ex cathedra* authority on September 8. "Up to the present they have not been so. If they are to be so in the future, it would be well to have the decision made by a body more regularly selected than this self-admittedly unofficial 'round table conference.' " Of French-language newspapers, the reaction of *Le Devoir* (13 septembre) to the Conservatives' meeting and to the acquiescence of the *Canadien* delegates to the resolutions on conscription was the most blunt and most accurate: "Chez nous, le parti conservateur est mort."

To Hanson, however, Port Hope was a forward step. "It goes a long way in social legislation," he wrote, "but I think that is all to the good." In a postscript, he added that "I hope [Meighen] will not be too reactionary in regard to it.[92]

This was a vain hope. Meighen was not greatly disturbed by the press reports of the conference, but on his first detailed examination of the resolutions several weeks later he was troubled. The stand on social security, he wrote to Milner,

is flagrant and mischievous dishonesty. Plainly it is an attempt to outbid the C.C.F. and out-King King. Throughout King's history he has made it a habit to picture what a Paradise the people want and say that that is what he stands for. . . . In this Clause, we enter the race and we cast away all the traditions of sanity and wisdom which have made us what we are, and which today are more vital to us than ever, if we are really to serve Canada. This Clause throws self-reliance into the discard. . . . It is my solemn belief that the main cause of the progressive decrepitude of nations is just too much of Clause 25.

"The whole situation," he continued, "makes my position most difficult," and he could only regret that "you people at Port Hope" had underestimated the all-controlling demands of the war and considered it only a mere element in the present difficulties of the country.[93] By the time this letter was written in October, however, Meighen had already committed himself to an irrevocable course of action.

The leader had been considering the possibility of a convention since the summer, and after Port Hope he pressed ahead with his plans. The Port Hope delegates eagerly welcomed this. "I am more than ever convinced that there can be no progress whatever in party reconstruction until the air, both as to leadership and policy, is cleared by a National Convention," R. A. Bell, who had been a Port Hope delegate, wrote to Hanson. "This . . . is the view of practically everyone who attended the

[92]Hanson Papers, File O-160, Hanson to Bell, Sept. 9, 1942.
[93]Bennett Papers, Notable Persons File, Meighen to Milner, Oct. 17, 1942 (copy).

Port Hope Conference."[94] Some Members of Parliament shared this view. "Our biggest problem is leadership," one New Brunswick M.P. wrote. "In spite of the ability, integrity and patriotism of Mr. Meighen, I do not think we are going to get anywhere under his leadership." "I have hardly met a person who wants him to stay," Grote Stirling remarked to Hanson.[95] Meighen himself was searching for an exit, but first he had to lay the groundwork.

The plans for a convention were first discussed in Montreal on September 17, 1942. There, Meighen met with Hanson and Senator Ballantyne of Montreal, now Conservative leader in the Senate and a financial power in the party, and selected a preliminary committee to make arrangements for a convention in late November. Milner, the chairman at Port Hope, was asked to perform a similar task for the convention, and Bell was named to head the convention secretariat.[96] The plans were revealed publicly on September 23, 1942, when Meighen announced that a convention to consider the "whole subject of leadership and policy" would be held. The party, he said in his press release, "has pressed unremittingly for a broadening of the basis of government in Canada," but nothing had been accomplished. "Instead of moving toward unity we have drifted the other way."

The time has come now when an opportunity should be given not only to Conservatives but to all Canadians who think as we do about this war . . . to get together and make a united effort to bring better things about.

It surely is time a great organization of the people was forged, which knows its mind, has definite principles—which is animated by an unwavering resolve to do the right and which fears not to demand of this country the universal service which alone can save us.

Therefore, it is my hope that the doors of the coming convention will be open to all citizens, who, regardless of former party affiliations, are animated by these principles and resolved to give them effect.[97]

As Meighen's statement made clear, his policy of conscription and national government remained constant and unchanging. The one new wrinkle was the insistence on an "open door" policy for the convention.

Meighen pressed this theme upon the interim committee when it met in Ottawa on September 25. The committee accepted his directive and

[94]Bell Papers, Vol. 1, Bell to Hanson, Sept. 11, 1942.
[95]Hanson Papers, File O-160-W, D. K. Hazen, M.P. to Hanson, Sept. 12, 1942; File MP-133, Stirling to Hanson, Oct. 5, 1942.
[96]*Ibid.*, File O-160, Hanson to G. B. Foster, Sept. 18, 1942; Meighen Papers, Meighen to Milner, Sept. 18, 1942. Progressive Conservative Party Files, Convention Documents, 1942, "Minutes of Interim Convention Committee, September 25, 1942," lists the members of this committee. (Cited hereafter as Convention Documents, 1942.)
[97]Convention Documents, "Text of Statement . . . September the 23rd, 1942."

also made arrangements for the formation of a broadly representative National Convention Committee and for its first meeting in Ottawa on October 6.[98] The National Committee determined finally on Winnipeg as the convention site and on December 9–11, 1942, as the time. A Resolutions and Policy Committee of thirteen members was formed under Cecil G. Frost of Lindsay, Ontario, as chairman and Finlayson as secretary. Eight of the members, including the chairman and the secretary, had been at Port Hope.[99] The open-door policy was accepted, and authority was granted for the issue of "voting credentials as delegates-at-large to individuals and representatives of organizations not previously associated with the Conservative party."[100] Each constituency was declared eligible to send three voting delegates and three alternates to Winnipeg, and provision was made for the selection of ex-officio delegates and delegates-at-large.[101] In all, more than 1250 persons were entitled to attend the convention.[102] The only question yet unsettled was the leadership.

There was no shortage of contenders for the post. John Diefenbaker and Howard Green from the parliamentary caucus were evidently preparing to contest the leadership, and J. H. Harris, M.P., of Toronto, an unsuccessful candidate at the 1938 convention, was rumoured to be considering another try. George Drew and Sidney Smith were believed to be interested, and Murdoch MacPherson was widely considered as the favourite of the Port Hope delegates.[103] Every Conservative had his

[98]*Ibid.*, "Minutes of Interim Committee."

[99]*Ibid.*, "Resolutions and Policy Committee."

[100]*Ibid.*, "Minutes of First Meeting of National Convention Committee . . . October 6, 1942." This policy was a dismal failure. Meighen sent out a number of letters to such organizations as the Canadian Legion, the Trades and Labour Congress, and the Canadian Federation of Agriculture, but got no results. Meighen Papers, letters, Oct. 8–14, 1942. Apparently only 8 people attended the convention in this category (Bell, "Conservative National Conventions," p. 104).

[101]Ex-officio delegates included Conservative Privy Councillors, M.P.s, senators, provincial legislators, and members of the National Convention Committee and its subcommittees. Delegates-at-large were to be selected by provincial associations. Each province was entitled to as many delegates as that province had federal constituencies. The delegates were to be selected so as to ensure broad representation. Youth delegates also were included in this category. Riding delegates were to be selected at meetings of the constituency associations. All delegates could vote. See Convention Documents, "Minutes, Oct. 6, 1942"; John W. Lederle, "National Party Conventions: Canada Shows the Way," *Southwestern Social Science Quarterly*, XXV (Sept., 1944), 124.

[102]Mrs. Bell has calculated the numbers of delegates as follows: constituency —735; ex-officio—213; at-large—310; total—1258. In all, 931 delegates attended. Bell, "Conservative National Conventions," Table V.

[103]Hanson Papers, File MP-120, H. R. Jackman to Hanson, Nov. 5, 1942; file P-450-Personal, Bell to Hanson, Nov. 16, 1942; E. A. Corbett, *Sidney Earle Smith* (Toronto, 1961), pp. 29–31.

candidate, but none of those mentioned was without his liabilities. Viscount Bennet, in Canada for a visit in October, canvassed the leadership situation with his friends and scribbled a note to Meighen on his findings:

There is no one in P.E.I. or Quebec. In Ont. there is Drew, Macdonnell and yourself. In Sask. Diefenbaker and MacPherson. In Alberta no one, and Maitland [Conservative leader] and Green in B.C. . . . Drew has difficulties to overcome that are too great to enable him to succeed. Diefenbaker . . . too inexperienced. . . . As for MacPherson . . . he has a *blackmark* against him in the Roman church. . . . So far as Green and Maitland are concerned I do not think they are seriously regarded. That leaves Man. and there is just one man there. I think that your views are the same: and I am convinced he must be secured for the sake of Canada and the Empire altogether apart from the party. If not you must again sacrifice yourself.[104]

The "one man" in Manitoba was John Bracken, the premier of Manitoba, and Meighen agreed completely with this assessment of the situation.

Meighen had first approached Bracken shortly before the Ottawa conference of November 1941. His attempt to garner support for Bracken there had failed, and after Meighen himself had been dragooned into accepting the leadership, communication between the two had lapsed. After his defeat in York South, Meighen's thoughts again turned to Bracken, reinforced now by his belief that the Premier was the only man who could beat the C.C.F. "Mr. Bracken appealed to me," he wrote later, "because I was convinced that only the farming population of Canada could save this country from the C.C.F. avalanche which was growing at that time very rapidly, and that the leader should be a man who in a high degree had the confidence of the farmers of Canada. This qualification Mr. Bracken possessed in abundant measure."[105] In addition, and possibly more important, Meighen believed that Bracken felt as strongly as he did on the questions of conscription and national government. Under the direction of its leader, the Manitoba legislature had passed a resolution in December 1941 urging conscription for overseas service, and Bracken had called King's plebiscite "the crowning indignity."[106] It was also widely believed that while Bracken was not

[104]Meighen Papers, Bennett to Meighen, n.d. [Oct. 1942]. (The punctuation and spelling of this letter have been corrected.) Part of the letter is printed in Graham, *Meighen*, III, 141. MacPherson's "blackmark" originated in his actions as Attorney General of Saskatchewan in 1930 in sponsoring legislation directed against Catholic schools in the province (*The Canadian Annual Review of Public Affairs, 1929–1930*, Toronto, 1930, pp. 481–3).

[105]Meighen Papers, Meighen to L. G. Gravel, April 6, 1944. Cf. Dafoe Papers, Microfilm roll M-80, T. A. Crerar to Dafoe, Dec. 27, 1942, recounting a conversation with Meighen's friend, Gratton O'Leary of the *Ottawa Journal.*

[106]Pickersgill, *Mackenzie King Record*, I, 313–14; *Winnipeg Free Press*, Jan. 20, 1942, p. 1.

interested, as he said, "in partisan government at a time of war"[107] or in leading a national party, he was receptive to the suggestion of a national government.[108] This was the explanation for Meighen's insistence on an open convention. Not only would it now be possible for Bracken to be presented as a candidate for the leadership, but the open convention device could be used to play down the partisanship so distasteful to the prairie leader.

Meighen's plans to bring about the desired transfer of leadership had worked perfectly to this point. The convention was organized as he wished, and the Port Hope conference, despite his own reservations about the policy it had enunciated, could be expected to appeal to the progressive Bracken. The appointment of Milner as convention chairman, and the selection of Frost and Finlayson to head the Resolutions Committee would be, as Professor Graham notes, "a sign to Bracken that the spirit of Port Hope was very much to the fore and not just a peculiar aberration from the Conservative norm, that it was, indeed, a progressive Conservative party he was being asked to lead."[109] Meighen's problems now were twofold. First, he had to convince the Conservative party that it needed Bracken, and then he had to persuade a dubious Bracken that he wanted the Conservative party.

His early efforts at influencing Conservative leaders in Bracken's favour were not promising, and Meighen began to fear that the groundswell of opinion he was trying to create would not materialize. There were some notable converts, however, including Hanson. "A national drive for Bracken would do the trick," he wrote to Meighen. "I am convinced he has the confidence of the west and I feel certain he could be sold to the east."[110] George McCullagh joined the campaign, and Meighen sent him to Winnipeg to discuss agricultural policy with Bracken. "He will find me ready to go just as far as he," Meighen wrote the Toronto publisher, "and I think we both know what is practicable. He knows much better than I do what is useful."[111] Gradually, the ranks swelled,[112] and Meighen was ready now to eliminate the strongest potential candidate from the race—his good friend, Murdoch MacPherson.

Meighen telephoned the Regina lawyer on November 3, 1942, and

[107]Bracken quoted in *Winnipeg Free Press*, Sept. 24, 1942, p. 12.

[108]E.g., Hanson Papers, Personal Correspondence, Vol. 33, John Bird to Hanson, Nov. 18, 1942; Pickersgill, *Mackenzie King Record*, I, 453–4; *Winnipeg Free Press*, Nov. 25, 1942, p. 6.

[109]Graham, *Meighen*, 140–1.

[110]Hanson Papers, File P-450-M, Hanson to Meighen, Oct. 9, 1942.

[111]Meighen Papers, Meighen to McCullagh, Oct. 17, 1942.

[112]Bell Papers, Vol. 1, Bell to Milner, Nov. 12, 1942; Hanson Papers, File MP-104, P. C. Black, M.P., to Hanson, Nov. 12, 1942, and File P-450-Personal, Hanson to Bell, Nov. 13, 1942.

asked him to fly to Toronto for the next day.[113] Their meeting, with Milner in attendance, was cordial. Meighen told MacPherson that Bennett agreed with him on the party's need for Bracken, and he asked the candidate to withdraw in Bracken's favour. MacPherson indicated that he was not unwilling to step aside, but he asked to be allowed to consult his backers before giving a final decision. Upon his return to the West, however, MacPherson wrote that his supporters both in Calgary and Winnipeg were "emphatic" in urging him to remain in contention. He heard from Winnipeg friends, he said to Meighen,

that Bracken had to be counted out; that if there was a unanimous request from the Convention for Bracken, Bracken might consider it, but that Bracken knew . . . that there was no possible chance of an absolutely unanimous request . . . . [his friend] said that he was satisfied beyond question that it was just out of the question to consider Bracken's name further as a practical matter.[114]

This was a heavy blow to the Tory leader. "I am meeting with cruel disappointments in my plans for the Convention," he wrote to his son. "Frankly it does not look to me now as if the door of hope is going to be opened at Winnipeg. Perhaps I am too blue today. . . . Oh how I wish that event was over!"[115]

The very next day, however, Meighen wrote to Bracken. "Well, to start with," he began,

I am still, and more resolutely than ever, of the mind I was when I saw you a year ago. The reason I am more resolute is that the crisis now is very much closer and it is much plainer than it was then that the crisis points to you and to you only. . . .
. . . I can say definitely that I have not met one single man in Eastern Canada with whom I have talked—and they have been very many—with whom I had to use one single argument to produce conviction.

The West, Meighen believed, would be equally enthusiastic, but there were many there with leadership ambitions:

There is no doubt—and I confess it frankly—that there is a feeling in the West that you will not accept, and as a result of that feeling, followings tend to gather behind other favourites, and the favourites themselves no doubt begin to generate views of great things to come. What I do want to impress, though, in the strongest terms I can use is that these factors are in no sense detracting factors. It would really not be a healthy situation if some, at least, of the usual competitive features of Conventions did not appear. I think it

---

[113]Meighen Papers, MacPherson to Meighen, Nov. 3, 1942.
[114]*Ibid.*, Nov. 15, 1942.
[115]Meighen to his son, Ted, Nov. 16, 1942, quoted in Graham, *Meighen*, III, 142.

far better if they do appear, providing, of course, the favourable trend is overwhelming. . . . I do not know what is going to happen to our country if you fail us, and I cannot believe for a moment you will fail us. . . .

If you will only give the word, we will do the rest in loyal association with you, and when this world travail is over, you will always know that you heeded the call of duty in its sternest tones.[116]

On November 22, accompanied by Hugh Mackay, Conservative leader in New Brunswick, and Gordon Graydon, the M.P. for Peel (Ontario), Meighen secretly travelled to Winnipeg, hoping to persuade Bracken to heed the call.

John Bracken had never wanted to enter politics. Born in 1883, he spent his young manhood working as a field representative for the federal Department of Agriculture, and he later became Professor of Field Husbandry at the University of Saskatchewan. In 1920, he accepted the post of president of the Manitoba Agricultural College, and it was while he held this position that he was asked to become premier of Manitoba. Western Canada had gone through a period of political ferment after the Great War as a profound revolt against "partyism" and high tariffs swept the prairie provinces, and there was a massive rejection of the old parties. One casualty was the Liberal government of Manitoba, and a farmer slate was returned with a narrow majority in 1922. Without a leader, the United Farmers of Manitoba turned to Bracken who, although he had no political experience, had a reputation as a solid, enlightened thinker. The offer came as a complete surprise to Bracken, but after much hesitation he accepted the proffered post as a "challenge."[117]

Within a short time, the austere Bracken restored order to Manitoba's hitherto chaotic administration, won a reputation for efficiency, and established a viable and popular government which had held office continuously from 1922. In 1932, under the stress of the depression, he merged his party with the provincial Liberals and henceforth campaigned as a Liberal-Progressive. The alliance was uneasy, and Bracken became increasingly restive under the federal leadership of Mackenzie King. First came the depression years and repeated trips to Ottawa to seek aid for the wheat farmer. With the outbreak of the war, the problem was exacerbated, for King seemed unwilling or unable to face the problems created by Manitoba's huge wheat surplus.[118] In addition, Bracken's

[116]Meighen Papers, Meighen to Bracken, Nov. 17, 1942. The letter is printed in part in Graham, *Meighen*, III, 142–3.

[117]The Hon. John Bracken Interview, June 1, 1963; Paul F. Sharp, *Agrarian Revolt in Western Canada* (Minneapolis, 1948), p. 169; *The Canadian Annual Review of Public Affairs, 1922* (Toronto, 1923), pp. 769–77.

[118]See "Wheat," *Canadian Forum*, XX (Oct., 1940), 197; "Wheat," *Canadian Forum*, XXI (April, 1941), 4; G. E. Britnell and V. C. Fowke, *Canadian Agriculture in War and Peace* (Stanford, 1962), pp. 200ff.

decision in November 1940 to form a coalition from representatives of all parties in the legislature—partisan politics had no place in wartime, he said—found scant favour in Ottawa.[119] The Manitoba premier was ready to break his tenuous ties with the Liberal party, and after Meighen's initial approach in November 1941, his interest was piqued.

Bracken was a complex individual—dour, humourless, laconic, but creating an overriding impression of sincerity and efficiency. To John Dafoe, a shrewd and generally sympathetic observer of his premier, Bracken remained something of an enigma. "I have been cooperating in a general way with J. B. for twenty years," he wrote to J. M. Macdonnell in July 1942,

and in that time have been of service to him at times and have helped to save his hide upon certain critical occasions. I have no regrets about this for there has never been a time in those two decades that anyone offered who could be preferred to him; and I don't know anyone who is. I don't know that he would subordinate the public interests to his own but he shows great ingenuity in leaning them up together. He is silent, secretive and selfish—and I am pretty sure jealous-minded as well. An old political hand who has had plenty of contacts with him and has also done him service, told me only yesterday that he was sure John was shaping his course to sign on with the C.C.F. at the next Dominion election, if the prospects of that party improve as they will, as the Manitoba leader. I find it possible to believe this. There have been signs that he is interested in the wider field and if so any road that leads to it would be attractive.[120]

Bracken was a man of many parts, playing his own hand in his own fashion, and the Conservatives who travelled west to speak with him soon discovered this.

The secrecy of Meighen's arrival in Winnipeg on November 24 was lost immediately when he was recognized by a reporter at the railway station.[121] The unwelcome publicity forced the Conservative leader to be extremely circumspect, and Bracken was first approached through intermediaries and then by Graydon and Milner (who was in Winnipeg to make final arrangements for the convention[122]). The discussions with Bracken were long, tedious, and inconclusive. The Premier allegedly demanded three conditions: that he be given the leadership without a

---

[119]Gardiner Papers, A. M. Shinbane to Gardiner, July 12 and July 19, 1940, and Gardiner to W. L. M. King, July 22, 1940; Hanson Papers, File P-450-HB-1, Bell to Hanson, Oct. 23, 1940, and File P-306, Errick Willis, M.L.A., to Hanson, Nov. 2, 1940; C.C.F. Records, Vol. 61, F. R. Scott to David Lewis, Aug. 15, 1940.
[120]Dafoe Papers, Microfilm roll M-80, Dafoe to Macdonnell, July 31, 1942.
[121]*Winnipeg Free Press*, Nov. 24, 1942, p. 1.
[122]*Ibid.*, Nov. 30, 1942, p. 7.

convention fight; that the name of the party be changed to Progressive Conservative; and that a platform similar in spirit to that produced by Port Hope be adopted by the convention. Only the first of these conditions was impossible, but Bracken was guaranteed an easy victory over MacPherson. The Manitoba leader, while not committing himself, indicated that he might, perhaps, contest the leadership in these circumstances. This was heartening to Meighen. ". . . things do look more— much more hopeful now," he wrote his son. "If I can succeed it will be one of the biggest things I have done. Others (some) have helped much particularly lately. But I was alone for so long."[123] There were still obstacles, but Meighen's plan remained viable. The most important hurdle, Bracken's consent, had not yet been cleared, but he was interested. MacPherson had refused to withdraw; this was unfortunate, but he could be beaten.

The immensely practical arguments advanced by Meighen in support of his candidate now began to produce results. The entire party agreed that the C.C.F. was the real threat, and the West did seem likely to respond to a progressive platform espoused by its own John Bracken. Already some of the Port Hope delegates, erstwhile MacPherson supporters, were beginning to look on Bracken as their candidate,[124] and Meighen was exerting all his still considerable powers on Bracken's behalf,[125] even arranging for George Drew to nominate Bracken.[126]

It soon began to appear that candidates other than MacPherson would contest the leadership. Significantly, every hopeful was from the West, the clearest possible proof that Meighen's reasoning was shared within the party. On December 2, John Diefenbaker, the M.P. from Lake Centre, Saskatchewan, announced that he would be a candidate. The decision was made, the maverick M.P. said, "when I heard the convention was going to be a cut and dried affair."[127] Within a few days, Diefenbaker's example was followed by Howard Green.[128] Sidney Smith was being widely mentioned as a contender, but as president of the provincially-supported University of Manitoba his position was a delicate one, since it was possible that the Premier might be a candidate.

[123]Meighen to his son, Ted, Nov. 27, 1942, quoted in Graham, *Meighen*, III, 144.

[124]Macdonnell Interview, July 10, 1963. Cf. *Winnipeg Free Press*, Nov. 27, 1942, p. 7.

[125]Finlayson Interview, June 1, 1963. Finlayson said that Milner, Mackay, and Macdonnell had been personally converted by Meighen.

[126]Bracken Interview, June 1, 1963.

[127]*Winnipeg Free Press*, Dec. 3, p. 3, and Dec. 8, 1942, p. 15; Peter Newman, *Renegade in Power: The Diefenbaker Years* (Toronto, 1963), p. 26.

[128]*Winnipeg Free Press*, Dec. 8, 1942, p. 15.

Smith would be unable to make his position clear until Bracken made up his mind.[129] The remaining candidate was the British Columbian, H. H. Stevens, the leader of the breakaway Reconstruction party of 1935. Returning as a penitent, Stevens was given no chance of winning significant support.

While the early arrivals among the leadership contestants were establishing themselves in Winnipeg on Monday, December 7, the first meetings of the convention Resolutions and Policy Committee were being held. The committee's task had been simplified by Port Hope and by the work of the pre-convention group under Finlayson. As a result a platform very similar to that produced at the Port Hope conference was virtually completed by the next evening.[130]

This draft platform was presented to Bracken for his approval on Tuesday night by a delegation of fifteen Conservatives. For six hours, the visitors sat in Bracken's living room while the Premier alternately read the prepared resolutions and cross-examined the delegation members.[131] At last, at 2:00 A.M., Bracken announced that he was satisfied with the policy and especially with its agricultural planks. He was, he hastened to add, still in a quandary, for he had come to believe that he could not afford to emerge as a sudden convert to Conservatism. Nor was he prepared to engage in a fight merely to head the Tory party. If the leadership had been unanimously offered to him, he would have accepted this as a token of the party's changed views. But with the prospect of a bitter convention struggle looming, he must insist on a definite gesture from the party. If the party's name could be altered to Progressive Conservative *before* the nominations were filed on Thursday night, he would run; if not, he would decline to enter the race.[132]

Bracken's reasoning was both shrewd and sensible. Having had no prior ties with the Conservative party, he wanted definite assurances that he was the choice of the whole party and not merely the selection of a few. The change of name would provide proof of this and would also

---

[129]Corbett, *Smith*, p. 30.

[130]Lederle, "National Party Conventions," p. 127; Toronto *Globe and Mail*, Dec. 9, 1942. The platform was printed and given wide circulation. *Freedom, Security, Opportunity and the British Partnership, Policy of the Progressive Conservative Party Adopted . . . 1942* (Ottawa, n.d.). Part of it may be found in Appendix 3.

[131]F. G. Gardiner Interview, Sept. 8, 1964. Gardiner was one of those in attendance. Toronto *Globe and Mail*, Dec. 10, 1942, p. 2; Montreal *Gazette*, Dec. 9, 1942, p. 1.

[132]Montreal *Gazette*, Dec. 15, 1942, p. 17; Toronto *Globe and Mail*, Dec. 12, 1942, p. 17; "The New Conservatism," *Round Table*, XXXIII (March, 1943), p. 173.

indicate to the country that the party had moved into the middle of the road. If this condition were not met, his Progressive supporters would not join the party, whereas he hoped they would rally to him under a new name, a new policy, and his leadership. There is nothing to indicate that the tired delegation found this condition unacceptable. Bracken earlier had indicated that he wanted the name changed, and it made little difference if this was done before or after the nominations. It was agreed that Bracken would send a letter setting out his conditions that morning.[133]

The letter was duly delivered, and its contents were read at the afternoon session of the first day of the proceedings. The leadership, Bracken said, had been presented to him as a challenge, and he believed he would have to accept if his candidature "could be effected in such a way that my political friends and associates of many years would feel that the principles for which we have unitedly stood were not being abandoned":

There is every indication that the principles and policies likely to be adopted by the convention will be progressive in character and will not differ substantially from my own convictions. . . .

If . . . the Conservative Party is becoming in fact the Progressive party that is indicated by the spirit of the Port Hope Report, there will be but little separating our respective views. . . .

If, therefore, the convention were prepared to give visible evidence of its progressive intent by association of these two names, Progressive and Conservative, I would be willing to become a candidate for the leadership.[134]

The letter, faithfully reflecting the discussions of Tuesday night, also represented Bracken's attempt to counter the charge that he was the candidate of the old guard—of Meighen and the "interests." His letter was aimed at the Port Hopefuls and at those who believed, as they did, that a progressive party was a necessity. But when the statement was read to the convention and a motion presented to adopt the new name, wild disorder broke out in the hall. Faced with a budding revolt, Milner, the chairman, quickly postponed debate until the next morning.[135]

Bracken's condition, and particularly the way it was presented, had created immediate resentment. Even those delegates eager to see him selected were dismayed by his ultimatum, and although many liked the proposed name, they deplored Bracken's tactics.[136] For Meighen, the

[133]Montreal *Gazette*, Dec. 9, 1942, p. 1; Toronto *Globe and Mail*, Dec. 10, 1942, p. 2; Bracken Interview, June 1, 1963.

[134]Progressive Conservative Party Files, Official Report (Unrevised) National Conservative Convention (1942) Winnipeg, Manitoba, December 9, 10, 11, 1942, pp. 58–9 (cited hereafter as Minutes, 1942).

[135]*Ibid.*, pp. 59–61.

[136]Bracken Interview, June 1, 1963.

day's events were shattering, and the carefully prepared plan to secure Bracken as leader seemed in danger of collapse. Incredibly, he had believed that Bracken's letter, at last making clear that he would run, would be greeted with cheers. Meighen and his supporters had not realized that the letter implied that the Conservatives were joining the Progressives rather than the reverse. To the average delegate, this was tantamount to saying that the Conservative party was dead, something he was not prepared to admit.[137]

On Thursday morning, the delegates again disrupted the proceedings. When Milner announced that a resolution had been filed proposing the adoption of the name Progressive Conservative, jeers and booing filled the hall. Again, Milner postponed the debate.[138] The resolution was finally presented in the afternoon by Earl Lawson of Toronto, the old guard candidate for the leadership at the 1938 convention who had been abandoned in the precipitate rush to MacPherson just prior to the vote. No friend of the old guard as a result, Lawson was a good choice to present the case for the name change. Reiterating his purity of motive again and again, he argued that the party should recognize the need for a progressive approach. The new name, he said, would project this view to the electorate.[139] Before his motion could be seconded, however, the floor was seized by those who opposed the motion, and speaker after speaker denounced the attempt to stampede the convention and "fix" the vote for Bracken.[140]

The opposition, led by Alan Cockeram of Toronto, the York South M.P. who had stepped aside for Meighen, and by Donald Fleming, a Toronto alderman prominent at Port Hope, argued that it would be a sign of weakness to change the party's name again. Scornful references were made to Manion, the "last Moses" who had promised victory, changed the party name, and lost everything. If the name change were approved, they maintained, the leadership race would be predetermined in Bracken's favour. The convention was in imminent danger of dissolution when J. M. Macdonnell, developing upon an earlier amendment to the motion, proposed that consideration of the suggested change be postponed until after the selection of the leader. The chairman had no choice other than to accept the recommendation, and the convention enthusiastically adopted Macdonnell's idea.[141]

[137]*Winnipeg Free Press*, Dec. 10, 1942, p. 13.
[138]Minutes, 1942, p. 77.
[139]*Ibid.*, pp. 147–53.
[140]Blair Fraser, "Bracken, the Leader," *Maclean's*, LVII (May 1, 1944), 10.
[141]Minutes, 1942, pp. 155–82, 182–3, 187.

The extent of the victory won by the delegates' revolt could not be underestimated. The ordinary delegate had become tired of conspiracies and plots, and although he was not really against the name change or even against Bracken, he was most certainly opposed to the ramrod methods being employed by his backers. Bracken's conditions had been rejected, to be sure, but the revolt had been directed at those attempting to force him upon the party, not at the Manitoba premier. If Bracken now wanted to be leader, it would have to be on the delegates' terms.

Bracken was plunged into indecision by the startling events of the afternoon session. Meighen made his final appeal to him between 6:45 and 7:30 P.M., but he could get no answer.[142] With the deadline for nominations at 8:00 P.M., the excitement was intense, and no one knew what Bracken's decision would be. Mrs. Bracken later described the events of the evening for her sons in the armed forces:

At four minutes to eight Mr. Smith of Calgary [Arthur L. Smith, a lawyer and an unsuccessful candidate for Parliament, who was to nominate Bracken] called and wanted to know where Jack was. . . . Mr. Smith asked frantically, "Mrs. Bracken, do you know what your husband is going to do? There are only four minutes to go and if he is not here soon, it will be too late. . . ." I told him that Dad had gone to the Auditorium to speak and be a candidate for the leadership. . . .

Douglas [a son] phoned me later on to say that everything had conspired to hold them up that night. Every traffic signal was against them, they got into a traffic jam, and arrived at one of the doors at five minutes to eight, but it was not at the right entrance and had a reporter that knew Jack not been there it is doubtful if the committee would have gotten him in time to sign his nomination papers. As it was he had just one minute to spare when the signatures were attached. . . .[143]

Bracken's entry into the main auditorium brought the delegates' uncertainty to an end. In the sudden release of tension, everyone "leaped to attention" while Bracken walked to the stage and took a seat alongside the other nominees. He came to seek the leadership, and although he obviously hoped the party's name would be changed, he came as a Conservative.[144]

The order of the nomination speeches was determined by ballot, and Bracken drew the first place. George Drew, who had earlier agreed to nominate the Premier, had backed off after the Wednesday fracas about

[142]Bennett Papers, Notable Persons File, Meighen to Bennett, Dec. 16, 1942.
[143]Mrs. Bracken to her sons, Dec. 13, 1942, quoted in Bell, "Conservative National Conventions," p. 38.
[144]*Winnipeg Free Press*, Dec. 11, 1942, p. 13.

the change of name,[145] and Bracken's nomination was moved by Arthur Smith and seconded by Gordon Graydon. At the close of the nomination speeches, the candidates spoke on their own behalf. In a short, stilted speech, evidently much affected by the tension of the day, Bracken stated that he was honoured to be considered for the leadership. He would be pleased if he were chosen, but not unhappy if he were not. His sole virtue, he told the convention, was that he spoke the "language of the common man," and he concluded by advising the delegates that "If you take me you take [my views] too."[146] The other candidates followed Bracken, and their oratory was equally dreary. "The speeches were terrible," one observer wrote, "the candidates at their worst."

Murdo [MacPherson] slouched in his chair like a weary hobo, while John D[iefenbaker] was so stiff and starched in his manner I could scarcely recognize him, and the wives were either crying or pulling hair off stage all the time the speeches were going on. . . . Poor Howard Green had such stage fright that suddenly in the midst of a sentence he let go the microphone, staggered backward, and fell in a faint, amid all the distinguished legs behind him. Dr. Bruce, rushing forward, tripped over a chair and fell flat on his face and had also to be picked up. . . .[147]

The scene could hardly have been an inspiring one.

The selection of the leader at last took place on Friday. The voting was by secret individual ballot, and a majority was necessary to win. On the first ballot the count was Bracken—420; Stevens—20; Diefenbaker —120; Green—80; and MacPherson—222.[148] When the results were announced, Stevens and Green announced their withdrawal from the race, but MacPherson's attempt to retire was shouted down by his supporters.[149] On the second ballot, Bracken received a majority,[150] and his selection was declared unanimous on the motion of the two defeated candidates. The victorious Bracken, freed from the anxiety of the past week, then proceeded to deliver a "magnificent" acceptance speech,[151] calling for teamwork and reiterating the progressive principles upon

[145]Drew's decision not to nominate Bracken caused a temporary break in relations with George McCullagh. Prior to the convention, the *Globe and Mail* built up Drew as a contender, presumably hoping to see his strength transferred to Bracken after the nomination speeches (Toronto *Globe and Mail*, Nov. 30, p. 6, and Dec. 3, 1942, p. 6).

[146]Minutes, 1942, pp. 275–82.

[147]Bennett Papers, Series H, Vol. 1, Evelyn S. Tufts to Miss Millar (Bennett's private secretary), Jan. 6, 1943; Newman, *Renegade in Power*, p. 27.

[148]Minutes, 1942, p. 361.

[149]*Ibid.*, pp. 361–3.

[150]Results were apparently not announced at the convention. *Ibid.*, Exhibit III, p. 410, lists the results as Bracken—538; MacPherson—255; Diefenbaker—79.

[151]Adamson Papers, Diary, Dec. 11, 1942.

which he would base his leadership.[152] Following the address, Alan Cockeram, the leader of the fight against the name change, came to the platform and announced that although he had not voted for Bracken he wished to move the adoption of the new party name. The motion creating the Progressive Conservative party was approved without debate by a resounding chorus of ayes from the floor.[153]

Incredibly, the results of the convention had seemingly satisfied everyone. Meighen was thrilled with his "wonderful" convention,[154] the Port Hope delegates had won both a progressive platform and a progressive leader, and the ordinary delegate had demonstrated that he was no cipher controlled from the back room. How this unanimous feeling of well-being had been created was something of a mystery. Half whimsically, half seriously, the editor of *Saturday Night* captured the perplexity of onlookers:

In the beginning there was a Junta, and the Junta had arranged to put something through. In the end something had been put through and it was what the Junta had arranged, in a sense. But the funny thing was that the Junta had not put it through. It sort of put itself through. Mr. Bracken is the leader of the party that the Convention turned the Conservative Party into. Mr. Bracken is the man that Mr. Meighen had decided should be the leader. But Mr. Bracken is not the leader because Mr. Meighen had decided that he should be, not at all.[155]

The selection of Bracken was nonetheless a triumph for Meighen. Nothing in his career as leader, one observer noted, "became him so much as the leaving of it. . . . his imposing of Bracken on the Tory party is maybe the most successful feat of leadership he has ever performed."[156]

But in getting Bracken, Meighen had forfeited his schemes for national government and conscription. There was no support at the convention for his persistent efforts to convert the Conservative party into an "all-Canadian league for war to the end"; the platform was moderate on the subject of compulsory service,[157] and the new leader did not even mention the subject in his acceptance speech.[158] Implicit in the events of

---

[152]Minutes, 1942, pp. 374–85.

[153]*Ibid.*, pp. 386–7; Adamson Papers, Diary, Dec. 11, 1942. Graham, *Meighen*, III, 150, mistakenly has the name change moved by Milner, the chairman.

[154]Bennett Papers, Notable Persons File, Meighen to Bennett, Dec. 16, 1942.

[155]B. K. Sandwell, "Without Bracken They Had Nothing," *Saturday Night*, LVIII (Dec. 26, 1942), p. 14.

[156]P.A.C., A. K. Cameron Papers, M.G. 27, Vol. 35, Cameron to the Hon. T. A. Crerar, Dec. 12, 1942.

[157]Pickersgill, *Mackenzie King Record*, I, 458, gives King's reaction. He felt "wholly vindicated in my stand re conscription, seeing that the word has been carefully kept out of any declaration of policy. . . ."

[158]The speech is in John Bracken, *John Bracken Says* (Toronto, 1944), pp. 3–8.

December 9 to 11 was the recognition that the war was Mackenzie King's to run and that the proper task of the Conservative party was to concentrate on scuppering the C.C.F. Meighen and his backers had won their fight to make Bracken leader, but in doing so they had been forced into concessions on policy and had abandoned the ideological field to the party's progressives. For the moment at least, one writer suggested, "the Old Guard . . . have consciously decided that three-quarters of the loaf is better than no bread," and that Bracken is the "lesser of two evils, the other being a C.C.F. victory."[159] Whether the Progressive Conservative party would be allowed to live up to the promise of its name or its new leader's expectations remained to be proven.

[159]Armour Mackay, "Progressive Conservatives on the Middle Road," *Saturday Night*, LVIII (Dec. 19, 1942), 16.

7.   The Bracken Party

John Bracken's selection as the leader of the Progressive Conservative party produced tremendous optimism in the party ranks, but the euphoria of December 1942 evaporated quickly. Reorganization got off to a slow start, and Bracken left himself open to attack and subjected the party to another long period of absentee leadership when he declined to seek entry to the House of Commons. As the hopes of the progressives sagged, increasing pressure was exerted by the right-wing Tories after George Drew's victory in the Ontario provincial elections in August 1943. The resulting struggle apparently diluted the party's commitment to social security, and as the strength of the C.C.F. waxed, the Conservatives renewed their emphasis on free enterprise. Also pulled to the left by the socialist challenge, Mackenzie King's Liberals soon recaptured the middle-of-the-road position which they had temporarily lost after the Port Hope conference and the Winnipeg convention. The Bracken party had been overrun by events, and the hard-won initiative lost.

The immediate Conservative response to the new leader was very favourable. Bracken met in a long session with the Members of Parliament in Winnipeg on the day after his selection and greatly impressed his new colleagues. "Am tremendously impressed with Bracken," Captain Rodney Adamson, the member for York West (Ontario) wrote in his diary: "he will definitely take direction and insist that we work in the House. . . . Bracken insists on knowing the organization in the House. . . . I am very definitely for him. . . . Bracken tells me definitely to get out of the army. . . . Tremendously impressed that he gives very definite orders."[1] The reaction of the caucus was important, of course, but of more immediate consequence was Bracken's effect on contributors to the empty party coffers.[2] Milner wrote from Calgary that "in one

[1] Adamson Papers, Diary, Dec. 12, 1942; Bracken to Adamson, Jan. 4, 1943; Hanson Papers, File P-450-HB-3, Hanson to Bell, Dec. 17, 1942; Bell Papers, Vol. 1, Bell to Milner, Dec. 30, 1942.

[2] Bell Papers, Milner to Bell, Jan. 4, 1943; Hanson Papers, File O-100, Hanson to Milner, Jan. 4, 1943, and Hanson to Bell, Jan. 4, 1943.

afternoon we got $6,000.00. Without touching the people who would give $200.00 or less," he added, "we hope to make this a pot of about $10,000.00 which is substantial for this Province." R. B. Hanson was also finding a changed attitude among contributors, and he reported that he was thinking in terms of a party fund of "at least $250 M." One unnamed firm, he said, "was prepared to go 50 grand at once and the balance could be obtained without much trouble." As it turned out the early promise of rich financial support was largely illusory,[3] but for the moment, at least, the Bracken party was in clover.

The response of some western Liberals to the new Conservatism and its leader was predictable. To T. A. Crerar, King's Minister of Mines and Resources, "the marriage" of Bracken to the Conservative party "was clearly one of convenience. . . . To see Meighen and Charlie Ballantyne and Hanson in the guise of ardent reformers, converted overnight, is a spectacle to make the gods weep." The Speaker of the House of Commons, James A. Glen, M.P. for Marquette (Manitoba), found a "very unfavourable reaction" in his province to the new leader. "The Conservatives feel bitter that this man, who was their bitterest opponent for twenty years, is now their leader and the Liberals are as bitter as can be."[4]

J. W. Dafoe of the *Winnipeg Free Press*, one of the shrewdest observers of Canadian politics, took a more balanced view. Observing that the "Tories have embarked on a huge gamble with the risk of having the new wine play hob with the old bottles,"[5] he assessed the new political alignment. "I am watching things closely with a view of forming some kind of a working theory as to what the 'revolution' in the Conservative party is going to do for that party and to the other parties," he wrote to his friend Crerar:

If it is a revolution, the customary convulsions are singularly lacking. . . . But the Liberals do not seem to be much worried over losing Bracken . . . and it is evident that elements in the Conservative Party who counted for much in the past, are rather stumped by the new shift and the new leader. A switch of this character in the past would only have been possible if Bracken could have taken with him a formidable visible following drawn from leading members of the [Liberal] party; but this phenomenon appears to be wholly lacking. So far as I have heard, there has not been a single prominent Liberal here or anywhere else in the West who has stepped out

---

[3]Bell Interview, Aug. 24, 1964. In fact, Bell said, he had had to pay the expenses of one of Bracken's early tours out of his own pocket.

[4]A. K. Cameron Papers, Vol. 35, Crerar to Cameron, Dec. 14, 1942; Gardiner Papers, Glen to Gardiner, Dec. 28, 1942.

[5]Dafoe Papers, Microfilm roll M-80, Dafoe to Clifford Sifton, Dec. 19, 1942.

and said: "I follow John Bracken." . . . [Bracken] evidently looked forward to going into the other camp with a great company and with banners flying. This certainly has not happened. That there is a possible following from the rank and file as the issues develop is not questioned, but there is certainly no rush. . . .

Dafoe had pinpointed one of the chief problems that was to bedevil the new leader. Bracken's reputation for progressive thinking was unassailable—that of the Conservative party was not. He would have to demonstrate that he could make the Conservative party follow his lead before he could hope to attract his old supporters from the Liberal party. Dafoe continued with an assessment of the new leader's effect on the nation:

Granted that the Conservative party throughout Canada accepts Bracken's leadership, and that this leadership is in keeping with his past—two fairly large assumptions, the first in particular, the nationwide effect on balance may be good. I am thinking in particular of the discouragement that this course will give to the Toronto gang in their efforts to split the country on racial lines. I cannot see Bracken mouthing the Tory-Orange-Imperialist slogans. . . . This gang has been a greater danger to national unity than the Quebec extremists at the other end of the scale. Yet they formed the core of the junta that made Bracken's selection possible. The whole situation is very confusing.[6]

The situation was indeed very confusing. Aware of this,[7] Bracken almost instinctively shied away from entering the House of Commons and thus confronting his difficulties directly.

This question first arose at the new leader's meeting with caucus on December 12, 1942,[8] and it dominated party discussion for the next month and more. A plausible case could be made for his staying out of parliament. Milner, one of those advising Bracken, expressed this view: "Bracken would be better employed going through the country and, incidentally, visiting the army, than in contesting a by-election and wasting several months in the House of Commons," he said. "He meets people well and is particularly effective with small audiences. He could make a tremendous number of friends and it would be impossible for King or his Ministers in the House to answer him."[9] Arthur Meighen, evidently remembering York South, agreed with this view, as did a good many others in the party.[10]

[6]*Ibid.*, Dafoe to T. A. Crerar, Jan. 4, 1943.
[7]So Bracken indicated to Mackenzie King in conversation on Jan. 19, 1943. Pickersgill, *Mackenzie King Record*, I, 477.
[8]Adamson Papers, Diary, Dec. 12, 1942.
[9]Bell Papers, Vol. 1, Milner to Graydon, Dec. 28, 1942 (copy).
[10]Meighen Papers, Meighen to Bennett, April 26, 1943; Bell Papers, Vol. 1, Macdonnell to Bell, Jan. 30, enclosing Macdonnell to Milner, Jan. 30, 1943.

On the other hand, there were those who disagreed, believing that Bracken should either contest the vacant seat of Selkirk (Manitoba) or accept the offer of J. A. Ross, the member for Souris (Manitoba), to resign in his new leader's favour.[11] There were difficulties in both constituencies, but while it was possible that Bracken might not be able to win the formerly Liberal constituency of Selkirk, he should be able to carry Souris handily. "Otherwise," one Toronto Conservative said, "the thirty-five Western seats that we hope he can win as a Progressive Conservative must be more of a mirage than I think they are."[12] It was also natural and proper for the leader of the party to be in parliament, Macdonnell wrote, and if Bracken did not enter the House the public might begin to suspect that "slick politics" was behind his selection. Furthermore, the Opposition needed a leader, and if Bracken did not take charge, the C.C.F. leader, M. J. Coldwell, would become the inevitable focus of opposition to the government.[13] The final decision was Bracken's to make, and cautiously he decided not to risk an early test of his strength.[14] He was not a strong speaker, he ingenuously admitted to Mackenzie King in Ottawa on January 19, "and would find the House of Commons difficult."[15] Evidently Bracken agreed with Milner's fear that he "would not be an effective opposition leader."[16] Mackenzie King's appraisal was equally blunt but more critical in tone:

Bracken will be a failure [he told Bruce Hutchison of the Free Press papers in an interview], a "nice fellow" but little on the ball. Is making a fatal mistake in staying out of the House and going to curling matches. They don't get you anywhere and everybody says, when he appears and talks, why isn't he in Parliament? His constitutional duty to enter House. Is afraid to face government.[17]

Once this decision had been made, Bracken had to find a House leader. As early as December 19, he had Graydon write each M.P. to ask for recommendations. Despite the results of the poll which showed Graydon preferred by most and closely followed by Diefenbaker, Bracken apparently attempted to persuade Hanson to continue.[18] "I had had a very difficult experience for two sessions on my own and

[11]Montreal *Gazette*, Dec. 16, 1942, p. 1; Pickersgill, *Mackenzie King Record*, I, 477.
[12]Hanson Papers, File O-100, F. G. Gardiner to Hanson, Jan. 8, 1943.
[13]*Ibid.*, Memorandum by Macdonnell, Jan. 8, 1943.
[14]Bell Papers, Vol. 1, Bell to Hanson, Jan. 11, 1943.
[15]Pickersgill, *Mackenzie King Record*, I, 477.
[16]Bell Papers, Vol. 1, Milner to Macdonnell, Dec. 28, 1942.
[17]Dafoe Papers, Microfilm roll M-123, Memorandum, Hutchison to Dafoe, Feb. 15, 1943; Bruce Hutchison, *The Incredible Canadian* (Toronto, 1952), p. 320.
[18]Hanson Papers, Personal Correspondence, Graydon to Hanson, Dec. 19, 1942. Allowing for half and even one-third votes, Graydon had 12, Diefenbaker 10,

one under Mr. Meighen," Hanson later wrote, "and after full consideration I declined." Absentee leadership, the New Brunswick politician noted reflectively, "was very trying, especially where I found my own judgment at variance with the leader's."[19] Hanson's mandate had never been clear, and he had not always been a surefooted leader. On balance, however, his effect on the party had been salutary. He had pressed the policies in which he believed, and he had opposed those in the party who would have directed him into dangerous channels. When he at last put down his unwelcome burden on January 27, 1943, Hanson deserved well of his party.[20] His successor, Bracken decided, would be selected by the caucus at its meeting on the eve of the opening of the 1943 session.[21] "At 8:30," Rodney Adamson noted in his diary on January 27, "Caucus reconvenes and Gordon [Graydon] is chosen leader by one vote over John Diefenbaker. John voted for Gordon and Gordon voted for himself. This is a swell set."[22] The leadership was settled at last, but fundamental problems of organization, finance, and policy remained to be solved.

The Port Hopefuls were fully aware of the party's condition after months of inaction. "The situation at the moment as I see it is this," wrote Macdonnell: "At the present time two things could happen in the party. The first is that the Old Guard should continue in control. If that happens, notwithstanding Bracken's leadership, I believe we are done. The second, of course, is that we not only have 'new management' but a new organization and a new breath of life."[23] Macdonnell's strongest ally was Richard A. Bell, the 29-year-old organizer of the Winnipeg convention. Able and pragmatic, Bell had had a unique schooling in practical politics. At the age of 21, he had been assistant private secretary to the Minister of National Revenue in the last year of the Bennett administration, and he had served as assistant dominion organizer in the general election of 1935. From 1938 to 1940, he had been private secretary to Manion, and he had continued in this post with Hanson. His views on policy and organization, shaped during the party's most unfruitful years, were clear and definite.

The immediate need, as Bell saw it in the weeks after the convention, was for action. The "terrific" response to Bracken at last put the party in

Hanson 4½, Green 4, and Harris 2½. There were 32 replies. P.A.C., John Bracken Papers, Vol. 12, File 6.

[19]*Ibid.*, Hanson to L. P. Rollason, Dec. 18, 1944.

[20]*Ibid.*, File P-300, "Statement to the Press . . ." n.d. [January 27, 1943].

[21]*Ibid.*, Personal Correspondence, Hanson to Rollason, Dec. 18, 1944; Bell Interview, Aug. 24, 1964.

[22]Adamson Papers, Diary, Jan. 27, 1943. Although Adamson recorded this story the night of the vote, some Conservatives consider it apocryphal (Bell Interview, Aug. 24, 1964; Jackman Interview, Sept. 8, 1964).

[23]Bell Papers, Vol. 1, Macdonnell to Bell, Jan. 30, 1943.

a position to commence the foundation of true political organization with a confident hope of success. But if the impetus given Progressive Conservatism by the favourable publicity was not to be lost, organization would have to begin immediately. "Our curse in the past," he wrote to Milner, "has been that we have chosen a leader and then expected him, by his own unaided efforts, to accomplish miracles."[24] None could be found to disagree with Bell's view, but no one was willing to take the initiative. "I am a little diffident about sticking my neck out too far," Milner replied. "As you know, now that the Convention is over I have no official connection with the Party. . . ." Gordon Graydon, the National Chairman since May 1941 took a similar view in January 1943 and disclaimed any authority to "take the lead in questions of organization."[25] This was most discouraging to the anxious Bell. "I had hoped that something could be done without it coming from Mr. Bracken—in other words that action would be taken to help him," he said, "but apparently that is not possible."[26]

Even the financial organization made little headway. Macdonnell, increasingly frustrated by the inertia of his erstwhile Port Hope colleagues, pointed out the probable effects of this inactivity:

If we are not very quickly able to make it apparent that there is a new crowd taking hold, there will be widespread disappointment, inevitably a feeling that there has really been very little change except the advent of a new leader, and incidentally a feeling on the part of the leader that he is in a rather false position. . . .
While the raising of money is only one feature of this . . . [and] while I have the highest regard for Bunnie Foster and Ballantyne, and while I do not question the wisdom of . . . leaving the money-raising in their hands in Montreal, nevertheless we must face the fact that this will be construed as the continuation in control of the Old Guard. If that happens in Toronto also I think it will be a great misfortune.[27]

More important still, there was no co-ordination of fund-raising. In mid-February, Macdonnell wrote that certainly he did not know the party's financial position. "Does anyone know the full position? Is anyone firmly guiding matters or have we a situation where people are working in compartments, where one group is raising money without any very clear-cut idea as to what is to be done with it and where others

[24]*Ibid.*, Bell to Milner, Dec. 30, 1942.
[25]*Ibid.*, Milner to Bell, Jan. 4, 1943; Hanson Papers, File O-100, Bell to Hanson, Jan. 7, 1943.
[26]Hanson Papers, File O-100, Bell to Hanson, Jan. 7, 1943.
[27]Bell Papers, Vol. 1, Macdonnell to Milner, Jan. 30, 1943, enclosed in Macdonnell to Bell, Jan. 30, 1943.

are anxious that things should be done and have no means of knowing whether money is available?"[28] The opportunity for change seemed to be slipping away.

Although his own position was by no means clear,[29] Bell was making plans for a full-scale reorganization of the party. "There must be set-up," he wrote at the end of 1942, "an organization consisting of a full-time National Organizer or National Chairman . . . with two subdivisions, namely, a Publicity Bureau and a Research Bureau, headed by men who are able to really contribute to the Party. Personally," Bell added, "I think the Research Bureau is one of the most important features of the whole organization."[30] Accustomed to having a civil service at his fingertips, ready to do his research for him, Bracken would find it difficult to adjust unless an efficient office organization was created. A full-time public relations man was another necessity, and Bell wanted a monthly newspaper and a press service catering to rural weeklies.[31]

The young organizer next turned his attention to the lamentable state of the party's national organization. The convention had re-established the Dominion Conservative Association (now named the Dominion Progressive Conservative Association) on a constitutional basis, but Bell was dissatisfied with the multifold compromises necessary to appease the ineffectual John R. MacNicol, M.P., its president since the 1920's.[32] What was needed, he wrote, was a sweeping reconstruction, with the election of new national officers as the first step. Some provincial associations had not met for three years, their officers were inefficient or worse, and organization was non-existent in almost 200 of the 245 constituencies. A full-time organizer should be appointed and set to work finding provincial organizers and establishing provincial headquarters.[33] These plans, prepared by the ablest organizer in the party, were far-reaching, and Bracken could not be other than impressed.

On April 19, 1943—four months after the Winnipeg convention—Bracken selected Bell as the National Director of the party, giving him responsibility for all organizational matters.[34] Bell's first steps were to name a publicity director and a national advisory committee on publicity and public relations.[35] Plans were soon begun for a national monthly

[28]*Ibid.*, Macdonnell to Bell, Feb. 18, 1943.
[29]*Ibid.*, Feb. 12 and 18, 1943; Bell to Macdonnell, Feb. 15, 1943.
[30]*Ibid.*, Bell to L. D. M. Baxter, Dec. 28, 1942.
[31]*Ibid.*, Bell to Milner, Dec. 30, 1942.
[32]*Ibid.*
[33]*Ibid.*
[34]*Public Opinion*, II (May, 1944), 1.
[35]Progressive Conservative Party Files, File PEI-P-2, Bell to W. Grant, April 30, 1943.

newspaper, *Public Opinion*, and the first issue of eight pages was released on August 31. "It is named 'Public Opinion,' " the first issue stated, "because it is not meant to be partisan in any narrow sense, and because the name suggests what is intended."[36] The Dominion Progressive Conservative Association was reorganized, Gordon Graydon was elected president, and MacNicol was ushered out with praises, honours, and finality.[37] In addition, the formation of Bracken clubs—"non-partisan" political study groups—was begun across the country.[38] After surveys of each constituency, Bell next turned to the task of co-ordinating the federal and provincial organizations.[39]

The problem of reconciling the needs of the federal party with the demands and desires of the provincial organizations was to trouble the leader of the Progressive Conservative party to the end of the war. Each province seemed to require special treatment. In tiny Prince Edward Island, Bell constituted a federal organizing committee and gave it complete authority over the provincial headquarters and its expenditures.[40] This was perhaps the ideal state of affairs from the national party's point of view, but what was suitable for P.E.I. might not work elsewhere. In Manitoba, for example, the problem was to avoid drawing a "distinction between the Liberal Progressive supporters of Mr. Bracken provincially and the regular Conservative organization."[41] Organization in Bracken's home province, therefore, obviously required a different technique. Similar tensions existed in all of the provinces,[42] but only in Ontario were the difficulties so great as to pose a threat to the federal leadership. "I know the Ontario situation, Provincially, is complicated and a matter of great concern to you," Meighen wrote to Bracken in February 1943.[43] So it was. The most populous province and the traditional heart of Conservatism, Ontario had to be won if the party was to have a chance to form the government. Difficulties between the Ontario and the national leaders persisted from Bennett's day. Part of

[36]*Public Opinion*, I (Aug. 31, 1943), 1.

[37]*Ottawa Citizen*, March 15, 1943, pp. 1, 10.

[38]Bell Papers, Vol. 1, "Problems of Organization," n.d. [May, 1944]; Bell Interview, Aug. 24, 1964; Cameron Papers, Vol. 35, Crerar to Cameron, May 3, 1943. The Bracken clubs received a formal structure in 1944. *Public Opinion*, II (March, 1944), 6.

[39]Progressive Conservative Party Files, File Y-Y-1, Bell to G. Black, M.P., May 20, 1943; PEI-P-2, Bell to W. Grant, April 30, 1943.

[40]*Ibid.*, PEI-P-2, Bell to W. Grant, May 31, 1943.

[41]*Ibid.*, M-M-4, Bell to Errick Willis, Sept. 16, 1943.

[42]Bell Papers, Vol. 1, "Problems of Organization." This long memorandum by Bell, a brilliant examination of the party's position in the spring of 1944, discusses the state of each provincial organization in detail.

[43]Meighen Papers, Meighen to Bracken, Feb. 13, 1943. For George Drew's interesting comments on the Ontario situation, see Bracken Papers, Vol. 12, Drew to

this was a conflict of personalities. George Drew was not any easy man to co-operate with, and there were hard feelings toward him among some Ontario M.P.s. Much of the trouble sprang from the ambitions of the provincial leader and his cohorts. "Some of the Drew people," Bell wrote in a survey of the Ontario scene,

> are in too much of a hurry to advance the cause of their own leader in federal affairs and have not hesitated to say so at the same time either directly or inferentially damning the present federal leadership. In the opinion of a considerable number of the federal members, the basic trouble is the desire of the Ontario Party to have control of the representation in the House of Commons from Ontario after the next election as a means of controlling a future convention of the Party and determining the future leadership of the party.[44]

The problem reached a head after the Ontario election of August 1943.

The erratic Mitchell Hepburn had resigned as Ontario's premier in October 1942, although he had retained both his position as leader of the party and his portfolio as provincial treasurer.[45] His successor, Gordon Conant, lasted only until May 1943 when a party convention chose Harry Nixon to be premier and leader. King was pleased with the rise of Nixon, long his strongest supporter in the Ontario Cabinet,[46] but the new premier was no match for the attractive Drew and his well-oiled machine. "No preparation for campaign in constituencies," the watching Mackenzie King noted. "No literature. Next, no platform for campaign. Greatest weakness of all running on the record of the Liberals which is really a thoroughly bad record."[47] The election on August 4 saw the complete collapse of the Liberals whose strength fell from fifty-nine to fifteen seats in the ninety-seat legislature. The C.C.F. came from nowhere to win thirty-four seats, while Drew's Tories, doubling their representation at dissolution, won thirty-eight seats and a chance to form the government.

Drew's narrow victory—the first Conservative success in a federal or provincial general election in twelve years—was a tremendous boost to the new Progressive Conservative party. Prime Minister King observed

Bracken, December 17, 1942.

[44]Bell Papers, Vol. 1, "Problems of Organization."

[45]Hepburn resigned, he said, because he had learned that the "board of strategy" at Ottawa had decided to force a provincial election, believing that this would raise the racial issue in Ontario. This would then hold Quebec's wavering support for the King government against a common enemy to be created in Ontario (Hepburn Papers, Supplementary Files (private), 1942, Hepburn to E. J. Anderson, M.P.P., Nov. 18, 1942; Conant Papers, General Correspondence, 1943, Hepburn to Conant, March 3, 1943).

[46]Pickersgill, *Mackenzie King Record*, I, 492.

[47]*Ibid.*, p. 569.

that the results "show the effect of organization in campaigns, advertising, etc. . . ."[48] The Ontario organization was indeed well-run, well-directed, and well-financed,[49] and it received substantial aid from the federal party. "From the federal point of view," Bell had written the president of the Ontario Progressive Conservative Association in April, "a victory for George would be of immense importance both from the practical and the psychological point of view. . . . I think it behooves all of us who can make any contribution to do what we can to throw the greatest possible weight behind George."[50] As a result, no attempt was made to build up the federal organization in the province until after the election, and the full co-operation of the Members of Parliament from Ontario was given to the campaign.[51] Bracken had assisted his provincial lieutenant by undertaking an extensive two-week tour of rural Ontario,[52] and Howard Ferguson, Conservative premier of Ontario from 1923 to 1930, reportedly attributed twelve rural seats to the presence and reputation of Bracken. If this was so, this was sufficient justification for those responsible for the selection of Bracken.[53]

But Bracken's impressive success was largely obscured by the enormous new strength of the C.C.F. in Ontario. The socialists had received over 400,000 votes in the election, more than the party had received throughout all Canada in 1940. Most of their thirty-four seats lay in the industrial horseshoe around the western end of Lake Ontario and in the mining districts of the north.[54] Here was the proof of Meighen's contention that the C.C.F. was making inroads into the industrial areas of Canada. Especially striking, however, were the 100,000 votes the party had won in rural Ontario and the fact that the C.C.F. had captured the largest share of the soldiers' vote.[55] When the C.C.F. won two of four

[48]*Ibid.*

[49]Adamson Papers, Diary, Jan. 13 and March 27, 1943.

[50]Progressive Conservative Party Files, File O-0-5a, Bell to C. G. Frost, April 29, 1943.

[51]*Ibid.*, Bell to A. D. McKenzie, July 5, 1943.

[52]The itinerary is in *ibid.*, McKenzie to Bell, June 29, 1943.

[53]Macdonnell Interviews, July 10, 1963, and Sept. 5, 1964; Finlayson Interview, July 6, 1963. According to the itinerary, Bracken spoke in at least five rural constituencies. Of these Drew won three, all from the Liberals. The effect of a tour is difficult to assess, of course, but it is significant that some Ontario Conservatives believed that Bracken was of help.

[54]*New Commonwealth*, IX (Aug. 12, 1943), 1. *New Commonwealth* was the C.C.F. newspaper.

[55]E. B. Jolliffe, "The Ontario Front," *New Commonwealth*, IX (Oct. 28, 1943), 1. Rodney Adamson noted that he had given a lift to some hitch-hiking soldiers. They were "badly bitten," he said. "Say the soldiers in the last war were screwed and we are not going to be screwed in this. The attitude caused by the negative policy of McQuisling King. . . . Very serious situation." Adamson Papers, Diary, Aug. 7, 1943.

federal by-elections on August 9, 1943, and a Labour Progressive party candidate won a third, the increasing popularity of the left-wing parties was apparent. In addition, the movement was collecting money rapidly— 1943 was the C.C.F.'s most successful financial year to that time—and plans were in hand for a public campaign to raise $500,000 for the next election.[56] Dues-paying members were being signed up all across the country. In Ontario membership rose from 3,161 in March 1942 to 18,624 in February 1945. By 1945 membership in Saskatchewan had reached 31,858 or approximately 4 per cent of the population and 8 per cent of the electorate. "The C.C.F. membership in the province," S. M. Lipset noted with some awe, "has reached the equivalent of a national dues-paying membership of about 500,000 in Canada and six million in the United States."[57] The growth in C.C.F. membership was extraordinary by any standard. Unfortunately no comparative figures for the other parties are available.

The heart of the C.C.F. argument, used with great effect all across the nation, was expressed in a political pamphlet prepared in Saskatchewan. "Dear Mr. Ilsley," the broadside addressed King's Minister of Finance, "we have seen your government unable to find a few million dollars for Saskatchewan relief, and then hey presto! find a budget in 1943–1944 of $5,500,000,000. Why couldn't we find it in 1938?"[58] Wartime controls, the C.C.F. asserted, had produced good results. Why not continue them in peacetime? The basic lesson of the war, two C.C.F. spokesmen argued in a book published in 1943, was that capitalism had had to be abandoned for the sake of efficiency. National planning and centralized direction had been substituted for the inefficiencies of the prewar system.[59] A C.C.F. government, the social democrats maintained, would provide this centralized direction, and the workers, soldiers, and farmers would get a fair deal at last.

Portentous evidence of the C.C.F.'s success in popularizing their

[56]Sigmund Samuel Library, University of Toronto, Woodsworth Memorial Collection, C.C.F. Ontario Records, Minutes of Provincial Council and Executive Meetings, Vol. 2, "Financial Committee's Report, March 20–August 31, 1944," n.d.; C.C.F. Records, Vol. 1, Minutes, National Council Meeting, Sept. 5–6, 1943.
[57]C.C.F. Ontario Records, Minutes of Provincial Council, Vol. 1, "Report of Ontario Section, C.C.F.," n.d., and Vol. 2, Memorandum, "Approximate Membership," n.d.; S. M. Lipset, "Political Participation and the Organization of the Cooperative Commonwealth Federation in Saskatchewan," *Canadian Journal of Economics and Political Science*, XIV (May, 1948), 191.
[58]Gardiner Papers, "Dear Mr. Ilsley," Saskatchewan C.C.F. pamphlet, n.d.; Hanson Papers, Personal Correspondence, Vol. 35, H. R. Jackman to Hanson, July 31, 1943, attests to the effectiveness of this charge.
[59]David Lewis and F. R. Scott, *Make This Your Canada* (Toronto, 1943), pp. 5–12, 25.

policies came in a Canadian Institute of Public Opinion poll[60] released on September 30, 1943:

	Lib.	P.C.	C.C.F.	Social Credit and Others
National	28%	28%	29%	15%
Ontario	26	40	32	2
West	23	23	41	13

For the first time, the C.C.F. led the two old parties on a national basis. An even more striking phenomenon was the C.C.F. margin in the West, the area in which Bracken had been expected to rally the farmers to the Progressive Conservative party. The results were scarcely less shocking to the Liberals. The West was usually safe ground for the political machine of James Gardiner, King's Minister of Agriculture, but now even Gardiner's home province of Saskatchewan was on the verge of falling to the C.C.F.[61]

The panic in the Liberal and Conservative parties was equalled by the alarm of business and financial interests. The C.C.F., Meighen wrote, "are adopting the same venomous methods used by their corresponding numbers in Italy, Spain and France, and if they are not checked will produce the same results in Canada as has brought about the complete political bedevilment and wreck of those Nations."[62] Meighen's reactions were not untypical of those of Canadian businessmen. In mid-1942, the chartered banks had begun contemplating an advertising campaign to help counter the mushroom growth of the C.C.F.,[63] and by the summer of 1943 a number of well-financed "free enterprise" groups were in the field.[64] Whether these anti-socialist organizations were financed or

[60]*New Commonwealth*, IX (Oct. 14, 1943), 1.

[61]The Gardiner Papers are full of material on the rise of the C.C.F. in Saskatchewan. E.g., Gardiner to Hon. J. W. Estey, April 1, 1940; T. H. Wood to Gardiner, Sept. 8, 1943. The Conservatives, too, were worried about Saskatchewan. They had little strength in the province but feared the effect of a C.C.F. victory there on the rest of Canada. See Hanson Papers, File O-167, Hanson to D. C. Coleman, May 30, 1942; Hanson to Morris W. Wilson, May 30, 1942; Hanson to M. A. MacPherson, Oct. 20, 1942.

[62]Meighen Papers, Meighen to Bracken, July 29, 1943.

[63]Hanson Papers, File O-167, Vernon Knowles to Hanson, June 19, 1942; Jackson Dodds to Hanson, June 17, 1942; H. D. Burns to Hanson, June 17, 1942.

[64]See the discussion in the latter chapters of Gerald L. Caplan, "The Co-operative Commonwealth Federation in Ontario 1932–1945: A Study of Socialist and Anti-Socialist Politics," unpublished M.A. thesis, University of Toronto, 1961.

assisted in any way by the old parties is not clear,[65] but certainly there was a community of interest. The C.C.F. was on the march, and the capitalist parties would have to counter it as best they could. Mackenzie King's Liberals, if only because they held office, were in the best position to undermine the strength of the socialist movement.

Prime Minister King was troubled by the rising tide of socialism, but he hoped, as he recorded unctuously in his diary, that the election results might cause "some of our people to realize that labour has to be dealt with in a considerate way. In my heart, I am not sorry to see the mass of the people coming a little more into their own, but I do regret that it is not a Liberal party that is winning that position for them."[66] Mackenzie King, however, had not yet abandoned hope that his party could capture those who wished to press the pace of social reform. As early as October 1942, within a month of the Port Hope Conference, he had stated his conception of the "national minimum" objectives of social security:

useful employment for all who are willing to work, standards of nutrition and housing, adequate to ensure the health of the whole population; social insurance against privation resulting from unemployment, from accident, from the death of the breadwinner, from ill health and from old age. . . .
By placing the interests of the community before the interests of individuals or groups; by social control, in which government, labour and management all share, human well-being can be vastly increased.[67]

Perhaps the Prime Minister intended this expression of faith only as a pious hope for the future or as a hedge against public demands, or perhaps the war absorbed his energies, for little was done until August 1943. After the electoral defeats of that month, however, King at last was ready to move.[68]

The Prime Minister's thoughts were probably crystallized by a long,

[65]Suggestions that the Conservatives co-operate with these groups do not appear to have been followed up. Progressive Conservative Party Files, File M-5-G, Macdonnell to Bell, July 20, 1943, and reply, July 24, 1943; File H-4-G, Bell to D. M. Hogarth, Dec. 21, 1943.
[66]Pickersgill, *Mackenzie King Record*, I, 571. King's fears were shared by other Liberals. The Hon. C. G. Power wrote that "it would appear as if we would have to pull up our socks if we are not to have a debacle" (Dafoe Papers, Microfilm roll M-80, Power to Dafoe, Aug. 9, 1943). Cf. Gardiner Papers, T. H. Wood to Gardiner, Sept. 8, 1943. One Tory M.P. wrote that the Liberals "are about as well a licked crowd as you ever talked to" (Hanson Papers, Personal Correspondence, Vol. 36, A. C. Casselman to Hanson, Aug. 26, 1943).
[67]Address, Oct. 9, 1942, in W. L. M. King, *Canada and the Fight for Freedom* (New York, 1944), pp. 202–3.
[68]Norman Lambert Diaries, June 6, 1943.

perceptive memorandum[69] prepared by J. W. Pickersgill, one of his secretaries. "A large part of the pressure both from farmers and from
labour," Pickersgill said,

arises not from discontent with their present situation, but from fear of a
postwar depression with ruinously low prices and mass unemployment.
The Liberal Party should, therefore, stick firmly by its wartime controls
which have protected the standard of living of the less fortunate in the community but, at the same time, it should seek by positive, concrete measures to
remove this fear of the future.

This was probably extraordinary advice for a civil servant to give, but
Pickersgill then went on to propose a floor under farm prices, a national
housing policy, family allowances, and detailed planning to ease the
strain of the eventual return to a peacetime economy. "From a political
standpoint," he continued, "parties in opposition can afford to rest on
their promises; that is really all they have to offer."

From a party in power, promises are useless; programs, speeches, and committees are not going to make much impression on the electorate. The
voters know that the government in office has the power to act and they are
going to judge it largely on the concrete, tangible evidences of action. . . .
. . . once the war is won, the voters are not going to vote for a political
party merely because it did a good job in winning the war. They are going
to vote for the party they think is most likely to do what is needed to provide
the maximum employment and a measure of social insurance in the future.
The record of the government will help it only if that record is joined to a
program already partly carried out. . . .

Pickersgill's skilful memorandum must have struck a responsive chord
with Mackenzie King; within the month the Liberal party began reshap-
ing its platform and policies.

At a cabinet meeting on September 1, 1943, King arranged for a full
caucus on the twenty-fourth to discuss the political situation and for a
meeting of the National Liberal Federation, the first since August 1939.
"I anticipate," he wrote to his ministers, "possible decisions of far-
reaching consequence. . . ."[70] At the caucus, the law was handed down.
Senator Lambert, former president of the National Federation, recorded
the scene in his diary. "General caucus all day. P.M. started out by
raising particular hell about the way members of the party had allowed
him to be abused by Hepburn and others during the past 6 years: that
he had to have an organization; and that he would quit if he didn't
get it. The result of the recent elections he blamed on lack of organiza-

---

[69]J. W. Pickersgill, *The Liberal Party* (Toronto, 1962), pp. 32–5.
[70]Gardiner Papers, King to Gardiner, Sept. 2, 1943.

tion. . . ."[71] With King's words as spur, the Liberal organization was overhauled and placed in operation again. J. G. Gardiner, probably the most efficient machine politician in the country, was named national organizer in December.[72] The National Liberal Federation also produced a series of resolutions—not "as a programme settled by the Liberal party," King said, "but merely as some suggestions from the Advisory Council to the Government"—very similar to those proposed earlier by Pickersgill.[73] Despite the Prime Minister's disclaimer, most of the Federation's resolutions were presented to parliament and the nation in the Speech from the Throne which opened the 1944 session.[74] The centre of gravity of Canadian politics was being moved to the left. Standing squarely on a platform of social security, the Liberals evidently intended to make a fight of the next general election whenever it might come.[75]

Mackenzie King's refurbished Liberalism altered the political situation once again. His proposals were "revolutionary without being destructive," one commentator noted. They go "far to the moderate left, not too far from the moderate right." Most important, as Pickersgill's memorandum had predicted, the Liberal programme left Bracken's Progressive Conservatives little timber with which to build an election platform.[76]

The startling political changes in the late summer of 1943 regenerated the long-dormant right wing of the Conservative party. Predictably, the revival began in George Drew's Ontario. The federal organization there had gained momentum after the August elections, but obstacles were numerous. After the appointment of an able organizer, for example, the provincial Conservative association complained that their executive had not been consulted about his nomination.[77] Powerful figures in the party, Macdonnell also cautioned Bell, objected to the formation of "two

[71]Lambert Diaries, Sept. 24, 1943.

[72]*Ibid.*, Dec. 28, 1943.

[73]Pickersgill, *Mackenzie King Record*, I, 585.

[74]House of Commons, *Debates*, Jan. 27, 1944, p. 2.

[75]"Had I wished to have been perfectly certain of another term of office," Mackenzie King wrote Roosevelt in October 1943, "I would have dissolved Parliament this autumn and left it to the electorate to say to whom they wished to entrust the continued direction of Canada's war effort. However, I have viewed my duty as seeing should that be possible, the war through to a victorious close, regardless of the consequences which may follow." Roosevelt Papers, P.S.F., Diplomatic Correspondence-Canada, King to Roosevelt, Oct. 26, 1943.

[76]G. C. Whittaker, "Canada's New Deal Puts All Other New Deals in the Shade," *Saturday Night*, LIX (Feb. 5, 1944), 11. Pickersgill's memorandum had predicted that his suggestions would "put the other parties on the defensive" (Pickersgill, *Liberal Party*, p. 36).

[77]Progressive Conservative Party Files, File O-0-5a, Frost to Bell, Sept. 9, 1943.

full fledged and potentially competing organizations in Ontario."[78] Bell discounted these and similar complaints at first,[79] but in November 1943 their originators attempted to place the leaders of the Ontario organization in effective control of the national party.

The plan, as broached in "deepest secrecy" to Bell by Henry Borden, a Toronto corporation lawyer and Sir Robert's nephew, called for a national organization committee to be set up in Toronto. Borden was to be chairman. Other members were to be J. H. Gundy, president of the investment house of Wood Gundy and Bracken's national financial chairman; E. W. Bickle, a stockbroker and Drew's chief fund-raiser; James S. Duncan, the president of Massey-Harris; and Alex McKenzie, Drew's organizer. Bell, who was known to have Bracken's ear and who, it was hoped, could persuade him to agree to the plan, was also to be on the committee. While party headquarters would remain in Ottawa, the real seat of power would be in Toronto. The planners' goal was to effect liaison with the numerous "private enterprise committees" springing up to counter socialism and to direct their activities to the advantage of the party. The Premier of Ontario, Bell was told, had stated that "this was what he and others intended to propose to you. . . ."[80]

These were astonishing and dangerous proposals, and Bell did his best to counter them in his letter to Bracken.[81] The scheme ignored the executive of the Dominion Progressive Conservative Association, he said, and would create widespread resentment among the rank and file of that newly reorganized body. In addition, "none of the men mentioned above have [*sic*] ever contested public office of any kind, and none, except McKenzie and myself, have [*sic*] ever belonged to a political association. . . ." With the same two exceptions, Bell went on, "no member of the committee can be considered as belonging to the so-called common folk."

Except for myself, no member of the committee has any conception of the problem of the farmer. . . . If not from these . . . classes where are we to get our vote? . . .

It does not require much imagination to conceive what either Mackenzie King or M. J. Coldwell would do on the hustings to a committee which, with two exceptions, consists of men whose income is not less than $50,000.00 per annum and whose accumulated wealth would be at least as great as an annual value of the farm crops from the whole of my county of Carleton. . . .

[78]*Ibid.*, File M-5-G, Macdonnell to Bell, Oct. 2, 1943.
[79]*Ibid.*, Bell to Macdonnell, Oct. 15, 1943.
[80]Bell Papers, Vol. 1, Bell to Bracken, Nov. 24, 1943.
[81]*Ibid.*

The interest of these men is based not on the belief that the Progressive Conservative Party, under your leadership, can build a greater Canada but only upon fear of the C.C.F. and the bulldog determination to retain at any cost their favoured position in society. . . .

Toronto, Bell continued, was hated throughout the nation. "The Quebecer [*sic*] would consider that the Party had sold out to the imperialist orange elements, the Westerner, that we had sold out to Bay Street finance." And again, the loyalties of this committee would certainly not be to the party as a whole and its leader:

The first criterion of any organization committee or an organizer is loyalty to the party leader and to him alone. Is it unfair to say that Bickle and McKenzie's primary loyalty is to Drew? Indeed this is as it should be. Is it unfair to point out that Duncan is a most intimate friend and admirer of Drew; that Gundy kicks with the same foot as McCullagh; that Borden on this matter can be called nondescript? Would it be surprising if the real boss of such a committee and through it the real boss of substantial activity in the Party should turn out to be the Premier of Ontario? One hesitates to draw distinction between a provincial and a federal leader in questions of loyalty but I know something from past experience of the arrogance and arbitrary claim to power of some men in Toronto and I am anxious that they should not be in any position to frustrate the will of the federal leader.

Bell admitted that there were still some things wrong with his federal organization, but these could be fixed, he said, if "we can get the support which you were promised when you took over the leadership and which we have been promised from time to time since then. If the adoption of a proposal of this sort is a condition precedent to getting adequate practical support, then we are placed in a most embarrassing and difficult position. . . ." Just how the Toronto proposals were presented to Bracken is unclear, but there is no doubt that the party leader refused to consider them. That such suggestions could be seriously made, however, did not augur well for the future.

The Toronto scheme was symptomatic of the discomfiture of the party. The new uneasiness was also immediately evident in the House of Commons. There Mackenzie King was adopting Bracken's programme (although the Prime Minister would not have acknowledged his paternity) and stealing the party's thunder. As Gordon Graydon, the House leader, asked in his first speech of the 1944 session of parliament,

Why did the government wait until after a call from Canada's next prime minister to adopt a policy of putting a floor under the prices of agricultural products?
It is extremely significant that the government should have waited until after it had been in power for eight years, and until the plan had been

incorporated as part of the Progressive Conservative agricultural policy, before undertaking to establish floor prices for farm products.[82]

"Our party," Graydon said in defining the platform of Progressive Conservatism, "stands for a programme of rational reform, as opposed to a policy on the one hand, of rigid reaction, and a policy on the other hand, of reckless revolution. Our party stands pledged to remove the abuses and reform the present system."[83] Earlier John Bracken had used similar words to chart his party's midway course between "piecemeal politics leaning toward reaction" and "socialism."[84]

The Progressive Conservative party was in the centre of the political spectrum, Bracken and Graydon agreed, flanked by revolution and reaction. Bracken, who had been touring the nation making speeches and expanding upon the platforms written at Port Hope and Winnipeg, had certainly tried to keep his party in the political centre.[85] The resurgence of the Tory old guard was threatening this posture from within the party, however, and the Speech from the Throne was an indication that King was readying the Liberals for an attack from without. Graydon himself had admitted that King had stolen part of the Conservative platform. How then could the Liberals be called reactionaries? If the Prime Minister really intended to transform the generalities of the Throne Speech into legislation, the Progressive Conservatives would be placed in an unhappy position. The choice would be between saying "Me, too!" while the Liberals took the credit for enacting a whole series of progressive measures into law, or of emphasizing other things such as conscription and free enterprise. The first parliamentary test came on the issue of the "baby bonus."

Family allowances had first been proposed seriously to the government in a report submitted by the National War Labour Board in August 1943.[86] By paying a minimum of $5.00 a month for each child under 16 years of age, the government hoped to "aid in ensuring a minimum of well-being to the children of the nation and to help gain for them a closer approach to equality of opportunity in the battle of life. . . ."[87] The cost of the scheme was estimated at some $250 millions each year, an amount equivalent to a 50 per cent increase in the prewar

[82]House of Commons, *Debates*, Jan. 31, 1944, p. 20.
[83]*Ibid.*, p. 26.
[84]Address at Hamilton, Ontario, Dec. 10, 1943, reprinted in Bracken, *Bracken Says*, p. 58.
[85]For example, see the speeches in *ibid.*
[86]The Hon. C. P. McTague Interview, June 1, 1965. McTague was chairman of the Board. Grant Dexter, *Family Allowances*, reprinted from the *Winnipeg Free Press* (Winnipeg, n.d.).
[87]House of Commons, *Debates*, Jan. 27, 1944, p. 2. The plan paid $5 for children under 5, $6 for children 6 to 9, $7 for children 10 to 12, and $8 for children 13 to 16 years of age.

national budget. This was far-reaching social legislation. The reaction of the Conservative party to the plan varied with the speaker. Dr. Bruce, for example, regarded the measure as "a bribe of the most brazen character, made chiefly to one province and paid for by the taxes of the rest," a charge for which he was expelled from the House for one day.[88] With the birth rate higher in Quebec than in the rest of Canada,[89] Bruce said, the legislation amounted to the subsidization of large families in French Canada. To the Toronto M.P. this was particularly shocking, for it would result "in bonusing families who have been unwilling to defend their country."[90] Premier Drew of Ontario presumably shared this view. In a bitter attack on the legislation, he warned that "one isolationist Province" must not be permitted "to dominate the destiny of a divided Canada. . . . Canada is now and will remain British North America."[91] The emphasis was clearly on the "British."

Though Bracken had earlier labelled the baby bonus a "political bribe," saying that "all this fanfare looks like an election bait to gain the support of the electors, or to fool them, or to do both,"[92] it was evident that such Progressive Conservative members as John Diefenbaker and Howard Green strongly favoured the measure. Rodney Adamson, the member for York West, recorded his impression of the decisive caucus on July 26, 1944, that determined the party's attitude to family allowances: "Long caucus about family allowances. I take stand against them. . . . Bracken is anti also but bows to Howard Green, Diefenbaker, the Western and Maritime Members. Perhaps this is good strategy. I say I will not vote for measure and will stay away."[93] Perhaps it was good strategy to vote for the baby bonus, and no Conservative—indeed, no Member of Parliament whatever his party—voted against the legislation.[94] With the exception of Dr. Bruce, the party's spokesmen did not oppose the measure in bitter fashion but relied on constitutional and financial arguments.[95] However sound these arguments, and however

---

[88]*Ibid.*, July 31, 1944, p. 5677.

[89]*Ottawa Citizen*, Dec. 22, 1965, p. 7, cites the birth rate in 1945 as 29.3 per thousand in Quebec and 24.3 nationally. (This article was one of a four-part series on the background of the bonus.)

[90]*Ibid.*; Bruce Papers, Bruce to Graydon, July 20, 1944; H. A. Bruce, *Varied Operations* (Toronto, 1958), p. 328.

[91]Toronto *Globe and Mail*, Aug. 10, 1944, p. 1.

[92]*Toronto Daily Star*, June 24, 1944, p. 2.

[93]Adamson Papers, Diary, July 26, 1944; Green Interview, Aug. 23, 1966. According to Gordon Graydon's notes of this caucus discussion, at least nine Members flatly opposed the bill while two more had doubts. P.A.C., Graydon Papers, Vol. 22, Social Security File, "notes of caucus stand re family allowances," n.d.

[94]House of Commons, *Debates*, July 28, 1944, pp. 5538–9. The vote on second reading was 139–0.

[95]E.g., H. R. Jackman in *ibid.*, Feb. 8, 1944, p. 271; J. G. Diefenbaker in *ibid.*, July 27, 1944, p. 5460. Cf. Meighen Papers, Meighen to George McCullagh, July 26, 1944.

much it was the duty of the Opposition to oppose, the impression was created that the Progressive Conservatives were less than enthusiastic about social welfare measures. This was grist for the propaganda mills of the other parties.[96]

Other issues, too, affected the new image the party was trying so hard to project. Bracken met with some success in bringing new men into the party, but not the success for which he had hoped.[97] There was unending grumbling from Queen's Park in Toronto, the headquarters of Drew's provincial administration, and from some Ontario Members of Parliament about the party's organizational work.[98] Resentment in the caucus, fed by Bracken's refusal to seek a seat, was also growing. "This is the end of the Conservative Party," Rodney Adamson grumbled at Bracken's decision not to contest a by-election scheduled for August 1943. "Bracken is frightened to run and is an absolutely useless leader. . . . The Conservative Party as a political force is ended, killed by the political appeasement of Bracken."[99] The Liberals, of course, took advantage of the situation and drew evident glee from chiding the Conservatives on the whereabouts of their absent leader. This made the problem worse. "To caucus," Adamson recorded on January 27, 1944. "Graydon resigns, but carries on. He is fed up and throws down the gauntlet to be in the House or else."[100]

The waters were further muddied by the recrudescence of the old issue of empire centralization. Speaking in Toronto on January 24, 1944, Lord Halifax, the British ambassador in Washington, advanced his conception of the proper role for Canada and the other dominions. The right of each Commonwealth member to determine its own course in external affairs, Halifax told an audience that included both John Bracken and George Drew,

may mean a gain or it may mean a loss. It is plainly a loss if . . . the responsibility for action which represents that unity is not visibly shared by all. It is an immeasurable gain if on vital issues we can achieve a common foreign policy expressed not by a single voice but by the unison of many. . . .

---

[96]E.g., Dexter, *Family Allowances*; "Family Allowance Feud," *Canadian Forum*, XXIV (Sept., 1944), 23–4; G. C. Whittaker, "Pity We Shan't Have a Conference. . . ," *Saturday Night*, LIX (Aug. 26, 1944), 8.

[97]The Liberals believed Bracken was making headway; the Conservatives knew he wasn't (Gardiner Papers, T. H. Wood to Gardiner, March 7, 1944; Bell Interview, Aug. 24, 1964).

[98]Adamson Papers, Diary, Jan. 4, 8, 9, 11, 1944.

[99]*Ibid.*, June 30, 1943. Cf. Pickersgill, *Mackenzie King Record*, I, 566.

[100]Adamson Papers, Diary, Jan. 27, 1944. For Liberal comment, see House of Commons, *Debates*, Feb. 11, 1943, p. 328; July 5, 1943, p. 4330; Jan. 31, 1944, pp. 30–1; Feb. 21, 1944, pp. 690–1.

. . . We see three great powers, the United States, Russia and China. . . .
Side by side with them is the United Kingdom. . . .
   In the company of these Titans, Britain, apart from the rest of the Commonwealth and Empire, could hardly claim equal partnership. . . .
   . . . Not Great Britain only, but the British Commonwealth and Empire must be the fourth power. . . .[101]

Halifax's speech, seemingly an expression of official British opinion,[102] had been delivered without any advance warning of its explosive contents to the Canadian government. Predictably, Mackenzie King was horrified. That Canada, situated geographically as she was between the Soviet Union and the United States and a member of the Commonwealth, could support such a conception of the postwar world was unthinkable. As the Prime Minister noted in his diary, "again it has fallen to my lot to have to make the most difficult of all the fights. This perpetual struggle to save the Empire despite all that Tories' policies will do. . . ."[103]

But Canadian Tories no longer viewed empire relations as they had a few years earlier, and Bracken was as aware as was King of the political dangers inherent in the policies enunciated by Halifax. His first reactions were properly cautious, and the Progressive Conservative leader confined himself to the hope that the Ambassador's remarks "will not become the subject of small political discussion."[104] In the House of Commons, Gordon Graydon too was vague, calling for a "greater and more powerful British Commonwealth," while stressing that Conservatives would yield to no one in their desire to achieve for Canada "her maximum national stature."[105]

Although the party leadership was careful to straddle the fence,[106] private members felt no hesitation in speaking out for the British policies. Howard Green, for example, one of the few Conservatives to comment on foreign policy at any time, stated flatly in a Vancouver speech that Conservative policy was based on Halifax's ideas.[107] Arthur Meighen, who had deliberately faded into the background after the Winnipeg convention, also had strong views on the future of the empire, and he

---

[101]"Speech of Lord Halifax to the Toronto Board of Trade, Jan. 24, 1944," *International Conciliation*, No. 398 (March, 1944), 226.

[102]Massey, *What's Past is Prologue*, pp. 393–4.

[103]Pickersgill, *Mackenzie King Record*, I, 637.

[104]Quoted in "Canada—Discussion of Commonwealth Relations," *Round Table*, XXIV (June, 1944), 271; Bracken Interview, June 1, 1963.

[105]House of Commons, *Debates*, Jan. 31, 1944, pp. 20, 26.

[106]A course that had been advised even before the Halifax address. Progressive Conservative Party Files, File M-5-G, Macdonnell to Bracken, Dec. 31, 1943, and reply, Bell to Macdonnell, Jan. 4, 1944.

[107]Bruce Hutchison, in *Christian Science Monitor*, April 22, 1944, p. 11.

commented tartly to Bennett in late February that "no very definite statement . . . has been made as yet by Mr. Bracken. I feel confident his views are the same as our own."[108] To be certain of this, however, Meighen took the opportunity to write to Bracken, urging him to foster discussion of the Halifax proposals "so that an unworthy course may not be taken . . . behind the backs of the Canadian people."[109] At last, in April, Bracken issued a statement to counter the "misrepresentations" of his views on Canada's position and proper function in the British Commonwealth.[110]

The lengthy statement was skilfully enough worded to mollify everyone.[111] But once his verbiage was penetrated, Bracken could be seen to have urged nothing more than "closer cooperation with the other Commonwealth nations" and to have denounced anything that would detract from "our sovereign rights." This was pallid stuff for the fire-eating imperialists but, incredibly, Bracken's ambiguities seemed to satisfy many Conservatives. Meighen, for one, wrote to a friend that he could think of "no endorsation of Lord Halifax's speech more complete and definite than Mr. Bracken's statement. It seems to have confused the enemy, . . ." he added in a splendid understatement.[112] But other Conservatives were still dissatisfied, and all the resentment over Bracken's leadership and policies culminated in an attempt, stage-managed by Drew's organizer, Alex McKenzie, to have Rodney Adamson elected as president of the Dominion Progressive Conservative Association at its second annual meeting in March 1944.[113] Bracken, however, managed to have his nominee, P. D. McArthur, president of the Dairy Farmers of Canada, selected, and the crisis blew over. With rumours of dissatisfaction with his leadership persisting throughout the summer of 1944, Bracken finally felt obliged to make an extraordinary statement on the radio network of the Canadian Broadcasting Corporation:

Speaking of leadership reminds me that a rumour is abroad concerning the leadership of this Party. The rumours are to the effect that efforts are being made to dominate me by a certain business group or groups. May I say

---

[108]Bennett Papers, Notable Persons File, Meighen to Bennett, Feb. 26, 1944.
[109]Meighen Papers, Meighen to Bracken, Feb. 17, 1944.
[110]*Toronto Daily Star*, April 18, 1944.
[111]Bracken later expressed his views in an article in *Maclean's*. King gleefully read long extracts into Hansard, remarking at his delight that he and Bracken were so close in their attitudes (House of Commons, *Debates*, Aug. 4, 1944, p. 5966).
[112]Meighen Papers, Meighen to Lawrence Hunt, April 25, 1944.
[113]Adamson Papers, Diary, Feb. 15, 25, 28, and March 1, 3, 1944.

emphatically there has been no domination; there has been no attempt at domination; and domination, if attempted by any one section anywhere will not be allowed.

As for ousting me, no one has tried that; and they wouldn't succeed if they did; and in any event, there are no aspirants that I know of. When I accepted the leadership of the Progressive Conservative Party, I accepted it from a National Convention. . . .[114]

Whatever the stories about the leadership, the party was having no difficulty in finding the money with which to finance its growing national organization. One of Bell's jobs as national director was "to play the major role in negotiating for enough money to maintain the party between elections," and in this role he was brilliantly successful.[115] In 1943, and after some early problems, the party spent more than $170,000, and the following year increased this to more than $475,000.[116] Though the party was in its best financial condition since the palmy days of Bennett, difficulties with fund-raising persisted. The Toronto situation was agitated with the perpetual squabbles between the various cliques, and the Montreal committee needed new blood.[117] This state of affairs was not resolved until John S. D. Tory, a leading Toronto barrister, took over as chairman of the party's National Finance Committee in mid-1944. A non-practising Liberal until early 1944, Tory became the most successful financial chairman the party had ever had, and he assumed responsibility not only for the collection of funds but also for deciding the party's over-all budget.[118]

The Progressive Conservative party's success in financing its operations also posed problems. Macdonnell, for one, believed it would be fatal for the party to remain dependent on "a few rich men," and certainly this had opened the party to attacks from its political opponents.[119] Bracken and Bell were aware of this and launched an ambitious experiment aimed at reducing the party's dependence on wealthy contributors. The idea of a "Popular Finance Campaign"—the first serious attempt by a major Canadian party to raise money by popular subscription—had originated with Bell in December 1942, and he had expanded upon it throughout the following year.[120] In October 1943 a

[114]*Public Opinion*, II (Aug., 1944), 2.

[115]Williams, *Conservative Party of Canada, 1920–1949*, pp. 148–9.

[116]Progressive Conservative Party Files, Financial Statements.

[117]Bell Papers, Vol. 1, "Problems of Organization."

[118]Bell Interview, Aug. 24, 1964; Progressive Conservative Party Files, File Y-Y-1, Bell to Tory, Oct. 20, 1944.

[119]Progressive Conservative Party Files, File M-5-G, Macdonnell to Bell, July 20, 1943.

[120]Bell Papers, Vol. 1, Bell to Milner, December 30, 1942; Progressive Conservative Party Files, File M-5-G, Bell to Macdonnell, July 24, 1943.

trial run was held in *Public Opinion*, the party's monthly newspaper, and in the early new year the campaign was carried to the daily and weekly press.[121] The purpose of the campaign, aside from the obvious hope that it would discover hitherto untapped financial resources, was frankly to counter the C.C.F. charge that the Conservative party was the party of the "interests."[122] The theme, party headquarters decided, would be "to establish the party's position as the sole custodian of political liberty and economic opportunity. Both the Liberals and the C.C.F.," the strategists believed, "lay emphasis on security rather than opportunity and herein lies the one palpable difference between the Progressive Conservatives and their political opponents." The Popular Finance Campaign would "sell people a share in the future of their country and an insurance policy to protect their political heritage and their freedom of opportunity."[123]

The fund-raising drive was a dismal failure. An elaborate and detailed advertising campaign was produced by McConnell, Eastman and Company,[124] a major agency, and an impressive organizational structure was raised to administer the anticipated $1 million in receipts. But the money collected did not even meet overhead, and Bell later described the scheme as "the most disappointing project" with which he had ever been closely associated.[125] The collapse of the Popular Finance Campaign could only increase the Conservative party's dependence upon the contributions of business and financial interests.

The party suffered another blow on June 15, 1944, when the C.C.F. scored a sweeping victory in Saskatchewan, winning a clear majority of the popular vote and capturing forty-seven of the fifty-five seats in the legislature. The Conservatives had put forward forty candidates, but they had failed to win a single seat. Worse yet, despite an attractive,

[121]Bell Papers, Vol. 1, Memorandum, "Progressive Conservative Campaign Fund," n.d.

[122]"I agree with you," Bell wrote to H. H. Stevens in October 1944, "that one of our greatest handicaps is the continual linking up of our Party with the reactionary Toronto interests. The deliberate campaign of the other parties in this particular has met with a considerable measure of success and the speeches of some of our friends have served only to promote that idea." Stevens Papers, Vol. 158, Oct. 26, 1944.

[123]Bell Papers, Vol. 1, "Memorandum re: Public Finance," n.d. The preparations for the campaign are dealt with more fully in J. L. Granatstein, "Conservative Party Finances, 1939–45," in Canada, Secretary of State, Committee on Election Expenses, *Studies in Canadian Party Finance* (Ottawa, 1967), pp. 297–301.

[124]Bell Papers, Vol. 1, G. C. Dixon to J. C. Reade, April 11, 1944.

[125]Bell Interview, Aug. 24, 1964.

young leader in Rupert Ramsay and the presence of prominent agriculturists in their ranks, the Conservative candidate in every riding had run third and lost his deposit.[126] Apparently neither the tag "Progressive Conservative" nor John Bracken's reputation were of much value on the prairies—at least provincially.

The failure in Saskatchewan, Bracken's "backyard," for all practical purposes ended the brief Conservative flirtation with the doctrines of the welfare state. The sudden changes in the political situation and the amazing resurgence of the right-wing Tories had resulted in a renewed power struggle. With their solid base in Ontario, the demands of the right could not be denied for long. Bracken had had his chance to offer the Progressive Conservative brand of social welfare, and the results had been less than successful. More important still, Mackenzie King had regained his accustomed position smack in the middle of the political road. Now, if the C.C.F. were to be stopped and the party put into office, different issues would have to be dusted off. What better issue could there be than conscription?

[126]Figures from *Canadian Parliamentary Guide, 1945*; Carlyle King, "CCF Sweeps Saskatchewan," *Canadian Forum*, XXIV (July, 1944), 79. See T. A. Crerar's comments on the significance of the result for the Tories. Douglas Library, Queen's University, T. A. Crerar Papers, Crerar to Grant Dexter, June 17, 1944.

8.

Conscription Again:
The Election of 1945

The Conservative party had been driven from the political centre and robbed of its chief issue by Mackenzie King's adoption of social welfare. The efforts of the party's progressives at the Port Hope conference and the Winnipeg convention seemed to have lost their meaning. In these circumstances, the party had little choice other than to fall back on a policy of conscription. The opportunity for this was not long in coming, for after D-day casualties mounted rapidly, and a genuine shortage of trained infantry arose. The ensuing crisis came close to toppling the King government, and the Conservative party had a popular issue for the first time in the war. But conscription was a two-edged sword, and what was popular in English-speaking Canada was hated in Quebec. The party thus fought the election of June 1945 as an English-speaking party, putting its pledge of conscription for the Pacific war on the line against the social security platforms of the Liberals and the C.C.F. The results of the voting demonstrated that conscription was no more effective against social welfare than it had been in February 1942.

The conscriptionist cry had been muted during Bracken's first eighteen months of leadership. His strongest speech had been delivered in Toronto on July 2, 1943. The war policy of the King government, he said then, "having been in too many of its aspects prompted by political cowardice, could not fail to result in the chaotic and . . . disgracefully wasteful conditions which now prevail. . . ."[1] These were forceful words, but they were aimed more at the government's allocation of civilian manpower than at its stand on military service. This was deliberate policy. Bracken believed that King should be made to pull his own chestnuts out of the fire. In addition, the party was already confident of its strength in conscriptionist Ontario; it was now trying to find support in Quebec and in the immigrant-populated provinces of the West, both areas in which a call for conscription would not help the party's prospects.[2] Four

[1]Bracken, *Bracken Says*, p. 26.
[2]Macdonnell Interview, July 10, 1963; Finlayson Interview, July 6, 1963.

days after the C.C.F. victory in the Saskatchewan election, however, the Conservative party altered its course again. The C.C.F. success had apparently convinced some in the party that a new issue was needed, and with Canadian troops now heavily engaged in both Italy and Normandy, that issue seemed to be conscription.

The party's pace was forced by the Hon. C. P. McTague, who had been chairman of the National War Labour Board and a justice of the Ontario Supreme Court until his resignation from these positions to become National Chairman of the Progressive Conservative party on April 24, 1944. Addressing his own nomination meeting in Guelph, Ontario, on June 19, with Bracken at his side on the platform, the Toronto Tory dealt bluntly with the manpower question:

Now as to where *this party stands on this matter*, let me state in simple unequivocal terms. To our army overseas and their relatives here we say you should have reinforcements now, and they are all available now, from the trained troops not now and never required for home defence, so-called. . . . National honour demands that without an hour's delay the necessary order in council should be passed making these reinforcements available. . . .

The government's persistence in leaving these trained soldiers of the home army in Canada, can only be construed as deference to the will of the minority in the Province of Quebec as voiced in the plebiscite. . . .[3]

There is some doubt whether or not Bracken knew that McTague intended to deal with manpower in these terms,[4] but he could not let this matter raised by one of his chief lieutenants drop without comment. "One point in particular in Mr. McTague's remarks I wish to support and endorse," he said.

He pointed out that since the war we have had many statements from the Department of National Defence as to the urgency of reinforcements, and he added, "National honour demands . . . these reinforcements [be made] available."

In this time of national emergency, surely there will be no Canadians who will find it in their heart to deny that appeal. Certainly it receives the endorsement of this party, and I would like to think of the great majority of people

---

[3]Quoted in Progressive Conservative Party, *Progressive Conservative Speaker's Handbook, 1945* (Ottawa, 1945), War Policy, Section I; *Ottawa Journal*, June 20, 1944, p. 13.

[4]McTague said that Bracken knew of his intent (Interview, June 1, 1965). In a radio address in December 1944 Bracken said he "had seen and approved" the speech (*Public Opinion*, III, Jan., 1945, 20). Others disagree (Bell Interview, July 15, 1964; Finlayson Interview, July 6, 1963). As early as June 14, it should be noted, Bracken had received a memorandum from H. H. Stevens urging a "showdown" on conscription. P.A.C., Gordon Graydon Papers, Vol. 5, Memorandum.

in all other parties as well.[5]

However, as was the case with the demands for compulsory service in 1941 and 1942, there was as yet no apparent shortage of reinforcements for the Canadian army overseas.[6]

The response of the Members of Parliament to McTague's initiative and Bracken's endorsement of it was almost unanimously unfavourable. Only Dr. Bruce was pleased. "I was delighted with the nomination speech of Charlie McTague which came as a complete surprise to our members here," he wrote his good friend and fellow conscriptionist, George McCullagh. "In fact some of our friends were foolish enough to express criticism because this had been done without consulting caucus."[7] Evidently the caucus went along with the idea that the party should put itself on record as favouring the employment of "Zombies" —as N.R.M.A. soldiers were now being called—overseas,[8] but there was no desire to go any further. "Arrive Ottawa," Rodney Adamson noted on July 24, 1944. "[Met] at station. . . . Caucus at 10. Important. It is the Globe [and Mail] group. Have asked Bracken to have us divide the House on conscription. Caucus is 100% against taking this suicidal step. Really a great show and a sock in the eye for the Toronto crowd."[9] Within three months, however, a genuine shortage of infantry reinforcements had developed overseas, and conscription once again dominated public discussion.

Signs of the coming crisis had been concealed by overly optimistic senior officers in the Canadian army overseas.[10] Reinforcement requirements had been based on a slavish copy of the British wastage rates calculated at the War Office. These estimated on a global basis that 48 per cent of total casualties would be infantrymen, whereas more than 75 per cent of the total casualties being reported in Italy and northwest Europe were infantrymen.[11] Now that the Luftwaffe was too weak to strafe the rearward elements of the invasion forces, casualties among

[5]Cited in Progressive Conservative Party Files, *War Policy, John Bracken on Record*, a mimeographed handout listing statements by Bracken on conscription.

[6]R. MacGregor Dawson, *The Conscription Crisis of 1944* (Toronto, 1961), pp. 13–14.

[7]Bruce Papers, Bruce to McCullagh, June 21, 1944.

[8]Graydon in House of Commons, *Debates*, July 11, 1944, p. 4711. The term "Zombie" was West Indian in origin and referred to mindless, soulless, walking dead.

[9]Adamson Papers, Diary, July 24, 1944.

[10]House of Commons, *Debates*, Nov. 27, 29, 1944, pp. 6598, 6660. On Aug. 3, 1944, the Chief of Staff, Canadian Military Headquarters, General Kenneth Stuart, reported to the cabinet that "while Army fighting for 12 months in Italy and two months in France, reinforcement situation very satisfactory. There were reinforcement personnel available for 3 months at intensive battle casualty rate." Ralston Papers, Vol. 44, L. Breen to Ralston, Aug. 29, 1945. (This is an extract from cabinet minutes.)

[11]H. D. G. Crerar Papers, 958.C.009 (D441), "Report on Survey of Reinforcement Situation. . . ," by Lt.-Gen. E. W. Sansom, pp. 2–3. The root of the problem,

units of the supporting arms and services were considerably fewer than estimated, so the American, British, and Canadian military authorities were busy converting the estimated surplus reinforcements for these corps into infantry. Conversion training often proved to be perfunctory, however, and Major Connie Smythe, a well-known Toronto sports promoter who had been commanding a light anti-aircraft battery in Normandy until wounded, charged following his return to Canada in September that some infantry reinforcements had "never thrown a grenade."[12] Since the Germans had not been crushed in Normandy and had managed to establish a new front closer to home, Colonel J. L. Ralston, the Minister of National Defence, had to be told during his annual autumn visit overseas that there had been a miscalculation: 15,000 additional trained infantrymen would have to be despatched from Canada before the end of 1944 to meet estimated needs in northwest Europe and Italy. Thoroughly disillusioned by the conditions he found overseas, Ralston returned to Ottawa on October 18, ready to demand that N.R.M.A. soldiers be sent overseas. "I must say to Council," the Minister told the startled cabinet, "that while I am ready to explore the situation further, as I see it at the moment, I feel that there is no alternative but for me to recommend the extension of service of N.R.M.A. personnel to overseas."[13]

Ralston's revelations shook King, the cabinet, and eventually the nation. The story of the crisis has been told elsewhere and only the broad outlines are needed here.[14] Immediately after Ralston's remarks, King indicated that he did not agree and polled his cabinet members. Three-quarters supported his position.[15] For the next two weeks, the cabinet wrestled with the problem, a serious split developing between

one expert on Canadian manpower problems has stated, "went back to the incorrect lessons which had been drawn from the early German success with blitzkrieg tactics. Recruiting posters had been too successful in urging young Canadians to become 'Captains of the Clouds,' 'Guardians of the Deep,' members of 'Canada's Mechanized Army,' or mere skilled tradesmen. . . . The 'poor bloody infantry' had received little attention unless it was from . . . veterans who advised their sons to join something that did not walk." Communication from Dr. J. Mackay Hitsman, Feb. 15, 1966.

[12]Toronto *Globe and Mail*, Sept. 19, 1944, p. 1.

[13]Dawson, *Conscription Crisis*, pp. 14–17; Ralston Papers, Untitled remarks to Council, October 24, 1944.

[14]Dawson, *Conscription Crisis*; J. W. Pickersgill and D. F. Forster, eds., *The Mackenzie King Record*. II. *1944–45* (Toronto, 1968), Chapters V–VIII. The Grant Dexter Papers at Queen's University contain three fascinating memoranda on the crisis, dated November 6 and 22, 1944, and January 9, 1945. The C. G. Power Papers, also at Queen's, contain Power's "Notes of Discussions on the Conscription Crisis, November, 1944." New material is also available in the T. A. Crerar Papers at Queen's. The author's forthcoming study, *Conscription in Canada* (with J. M. Hitsman) will examine the 1944 crisis in detail.

[15]Ralston Papers, "Notes for the Record on the recent crisis in the Government over reinforcements," Dec. 26, 1944.

conscriptionists and anti-conscriptionists. Led by Ralston, the conscriptionists maintained that King had promised to send the home defence
conscripts overseas "if necessary"; now, they maintained, conscription
was necessary.[16] Their opposition in the cabinet, similarly motivated by
the highest considerations, objected to this argument. The Hon. C. G.
Power, the Minister of National Defence for Air, a wounded veteran of
the Great War, and the father of a prisoner in a Japanese camp,
explained his reasoning for opposing Ralston in a heartsick memorandum written after the resolution of the crisis:

Conscription was a long way from being anywhere necessary at this stage.
It was certainly convenient to send the Zombies, but convenience should
give way before future National interest.
    Of course, we can argue interminably on the definition of "necessity"
and God knows we did. We will, in all probability never agree on this, but
"absolute necessity" in the logical sense had disappeared. The war is won
and none of the essential conditions which to the ordinary Liberal mind might
justify coercion, any longer exist. There remain other "necessities" not
fundamental, namely, prestige, interest in the Peace Conference, morale of
the troops, overwhelming and inflamed public opinion. I found none of
these sufficient to outweigh the serious and far reaching consequences to
Canada internally.
    I faced the prospect of a Government defeat in the House, and a Party
minority in the Country, and was not discouraged. I envisaged the prospect
of one-third of our population uncooperative, with a deep sense of injury,
and the prey to the worst elements amongst them, and worst of all hating
all other Canadians.
    Don't forget, the chief [Mackenzie King] was right when he hinted in a
phrase which he stole from Brooke Claxton: "Conscription in the mind of
the French Canadian, as such, is not so bad. It is because it is considered
to be a symbol of British domination that it is anathema. To them it means
being forced to fight for the 'maudit Anglais.' "[17]

In his desperate attempts to maintain the voluntary system and prevent
the racial split seen by Power, King ruthlessly sacked Ralston and
appointed General A. G. L. McNaughton in his stead. But the former
commander of the First Canadian Army failed to persuade the required
number of N.R.M.A. soldiers to convert voluntarily to general service.
At this point the cabinet was on the verge of dissolution. C. D. Howe,

[16]Col. Ralston was approached by representatives of the Conservative party at
this time and asked to cross the floor of the House. He refused. Information from
Mrs. Stuart B. Ralston. Mr. Henry Borden attempted to persuade Ralston to move
toward a national government in this period, according to one source (Confidential Interview, March 10, 1966).
    [17]Gardiner Papers, "Memorandum re Resignation of Charles G. Power. . . ,"
Dec. 10, 1944. The memorandum is printed in part in Ward, ed., *Power Memoirs*,
pp. 168–72, and some changes in punctuation have been made in that version.

the Minister of Munitions and Supply, was ready to break with King on November 22, as were T. A. Crerar and at least four other ministers. At the party caucus King stalled discussion on the crisis, and the dissident ministers met later that day.[18] Almost certainly aware of the rebels' meeting, the Prime Minister executed an astonishing *volte-face* and determined upon a brilliant half-measure. Only 16,000 conscripts, just enough to meet the shortage, would be sent overseas in the first instance. King's desperate expedient succeeded in maintaining his cabinet virtually intact. Though Power resigned in protest, the remainder, both pro- and anti-conscription, stayed.[19] The French-Canadian M.P.s, all pledged to oppose conscription, were in surprising numbers persuaded to support the Prime Minister's policy by what has been called "one of the greatest orations of the Canadian Parliament."[20] Turning his back to the Opposition benches, King appealed to his followers, his peroration a *cri de cœur*:

If there is anything to which I have devoted my political life, it is to try to promote unity, harmony and amity between the diverse elements of this country. My friends can desert me, they can remove their confidence from me, they can withdraw the trust they have placed in my hands, but never shall I deviate from that line of policy. Whatever may be the consequences, whether loss of prestige, loss of popularity, or loss of power, I feel that I am in the right, and I know that a time will come when every man will render me full justice on that score.[21]

The Quebec members may have voted for King, but neither their constituents nor the provincial legislators showed as much understanding of the Prime Minister's awful dilemma. Rioting erupted in Montreal and Quebec, speakers denounced the "tyranny of the majority," and in March 1945 the Quebec legislature passed a resolution censuring the federal government for enforcing conscription and regretting that "M. Mackenzie King ait renié ses engagements les plus sacrés à ce sujet."[22] The Liberal leader's policy had few defenders.

The Progressive Conservative party, however, had no difficulty in determining its course of action in the crisis. The Conservative press,

[18]Ralston Papers, "Notes for the record. . . ."
[19]Senator Lambert noted in his diary on November 23, the following scene in caucus: "At caucus at 11.30, P.M. explained his change of front; and J.G[ardiner] and Powers [*sic*] both disagreed with the P.M.s statement. Powers later resigned: but J.G. simply wanted assurance that full conscription was not being adopted" (Norman Lambert Papers).
[20]Ford, *As the World Wags On*, p. 185. Of fifty-seven French Canadian M.P.s voting on the question, twenty-three supported King.
[21]House of Commons, *Debates*, Nov. 27, 1944, pp. 6617–18.
[22]*Le Devoir*, 2 mars 1945.

led by the Montreal *Gazette* and the *Globe and Mail*, accused King of risking a military disaster in his attempts to win political advantage.[23] Conservative speakers charged the Prime Minister with "deliberately ruling according to the will of a minority. . . . Why did he not tell us at the time of the plebiscite in 1942," one Toronto Conservative demanded, "that he would not use the conscript army for fighting overseas if the Province of Quebec opposed it?"[24] "In the name of the Canadian people," John Bracken said in a statement released on November 13, 1944,

and for the protection of the men overseas, after due consideration and with the endorsation [*sic*] of the national committee of the Progressive Conservative party . . . , I call upon the government to fulfill its duty to our men overseas and to carry out the will of the people as expressed in the plebiscite by passing the necessary order-in-council and sending the available men in the Home Army as reinforcements forthwith.[25]

By this date, public opinion in English-speaking Canada was thoroughly aroused against the government and against Quebec, perhaps for the first time in the war.[26] Voices of moderation were few. J. M. Macdonnell was one such voice, pleading vainly for sympathy and understanding in dealing with Quebec:

Let us remember that the great bulk of them have been taught to think of us, not as real Canadians, but as Englishmen, Scotsmen . . . living in Canada. . . . The fact that the bulk of the Canadian Corps in the last war was British-born may give color to this view. . . . Can we not bring to an end this cause of strife which wicked men, not all of one party, have sought to keep alive for their own political advantage?[27]

No similar remarks were made in the House of Commons by Conservatives. Gordon Graydon moved the party's amendment to the Prime Minister's motion of confidence: "This house is of the opinion that the government has not made certain of adequate and continuous trained reinforcements by requiring all N.R.M.A. personnel whether now or hereafter enrolled to serve in any theatre of war and has failed to assure equality of service and sacrifice." When pressed by government members, Graydon later agreed that his amendment meant that the policy

[23]E.g., Montreal *Gazette*, Nov. 13, 1944, p. 8.

[24]Alderman Donald Fleming, quoted in Toronto *Globe and Mail*, Nov. 8, 1944, p. 4.

[25]Quoted in Progressive Conservative Party Files, *War Policy, John Bracken on Record*.

[26]See the compilation of press attitudes in Gardiner Papers, J. G. Fogo to Gardiner, Jan. 12, 1945.

[27]Quoted in Toronto *Globe and Mail*, Nov. 21, 1944, p. 4.

of his party was to use conscripts anywhere in the world, including Japan, China, and Manchuria.[28]

The Conservatives maintained the pressure of their criticism into February, throwing the full weight of the party into a by-election in Grey North (Ontario) where General McNaughton was seeking election to the House. There were suggestions that Bracken, still out of the House of Commons more than two years after his selection, should run in the February 5 election, but as usual there seemed to be serious drawbacks to this course. "The situation with respect to North Grey has caused all of us very great concern," Bell wrote to Hanson at the end of December 1944:

> The position was canvassed with the greatest of care both in its national aspect and in its local aspect. Due consideration had to be taken of the results in event of a defeat for Mr. Bracken and as well of the future prospect in Western Canada were Mr. Bracken to take an Eastern seat. . . . The decisive factor, however, was that the C.C.F. will likely nominate a candidate if Mr. Bracken does not run. On the other hand, were Mr. Bracken to run, there is no question whatever that the local C.C.F. would not nominate a candidate and would gang up to defeat our Leader. It would be a repetition of the circumstances in York South but in reverse. My own belief is that Mr. Bracken would win but the stakes are too high. . . .[29]

When Bracken decided not to risk defeat, Garfield Case, the mayor of Owen Sound and a man of genuinely undistinguished abilities,[30] was nominated. The C.C.F. then nominated a candidate, and a three-cornered election battle was under way.

McNaughton fought the election in amateur fashion. Despite warnings of its probable effect on the electorate from Arthur Roebuck, M.P., the Liberal party's Ontario campaign chairman, the dutiful general insisted on visiting the rural riding in a private, radio-equipped railway car so that he could maintain contact with National Defence Headquarters.[31] The press of work also restricted his time in the riding, and Roebuck began to sound pessimistic. "I shudder at the black eye involved in a loss," he said.[32] In addition, McNaughton's wife was a Roman Catholic, and this was used against him in the solidly Protestant

---

[28]House of Commons, *Debates*, Nov. 27, 1944, p. 6622, Dec. 7, 1944, p. 6890.

[29]Hanson Papers, Personal Correspondence, Bell to Hanson, Dec. 27, 1944. The exquisite irony of the situation was that McNaughton, shortly before he joined the government, allegedly had been approached by the Conservatives with Bracken's consent and asked to become leader of the party (Dawson, *Conscription Crisis*, p. 36).

[30]Bruce Papers, Bruce to D. M. Hogarth, Feb. 9, 1945.

[31]A. G. L. McNaughton Papers, Roebuck to McNaughton, Dec. 20, and reply, Dec. 24, 1944.   [32]*Ibid.*, Roebuck to McNaughton, Jan. 2, 1945.

constituency. The Conservative nominee was assisted by John Bracken, who came into the constituency for several days early in February. The Conservative leader's style was unaccustomedly hard-hitting, and he threw a devastating charge at the Minister of National Defence: "*Let him tell you why some of those* [N.R.M.A.] *men arrived in Britain without their rifles which they are expected to have.* Let him tell you about how they threw their rifles . . . their ammunition overboard. Let him tell you the truth, which is a condemnation of the complacency, the lack of leadership, the inept mishandling of the entire manpower problem in this nation."[33] Bracken's damning but completely unverified accusation was picked up by Senator Burton K. Wheeler of Montana in the United States Senate. Speaking about a reported death sentence of an American soldier for refusing to drill, Wheeler stated that "if that were to be done, between 16,000 and 18,000 Canadians would have to be hanged because of the fact that they refused to drill. Some of them apparently threw their arms overboard."[34] In fact, one conscript had thrown his rifle and two kitbags into the harbour as he boarded ship, but the Minister's rebuttal never caught up with the accusation.[35]

The result of the by-election was a victory of impressive proportions for the Conservative candidate. Case received 7,333 votes; McNaughton 6,097; and Godfrey, the C.C.F. candidate, 3,118. The party had succeeded in its strategy of making reinforcements the only issue, and it had won the election with this tactic.[36] It seemed significant that the C.C.F. candidate, who concentrated on postwar reconstruction and social security, got nowhere and, indeed, lost his deposit. The Conservative press was jubilant and only too happy to admit that Bracken had saved the day. The party leader, the *Ottawa Journal* noted, emerges "from this contest as a compelling national figure. . . . In many respects it is for him a great personal triumph."[37] Even one Liberal fund-raiser, while bemoaning the party's expenditure of $14,500 in Grey North, noted that the Conservative victory was the "first feather in Bracken's hat."[38]

[33]Bracken at Meaford, Ontario, Feb. 1, 1945, quoted in a Progressive Conservative press release, March 2, 1945, copy in McNaughton Papers. According to Norman Lambert's diary, Bracken's speech "was combined product of Geo McCullagh, Geo Drew, McTague, Rod [Finlayson] and Bracken" (Diary, Feb. 14, 1945). Lambert had a reliable source of information in Conservative ranks.
[34]Directorate of History, File 314.009 (D15), Col. G. V. Gurney, Military Attaché, Washington, to Secretary, Department of National Defence, Feb. 7, 1945.
[35]McNaughton Papers, Press release, Feb. 15, 1945.
[36]C.C.F. Ontario Records, Minutes of Provincial Council and Executive Meetings, Vol. 2, Provincial Executive Meeting, Feb. 13, 1945.
[37]*Ottawa Journal*, Feb. 7, 1945, p. 6. Cf. the comment in "North Grey in Retrospect," *Canadian Forum*, XXIV (March, 1945), 273, and McNaughton's reaction in McNaughton Papers, McNaughton to G. Whiting, Feb. 17, 1945.
[38]Lambert Diaries, Feb. 5, 28, 1945.

The party's harsh new attitude on manpower was not welcomed in Quebec, where Bracken's scrupulous tiptoeing around the conscription issue in 1943 and early 1944 had been appreciated. The Progressive Conservative party had devoted much time and money to organization in the French-speaking province, and there had been signs that this effort was beginning to pay dividends. One of Bracken's first extended trips as leader had been a tour of the province in March and April 1943, and consideration was given to the purchase of a French-language newspaper to present the Conservative view.[39] Late in 1943, a provincial organization committee, part of the "most complete and thorough organization scheme ever attempted by any party in that province," was formed.[40] Although a tacit if uneasy alliance with Maurice Duplessis and his Union Nationale seems to have been made, difficulties arose. "The fundamental problem," Bell wrote in a memorandum on the state of the provincial organization in the late spring of 1944,

arises out of the imminent provincial election. The Duplessis group have done their best to pull off some of our prominent friends so that they will be available for provincial campaigning. It is the belief of Duplessis and his group that these men should not compromise themselves in federal affairs until after a provincial election is over. It is their belief that association with the Bracken cause federally would do injury to their provincial chances. The result has been that it is very difficult to get the men who should be doing the work in Quebec to undertake to do it.[41]

Duplessis won the provincial election on August 8, 1944. His opposition to the war had lost him the election of 1939 but won a victory for him in 1944. "Malheureusement pour M. Godbout et son parti," Professor Brunet wrote, "la guerre se poursuivait toujours à l'automne de 1944 et les électeurs canadiens-français n'avaient pas perdu la mémoire." There was little comfort for the Conservatives in the Duplessis victory, however, for they had raised the conscription issue again by that date, and Duplessis henceforth showed little inclination to co-operate.[42]

Federally, the Quebec scene was confused by a multiplicity of parties and leaders, most nationalists, some radical in orientation, some merely hating Mackenzie King. If the Conservative party could organize these disparate groups, it might be possible to defeat the Liberals in the province. In some constituencies it might even be possible to split the

---

[39]Bell Papers, Vol. 1, "Expenditures—Tour of Quebec Province, March–April, 1943," and Milner to Macdonnell, Dec. 28, 1942 (copy); Bell Interview, Aug. 24, 1964.
[40]*Public Opinion*, II (Jan., 1944), 3.
[41]Bell Papers, Vol. 1, Memorandum, "Problems of Organization," n.d.
[42]Quinn, *The Union Nationale*, pp. 110–11; Michel Brunet, *La Présence anglaise et les Canadiens* (Montréal, 1958), p. 248.

vote and elect Conservatives.[43] With this in mind, the party carried out negotiations with P. J. A. Cardin, the former Liberal minister who had resigned from the cabinet on the question of Bill 80 in May 1942; with Camillien Houde, onetime leader of the Quebec Conservatives, mayor of Montreal on numerous occasions, and an internee from 1940 to 1944 for his statements urging his compatriots not to register in the national registration of 1940; and with Frédéric Dorion, a nationalist M.P. first elected to parliament in a 1942 by-election.[44] The negotiations were conducted in secret, but rumours of these or similar discussions had been current for months. Grant Dexter of the *Winnipeg Free Press* gave his interpretation of the party's Quebec strategy in a devastating series of columns which were subsequently reprinted and given wide publicity by the Liberal party. The articles compared the Conservatives' tactics of 1944 with those employed by the party in the successful elections of 1911 and 1930:

And so the traditional strategy of the Conservatives begins to take on form. The chief ingredients of success are that the Conservatives run no candidates in Quebec—except in English-speaking seats—but back the Nationalists with hard cash and promissory notes. In the past the notes have always been paid.

In English-speaking Canada, the strategy calls for attacks on the Liberals for pandering to Quebec.[45]

Whether such a strategy, if indeed this was the Conservative strategy, could be successful with passions aroused by the war was unknown. Certainly after the conscription crisis of 1944 and the Grey North by-election, it seemed obvious that no candidate running as a Progressive Conservative could hope to win in French-speaking Canada.

How well the party would do elsewhere in the Dominion in the general election of 1945 was also in some doubt. The strength of the C.C.F. in the West, as demonstrated by the Saskatchewan victory, could be expected to be substantial, and Social Credit's grasp on Alberta showed no signs of weakening. How much the strength of J. G. Gardiner's once-mighty Liberal machine had declined was also unknown, although Conservatives expected few Liberal ministers to retain their seats in the West.[46] In Ontario, the party was confident of increased support, and although there was still fear of C.C.F. gains in the indus-

[43]Hanson Papers, Personal Correspondence, Bell to Hanson, Aug. 25, 1943.
[44]Bell Papers, Vol. 1, Bona Arsenault to Bell, Oct. 6, 8, 1944.
[45]Grant Dexter, *And They Welcome Mr. Bracken* (Ottawa, n.d.), p. 9.
[46]Hanson Papers, Personal Correspondence, Hanson to Percy Black, M.P., Oct. 18, 1944.

trial areas, the massive, well-organized anti-socialist campaign was making progress.[47] As always, the Maritimes were a world apart, but the Conservatives were optimistic, except in the French-speaking areas of New Brunswick.[48]

In this unsettled political situation the Conservatives expected to have the largest number of seats, although few looked for a majority in the new parliament. In July 1944 Hanson foresaw his party as the largest group in the House, the C.C.F. with sixty seats, the Liberals with less than fifty, and a bloc of sixty members from Quebec of various nationalist hues. In February 1945 he was less optimistic. "If the Election is held before the Germans collapse," he said, "Bracken might win. But if peace comes soon and you lose the issue of reinforcements it might be otherwise."[49] As late as March 1945, Conservatives still saw their party winning most of the seats,[50] but the Liberals began to regain their confidence and their strength in the spring. The political correspondent for *Maclean's* reported that the Liberals now were expecting to win at least 110 seats and that they saw the Progressive Conservatives slumping badly. Bracken's story of soldiers tossing their rifles overboard had boomeranged, the Liberals maintained, when Senator Wheeler had picked it up in the United States Senate and blackened Canada's eye.[51] Nonetheless, the Conservatives were counting on a two-to-one majority of the soldiers' vote, and as this averaged out at some 4000 votes for each of the 245 constituencies, the benefits could be substantial.[52] But, as the commander of the First Canadian Army wrote to a friend in March 1945, "the political situation in Canada during recent months has made us all distinctly unhappy, when we found time to ponder over it. There is a general feeling of resentment among all ranks, over the situation," Crerar observed, "and no political party or persons or political life in Canada, stands high at present in the eyes of the Canadian Army Overseas."[53]

[47]E.g., Dunning Papers, V. Knowles to Dunning, Feb. 8, and reply, Feb. 9, 1944; Bruce Papers, McCullagh to Bruce, June 22, 1944; Dean E. McHenry, *The Third Force in Canada* (Berkeley, 1950), pp. 124–5; B. A. Trestrail, "Social Suicide" (n.p., n.d.), copy in Gardiner Papers.

[48]Hanson Papers, Personal Correspondence, Hanson to Sen. J. T. Haig, Aug. 30, 1944.

[49]*Ibid.*, Hanson to W. R. Givens, July 13, 1944; Hanson to Bell, Feb. 17, 1945.

[50]Bruce Papers, Bruce to D. M. Hogarth, March 2, 1945.

[51]"Backstage at Ottawa," *Maclean's*, LVIII (May 1, 1945), 15, 57.

[52]Progressive Conservative Party Files, File E-6-G, "Memorandum re Active Service Vote," Jan. 24, 1945; Hanson Papers, Personal Correspondence, Hanson to C. G. Dunn, May 2, 1945.

[53]H. D. G. Crerar Papers, 958.C.009 (D154), Crerar to J. B. Bickersteth, March 27, 1945.

The election date was announced on April 16, 1945.[54] Gambling that the war in Europe would be over by then, King selected June 11 as voting day. Parliament had met briefly in March and April to approve Canada's participation in the United Nations Conference on International Organization at San Francisco, and to the Prime Minister's relief, the war in Europe drew to its close shortly thereafter. Preparations for a division-sized Canadian Army Pacific Force, begun in 1944, were continued, but there was no appreciable enthusiasm anywhere in Canada for a major effort against Japan.[55] The election of 1945 was to be a "khaki" one, and the clash of parties, leaders, and policies would revolve around the issues of reconstruction.

The Liberals were fully aware of this. V-E day had finally ended the reinforcement issue as a burning political question, and although the nation's war effort had been a magnificent one, the Liberals chose to stress their programme of social security and full employment.[56] "Protect Your Social and Economic Gains," Liberal posters urged. "Build a New Social Order—Vote Liberal," "Liberal Policies Make Jobs," and "Liberal Family Allowances Provide Food, Education, Health, Security," were other favoured themes.[57] The Liberals were interested in countering the C.C.F. and their advertising reflected this. "The Liberal Party," Mackenzie King said in a radio broadcast,

has never accepted extreme positions. We do not believe that more employment and prosperity will be created by the mere fact of changing the ownership of property from individuals or corporations to the state. Nor do we believe that our free way of life is threatened by the ownership and development by the nation of certain great undertakings. For the Liberal Party, the test is what will best serve the general interest, rather than special interests, whether those special interests be the interests of a financial oligarchy or a particular class.[58]

If Mr. King could be believed, the Liberal party had squatter's rights to the middle of the road.

The Liberals' National Campaign Committee under the chairmanship of J. G. Gardiner had begun serious planning in January 1945.[59] The party's coffers benefited from the fear of the C.C.F. and from grateful

[54]House of Commons, *Debates*, April 16, 1945, p. 886.

[55]The extent of the preparations is perhaps best shown by the fact that Col. Stacey disposed of the Canadian Army Pacific Force in nine pages, *Official History of the Second World War*, I, 510–18.

[56]See National Liberal Committee, *Reference Handbook, 1945* (Ottawa, 1945), p. A-11. Copy in McNaughton Papers, File 970–30.

[57]National Liberal Committee, *Programme for Canada* (n.p., 1945).

[58]Radio broadcast, June 8, 1945, quoted in Pickersgill, *Liberal Party*, p. 31.

[59]Gardiner Papers, J. G. Fogo to Gardiner, Jan. 25, 1945.

war contractors, and there was little difficulty in finding the money needed to fight the election.[60] "I hear that the Grits tapped everyone whoever had a contract with Munitions and Supplies [*sic*]," Hanson said, not overstating the case at all. "It is said that the Government's 'slush' fund exceeded five million dollars."[61] The organization was efficient, and the party's prospects were better than anyone would have dared to hope in the midst of the conscription crisis a bare six months before. Even Quebec looked promising. "It is reported," an official of the National Liberal Committee wrote to Gardiner of the Quebec situation, "that considerably more King sentiment is evident now than was the case several weeks ago."[62] The Liberals seemed on the upswing.

The situation was reversed for the C.C.F. The high hopes of September 1943, when the party had led on the opinion polls, had faded under the combined impact of the Liberals' adoption of social welfare and the anti-socialist campaign. Many electors who had voted C.C.F. in Ontario in 1943, one Conservative was advised by an opinion-sampling agency, now refused to admit having done so.[63] In 1943, too, as the always practical Gardiner had observed, it was impossible "to scare people with Communism . . . at least so long as the battle [was] going on in Russia."[64] By May 1945, the wartime alliance with the Soviet Union already beginning to sour, there were no longer any compunctions against linking social democracy with communism. Some, of course, like the *Globe and Mail* in an editorial on May 25, 1945, entitled "Hitler Was A Socialist," continued to link Nazi ideology with the C.C.F. These attacks had some effect. The C.C.F. had done the spade work for social welfare, popularized the ideas, and forced the old parties to adjust their platforms and policies. Now it seemed as if the party's role was to be a radical bogey, useful only to frighten the electors into voting for the capitalist parties. The difficulties were reflected in C.C.F. finances. In 1943, plans had been drawn for a $500,000 campaign chest, but only some $80,000 nationally was raised for the election. Plans for a

[60]*Ibid.*, and May 5, 1945. For evidence of the availability of funds, see the Lambert Diaries, April–June, 1945.

[61]Hanson Papers, Personal Correspondence, Hanson to H. A. Bruce, June 14, 1945. The Lambert Diaries provide ample evidence to support Hanson's contention. March 15, 1944: "C.D.H[owe] spoke to me . . . about taking hold of finances of organization. I told him . . . I would help him organize the thing after certain lists were supplied from M[unitions] & S[upply]. . . ." March 16, 1944: "Prepared lists of 37 names of people who served Govt during last 4 years mainly through M&S who should be asked by CDH to help him."

[62]Gardiner Papers, J. G. Fogo to Gardiner, May 5, 1945.

[63]Adamson Papers, "Study of Public Opinion and Political Preference of Voters, West York," February 1945.

[64]Gardiner Papers, Gardiner to T. H. Wood, Oct. 1, 1943.

$300,000 fund in Ontario were similarly affected, and the provincial party managed to collect only $84,000. These sums,[65] though disappointing when compared with the party's roseate expectations, were nevertheless far more than the C.C.F. had previously attained. The socialists would make gains in the election, but at whose expense was still unclear.

The Conservatives had begun their election preparations in July 1944. The party had commissioned McKim Advertising Limited to plan the campaign themes—the first time this had been done in Canada— and in discussion with the headquarters staff and the caucus, a number of ideas were canvassed. Some M.Ps wanted "to go after Quebec"; others preferred to paint the Liberals and the C.C.F. as birds of a feather.[66] The consensus, however, was to concentrate on Bracken and to present the situation to the people as "Bracken or socialism." The campaign planners were aware that in the West the difficult task would be to overcome the popular belief, assiduously spread by the Liberal press, that Bracken was a "front" for the interests of the East.[67] The result of these early discussions was a campaign centred on the theme "Win with Bracken." Advertisements featured "John Bracken—The Man," "John Bracken—The Worker," "The Farmer," "The Progressive."[68] The advertising strategy was carefully co-ordinated, but the Liberals were able to charge that the Tories were selling their leader as if he were "a new breakfast food, or a new brand of soap."[69]

The party's campaign was an expensive one, but for the first time since the election of 1930 there was no difficulty with finances.[70] By May 28, 1945, with two weeks to go before the election and with fund-raising still in full swing,[71] the party had collected more than $550,000, almost evenly divided between Toronto and Montreal.[72] Of this sum, more than half had been committed to advertising, and this expense mounted rapidly as the election approached.[73] Substantial funds were

[65]C.C.F. Records, Vol. 1, Minutes of National Council Meeting, Sept. 7–9, 1945; C.C.F. Ontario Records, Minutes of Provincial Council and Executive Meetings, Vol. 2, Minutes of Provincial Council, May 15, 1945.

[66]Progressive Conservative Party Files, File P-2-G, "General Summary of Discussions on Progressive-Conservative Campaign," Appendix, July 26, 1944. The election advertising was handled by McConnell Eastman Limited once again, however.

[67]*Ibid.*, July 24, 1944.

[68]*Ibid.*, "Ads 1945 General Election"; File P-2-G, Ads.

[69]Mackenzie King, quoted in *Ottawa Journal*, June 9, 1945.

[70]Bell Interview, Aug. 24, 1964.

[71]Progressive Conservative Party Files, Financial Matters, Bell to various firms, May 31, 1945.

[72]*Ibid.*, Private Finances, Bell to Tory, May 28, 1945.

[73]*Ibid.*, Finances-General, M. Eastman to R. Brown, May 13, 1945.

also allotted to the constituencies. In Manitoba, for example, no riding received less than $1500 from the Winnipeg provincial headquarters, and one received $14,000. Most Manitoba candidates were assisted with speakers, free radio time, advertising paraphernalia, and organizing help.[74] In all the Conservatives spent at least $1,500,000 in the election.[75]

Other steps were taken to help the candidates. The military vote overseas was thoroughly canvassed, and gifts of cigarettes were sent along with campaign literature.[76] In addition, the party contracted for an entire issue of the "independent" monthly, *Canadian Veteran*, and arranged for wide distribution overseas and in Canada.[77] Conservative headquarters conducted "candidates' schools" in Ottawa and in several provincial capitals where the prospective parliamentarians were instructed on constituency organization, on the role of women and youth in the campaign, and on public relations and finances.[78] A national speakers' bureau was also established,[79] and preparations were made for the most effective use of the party's allotted free time on the national radio network.[80] In all, the party fielded 204 candidates (only twenty-nine of sixty-five seats were contested in Quebec), proudly boasting that more than half were veterans.[81] The Conservative campaign organization, in all its aspects, was probably as efficient as any in Canadian history to that time.

The selection of the issues upon which the party's fight for election would be based was not as successful. By force of circumstance perhaps more than by the convictions of its leader, the party found itself entering the campaign wedded to the twin policies of conscription and free enterprise. The Conservative commitment to free enterprise had never been in doubt. Both the Port Hope and the Winnipeg platforms had been explicit on this point. But after the Liberals turned in earnest to

[74]Bell Papers, Vol. 1, Doc [R. D. Guy] to Bell, June 15, 1945.

[75]Confidential source.

[76]Progressive Conservative Party Files, File E-6-G, "Memorandum re Active Service Vote," Jan. 24, 1945.

[77]*Ibid.*, File BC-B-2, Bell to C. B. Barker, Nov. 7, 1944. The Liberals were worried about the Conservatives' success overseas (Gardiner Papers, Gardiner to Fogo, March 26, 1945).

[78]Progressive Conservative Party Files, "Candidate Meeting Material"; Stevens Papers, Vol. 158, "Minutes of Federal Organizing Meeting, Vancouver, Jan. 27, 1945."

[79]Progressive Conservative Party Files, "National Speakers' Bureau," Bell to R. C. Levy, Jan. 15, 1945.

[80]The division of free time was Liberal—21 quarter-hours; Conservative—15; C.C.F.—14 (Gardiner Papers, Fogo to Gardiner, Feb. 6, 1945). Cf. Stevens Papers, Vol. 158, Minutes, Jan. 27, 1945.

[81]*Public Opinion*, III (June 4, 1945), 1; *Halifax Chronicle*, May 15, 1945, p. 1. R. A. Bell's assessment of the efficiency of the campaign staff is in P.A.C., John Bracken Papers, Vol. 3, Memorandum, Bell to Bracken, June 9, 1945.

social welfare, the party was virtually forced to concentrate on the aspects of policy that differentiated it from the government. "Mr. Bracken emphasizes," the party's *Speaker's Handbook* stated,

that, unlike either of its political opponents, the Progressive Conservative Party sets opportunity and prosperity as the goal which the nation should attain, rather than the rationed scarcity of the Socialistic state, or the elaborate and burdensome system of social security which the Liberal Party is seeking to create. Social security legislation is necessary to prevent the hazards of life bearing too heavily on any one person or group, but the main emphasis must be placed on reducing these hazards or eliminating them.

The functions of government, the Conservatives believed, were to provide leadership, give information, formulate policy, and regulate and correlate the efforts of the various economic groups in the community—not to administer every detail of life.[82] This was not a *laissez-faire* policy, but neither was it as progressive in spirit as the Port Hope or Winnipeg platforms. To the average Canadian, the Conservative message on social security must have sounded unenthusiastic. The Liberals and the C.C.F., on the other hand, were pulling out all the stops and frankly stressing the benefits they could offer. "Cash on hand is good payment," the Liberal *Halifax Chronicle-Herald* told its readers on May 16. "It is the sort of payment the Liberal party has made to the people of Canada during the last administration."

If time had weakened the Conservative party's commitment to social security, it had strengthened some Conservatives' attitudes to conscription. The rancour of the conscription crisis persisted, and the success of reinforcements as an election issue seemingly had been demonstrated in Grey North. Still, there was little enthusiasm for conscription in the party caucus. As Rodney Adamson noted in his diary:

March 20, 1945:—To caucus at 10. . . . the Globe and Mail want us to bring in amendment on Conscription on the San Francisco resolution [approving Canadian participation in the U.N. Conference there] of all places. Speak rather bitterly against this. Find out definitely it is McCullagh again. . . .
March 21, 1945:—Away to caucus at 10. . . . The George McCullagh amendment on conscription is turned down unanimously. Only Dr. Bruce makes a play for it. Eventually after two hours of discussion NO amendment is going to be made.[83]

In view of this opposition, Bracken's subsequent course was a curious

---

[82]*Progressive Conservative Speaker's Handbook, 1945*, Leadership, Section II.
[83]Adamson Papers, Diary, March 20, 21, 1945.

one. In his first major speech of the campaign on May 16, 1945, at Ottawa, he promulgated his Charter for a Better Canada. The portion of his speech that attracted the most attention, however, was his pledge to carry out Canada's "fair share of responsibility" in the Pacific and to use physically fit draftees to fill manpower requirements "insofar as Canadian troops have been promised or are needed."[84] Graydon had stated this to be Conservative policy in December 1944, but his pledge had been forgotten with the end of the war in Europe. With fatal timing, the Conservative party had again nailed conscription to the masthead. Possibly Bracken's speech was prompted by two reasons: first, conscription was still being demanded by influential figures in Toronto, led by McCullagh and his newspaper; and second, an anti-Quebec line was believed to have appeal in English Canada, and especially in Ontario.[85] This latter reason carried added weight because the date of a provincial election in Ontario had been carefully arranged to be one week before the federal election. If Drew could sweep Ontario, the effect would be felt on the national scene.

The call for conscription for the Pacific theatre served notice that the Conservatives had written off Quebec in the election. Indeed there was little left to write off. The party's hard-line policy had scattered French-speaking Conservatives, and *bleus* were now found in the Union Nationale, in the *nationaliste* Bloc Populaire Canadien, and in the Independent ranks. It came as no surprise, therefore, when Premier Duplessis announced that the Union Nationale supported no federal party, and when former Conservatives like Onésime Gagnon and Frédéric Dorion vehemently denounced Bracken as an imperialist.[86]

As a result there were few Conservatives in Quebec to object when Bracken deliberately flogged the race issue for all it was worth. "They have drained your firesides of your sons and they have deceived Quebec in this war," Bracken told an Ontario audience.

The Government has now announced that it will expect the war in the Pacific to be fought by those who volunteer. The Government's policy in this respect is but another bid for Quebec's support. . . . They are asking your sons to die in double the numbers of others and they are asking Quebec to continue to be misrepresented before the world. The patriotic among Canada's sons will again be asked to die for Canada, while others will stay at home to populate the land their brothers saved.[87]

[84]*Ottawa Journal*, May 16, 1945, p. 13; *Montreal Star*, May 16, 1945, p. 1.
[85]E.g., Adamson Papers, "Study of Public Opinion. . . ."
[86]*Le Devoir*, 16 mai 1945, pp. 2, 3; 6 juin 1945, p. 4.
[87]Montreal *Gazette*, May 17, 1945, p. 1.

Karl Homuth, one of the Conservative members who had steadfastly opposed compulsory service in caucus, followed his leader's line and now charged that the government had sown "dissension, dissatisfaction and disunity" because it "lacked the courage" to enforce conscription.[88] Mackenzie King had failed the people of Canada, the *Globe and Mail* trumpeted (May 18, 1945), "because he put cheap partisan politics ahead of the national interest." "Mr. King," the *Ottawa Journal* stated on June 5, "has been campaigning in Quebec, and winning support in Quebec, and continuing himself in office because of Quebec, through appeals to Quebec's prejudices. It is," the Conservative *Journal* concluded, "one of the ugly, tragic things of Canadian politics."

There was undoubtedly a substantial element of truth in the Conservative attacks, but their impact was weakened by the support the party gave to anti-conscriptionist Independents in Quebec. Attempts to unite the anti-King forces into a bloc led by P. J. A. Cardin had finally collapsed in the middle of May. This had been followed by an announcement from Paul Lafontaine, a principal Conservative organizer in Quebec, that the party would support thirty-three Independent candidates who differed with the official policy only on "points which are not essential."[89] Lafontaine had had no authority to make this statement, but he could not readily be disavowed. As a result, Bracken was compelled to issue yet another of his many statements of clarification:

In June last, at Guelph, . . . I stated that the Progressive Conservative party had no deal and would make no deal with any other political group and would not deceive either French or English. . . .
I now state again that this is still our position. . . .
There are some constituencies in the province of Quebec where, as has been announced, no Progressive Conservative candidate has been nominated. It does not follow that we support any candidate who has been nominated in those constituencies—the fact is that, in five of them we do not.
With respect to certain Independents in other Quebec constituencies . . . the party organization in Quebec has been frank and honest in stating its position. If in these latter constituencies there are candidates who support us on our policies of national unity . . . so much the better. If they differ with us in certain matters—such as, for example, our manpower policy—that is their privilege. . . .[90]

Bracken's statement gave the Liberals the opportunity they needed in French Canada. "I saw the defeat of Sir Wilfrid Laurier in 1911," Mackenzie King told a Montreal audience on June 3, "a defeat caused

[88]*Ottawa Journal*, May 2, 1945, p. 1.
[89]"Backstage at Ottawa," *Maclean's* LVIII (July 15, 1945), 15.
[90]*Winnipeg Free Press*, May 21, 1945, p. 4.

by the alliance of the nationalists of this province with the Tories of the other provinces."[91] A vote against King, the Liberals now could say, was a vote for Bracken—"le toryisme, voilà l'ennemi."[92] "Bracken et le parti conservateur," a Liberal newspaper advertisement blared, "ce sont les hauts tarifs et les petits salaires. C'est le parti ennemi-né de Québec, qui a trahi en 1911 et 1917. Il fait sa campagne sur le dos des Canadiens-français."[93] This was only the usual election exaggeration, but the situation in Quebec had altered greatly since 1944 and early 1945. The war was over, the conscription threat gone. "Personne ne pouvait nier," a French-Canadian historian later noted, "que Mackenzie King et ses collègues avaient tenté de ménager l'opinion canadienne-française avec un certain succès. Ils avaient au moins réussi à prévenir un conflit de races trop violent. La plupart des Canadiens français leur en étaient reconnaissants."[94]

The Conservative party's prospects in Quebec were non-existent, but the Ontario situation was much brighter. George Drew won a complete victory on June 4, taking sixty-six of ninety seats in the legislature. Significantly the C.C.F. was badly trounced, ending up with only eight representatives. The impetus the Ontario success gave to the federal party was squandered, however, when Drew, acting against Bracken's wishes,[95] flew to the West to campaign for the national party. "The federal issue," the victorious premier declared, "is exactly the same as was decided in Ontario. The issue is the same because the Dominion Liberal party through its open acceptance of support of the Communists has bound itself to the Socialist doctrines which are opposed to the principles of the Progressive Conservative party."[96] Drew's speeches put the cap on the West's conviction that, as the Liberals had charged, the Conservative party was controlled from Toronto. This impression was further strengthened when George McCullagh, an effective and persuasive speaker, rather than the halting Bracken, delivered the party's closing radio addresses of the campaign.[97]

The result of the election was clear cut, and the Mackenzie King government was returned to office with 127 seats and a narrow majority.

[91]Montreal *La Presse*, 4 juin 1945, p. 1.
[92]G. O. Rothney, "Quebec Saves Our King," *Canadian Forum*, XXV (July, 1945), 83.
[93]Montreal *La Presse*, 9 juin 1945, p. 23.
[94]Brunet, *La présence anglaise*, pp. 250–1.
[95]Bell Interview, Aug. 24, 1964.
[96]*Ottawa Journal*, June 5, 1945, p. 1.
[97]"The General Election," *Round Table*, XXXVI (Sept., 1945), 361; "The Meaning of the Elections," *Canadian Forum*, XXV (July, 1945), 81; Bell Interview, Aug. 24, 1964.

The C.C.F. won twenty-eight seats and polled more than 800,000 votes, but the social democrats were shut out east of the prairie provinces except for lone seats in New Brunswick and Nova Scotia.[98] The Conservatives increased their strength to sixty-eight, a gain of twenty-eight seats, but forty-eight of these were in Ontario constituencies. The party won seven seats in the Maritimes, two in Quebec, and five in British Columbia. It was in the West and overseas that disappointment was greatest. Bracken's country, the area in which the party had hoped for thirty-five seats, returned only five Conservatives, including, at last, the leader. Although Mackenzie King lost his own seat of Prince Albert (Saskatchewan) on overseas ballots, his party to everyone's surprise won the largest share of the military vote with the C.C.F. running a close second. For all their expectations, the Conservatives trailed both their opponents on the soldiers' vote.[99]

The pattern of the results finally demonstrated that Arthur Meighen's reasoning in 1942, if it had ever been correct, no longer had any validity in 1945. The old leader had been convinced that the C.C.F. would sweep the industrial areas, and he had selected Bracken to give the Conservative party an entrée to the farming sections of the country. But in fact the C.C.F. lost everything in Ontario, the Conservatives increased their strength there, and Bracken proved unable to do substantially better on the prairies than his predecessors. What had gone wrong?

The election itself had probably been lost because of the issues. Some had been forced upon the Conservatives; some they had chosen. Hanson saw the causes of the defeat as three: family allowances, conscription,

[98]The election results were as follows (1940 results in brackets):

	Lib.	P.C.	C.C.F.	S.C.	Other
P.E.I.	3(4)	1(0)	—	—	—
N.S.	8(10)	3(1)	1(1)	—	—
N.B.	7(5)	3(5)	1(0)	—	—
P.Q.	56(64)	2(1)	—	—	7
Ont.	34(57)	48(25)	—	—	—
Man.	10(15)	2(1)	5(1)	—	—
Sask.	2(12)	1(2)	18(5)	—	(2)
Alta.	2(7)	2(0)	—	13(10)	—
B.C.	5(10)	5(4)	4(1)	—	1(1)
Yukon	—	1(1)	—	—	—
TOTAL	127(184)	68(40)	29(8)	13(10)	8(3)

[99]The military vote was divided as follows: Liberal—118,537; C.C.F.—109,679; Conservative—87,530. Only 45 per cent of the eligible service personnel voted at all. Toronto *Globe and Mail*, June 20, 1945, p. 1.

and Liberal money. Family allowances were very popular in poorer districts, he said, and conscription for the Pacific was not. "The war ended too soon."[100] These views were shared by others in the party. The Manitoba organizer put conscription first on his list of reasons for the poor showing in Bracken's province,[101] as did a rural Ontario candidate.[102] Arthur Meighen, who had taken no part in the campaign, saw things differently and placed the blame on the "business element of Canada,"

whose sympathies were definitely with the Conservative party [but who] scuttled to cover in quite substantial numbers, thinking that a vote for King was more likely to result in a sure defeat for the C.C.F. than a vote for the Conservative Party, which, before the election, had so small a number in the house—only forty. This conduct those who are at all capable of an intelligent appraisement will now know to have been stupid.[103]

There were other reasons. John W. Dafoe had correctly appraised the party's problem in January 1943. The Conservatives, he said then, would have to accept Bracken's leadership, and this leadership would have to be in keeping with Bracken's past if he were to be a success. But, in the first place, the new leader proved unable to construct the entirely new organization he needed, and the Old Guard retained a large element of control. The resurgence of the party's right wing, led by the Toronto Tories, increased this problem and necessarily resulted in the tailoring of Progressive Conservative policies to fit the demands of this influential segment of the party. Had Bracken entered the House of Commons and won a name for himself there, this Toronto control might have slackened, but outside parliament he could do little.

The high hopes of December 1942 had been dashed. The Progressive Conservative party was once again in Opposition, and it was more than ever an Ontario party. The radical proposals of 1942 no longer seemed radical in 1945, so far had the political centre of gravity shifted in the intervening years, and Mackenzie King had forced the Conservatives out of the middle-of-the-road position they had held so briefly. The only satisfaction for the Conservatives was that the C.C.F. had been checked and that Bracken at last had a seat in the House of Commons. Before long, however, Bracken's suspected inadequacies as an Opposition leader would be apparent, and the former Manitoba premier would find himself a lonely western farmer leading an Ontario party.

[100]Hanson Papers, Personal Correspondence, Hanson to Bruce, June 14, 1945; Hanson to G. Black, M.P., June 29, 1945.
[101]Bell Papers, Vol. 1, R. D. Guy to Bell, June 15, 1945.
[102]Progressive Conservative Party Files, File O-H-2, A. Nicholson to Bracken, June 14, 1945.
[103]Meighen Papers, Meighen to L. Hunt, June 13, 1945.

9.   Conclusion

The Conservative party entered the Second World War under the leadership of R. J. Manion, committed to a policy opposing conscription for overseas military service and searching for a *rapprochement* with Quebec. Six years later, the Progressive Conservative party, led by John Bracken, fought the election of June 1945 as an English-speaking free enterprise party pledged to enforce conscription for the continuing war in the Pacific. Leaders had come and gone in the intervening years, policies had been made and abandoned. The party had come close to political extinction, but it had regenerated itself, driven by the belief that Conservatism was the only possible alternative to a postwar socialist government. The calculations, schemes, and changes in policy came to naught, however, and the party emerged from the war still in a minority in the House of Commons and still uncertain within itself concerning Conservatism's role in Canadian life. What had happened?

Conscription was the dominant issue of the war years, and the cause of most of the troubles of the Conservative party. Manion had declared against it in March 1939 and his policy had been continued after his political demise by R. B. Hanson. But there was no satisfaction for the Conservative party in this tactic of self-denial. Conscription had been the party's policy in 1917, and many of its followers, probably a majority, believed it should be so again. Certainly Arthur Meighen, the architect of conscription in the Great War and the Conservative of Conservatives, believed this. When the coup of November 1941 put him at the helm once again, he quickly converted the party into a vehicle for the support of conscription. Whether Meighen's backers had ulterior motives or not, his conscription campaign in early 1942 faced the Mackenzie King government with its most serious test until 1944. But the attempt to split the government foundered on Meighen's defeat in York South. Conscription and national government had been his only issues, and these had fallen before the social welfare attack of the C.C.F. Meighen's timing had been wrong. The war was not as close to Canadians as it was later to be. The army had not yet gone into action, there were still relatively few casualties, and the Americans were in the war now, thus ensuring eventual victory for the Allied cause.

Conscription was a dead issue to everyone but Meighen after the spring of 1942. The Port Hope Conference endorsed compulsory service, as did the Winnipeg convention, but these resolutions seemed mere obeisance to a cherished but no longer potent tenet of the party's credo. The issue was not revived until after D-day when C. P. McTague unexpectedly nailed conscription to the mast. Within a few months, emotions in English-speaking Canada were fully aroused by the reports from overseas, and the Conservative party for the first time in the war spoke clearly and with one voice. The reinforcements question won the Grey North by-election for the party in February 1945, but this victory deluded some Conservatives into thinking that conscription could win a general election. This hope was crushed by the end of the war in Europe, and the party's subsequent pledge of conscription for the Pacific was a liability in June 1945.

Conscription had killed the Conservatives during the Second World War. And yet, conscription was the only issue that could have toppled the government. The subject was charged with emotionalism, with racial feeling, with memories of 1917. If Mackenzie King, with his skilful temporizing, had not been in office; if Arthur Meighen had been a better politician and had won the York South by-election; if, deep within its soul, the Conservative party had not had scruples about using the race cry; if, in fact, the conscription crisis of 1917 had never taken place; if all these factors had not been present, and if the Conservative party had firmly demanded compulsory service throughout the war, then the result of the interparty struggle might have been different. As it was, for all its cultivation of expediency on this issue, the Conservative party again won a conscriptionist reputation and received nothing for its pains but defeat. Quebec remained a Liberal stronghold, and much of the rest of Canada chose to give its vote to others. But this is a purely political assessment. In terms of the future harmony of the nation, it was fortunate indeed that some Conservatives stood out against those who would have played upon the divisions between the two Canadian peoples.

The second great development of the war years was the emergence of Canadian social democracy as a potent force. The Co-operative Commonwealth Federation had been seven years old at the outbreak of the war in 1939, and its electoral support was severely limited. Even this support was virtually wiped out in the election of 1940 as the party suffered for its prewar isolationism and from a campaign that concentrated more on damning war profiteers than Nazis. But times change, and attitudes and policies with them. By early 1942, the C.C.F. had produced a suitably aggressive war policy and an attractive platform of social welfare measures. Its plea for support struck a responsive note among the working-class voters of York South, and Meighen's stunning defeat, a grievous blow to Conservatism, was the first sign of the new-found appeal of the C.C.F. By September 1943 the party had formed the Loyal Opposition in Ontario and led the old parties in the national opinion polls; the next year, the C.C.F. became the government in Saskatchewan, establishing the first socialist administration on the North American continent. In striking contrast to weak and divided socialism in the United States, the C.C.F. seemed close to national power.

The effect of the socialists' success was profound. The first to be hurt by the C.C.F. and the party most in need of resuscitation, the Conservatives reacted most quickly. Successful resistance to the demands of the C.C.F. required a partial incorporation of their programme. Led by J. M. Macdonnell, a most uncharacteristic Toronto Tory and next to Meighen probably the most influential Conservative of the war years, the party embarked on an ambitious and largely sincere attempt to remodel its attitudes and policies. The democratic strain in Toryism, evident in Meighen's early career, in Bennett's New Deal, in Stevens' Reconstruction party, again came to the fore and the Conservatives moved into the vital centre of Canadian political life. Although Bracken's selection was engineered by Meighen who saw the Manitoba premier primarily as the leader of a non-partisan conscriptionist movement, the new leader confirmed the party in its progressive role. If the Liberals had remained quiescent, the Bracken party might have succeeded in its attempts to hold the political centre, midway between Liberal "reaction" and C.C.F. "revolution."

Mackenzie King did not make his move until a year after the Winnipeg convention. His greatest advantage was that he was in office, able to give the electorate something more concrete than promises of eventual reform; his re-adoption of the Liberal principles of 1919 made social welfare legislation a reality and blunted the attacks of both opposition parties. The baby bonus was the first and most arresting of King's measures. When this was unwisely characterized as political bribery by Bracken, Drew, and Bruce, King must have known that he had nothing to fear from Progressive Conservatism. It was always a simple matter thereafter to paint the Tories as unchanged reactionaries masquerading as progressives. The centre of gravity of Canadian politics had been moved to the left by the pressures of the C.C.F. And Mackenzie

King had triumphed over both opposing parties and won back Liberalism's hold on the middle of the road.

Where did this leave the Conservative party? The long struggle between those who wished to make conscription and free enterprise the keystones of Conservative policy and those who wanted a party dedicated to social welfare seemingly had been resolved at the Winnipeg convention. There the Port Hopefuls had carried the day, winning a progressive leader and a platform that committed the party to the welfare state. But the gains of December 1942 had been frittered away. Bracken had declined to seek a seat in parliament; the party's financial organization had remained firmly in the hands of the old-line Toronto and Montreal crowd; and the vitally necessary sweeping reorganization of the party's machinery had been delayed until months after the Winnipeg convention. When the C.C.F. scored heavily in the Ontario elections of 1943 and showed impressive strength in the national opinion polls, and when the Liberals turned to a social welfare policy, the initiative slipped from Conservative hands. For all its progressive resolutions and for all its protestations of sincerity, the Conservative party was back in its accustomed position on the right of the Canadian political spectrum.

The resulting resurgence of the old guard Tories renewed the battle within the sorely tried party. The "Toronto scheme" of November 1943, a by-product of George Drew's success in Ontario, was the first overt challenge to Bracken's leadership. Still out of the House of Commons, Bracken survived this passage of arms. By the summer of 1944, however, he seemed to have lost all but the shadow of control over his party. The caucus overruled him on family allowances, and C. P. McTague foisted conscription on the party once again. The crisis of November 1944 and the Grey North by-election seemed to confirm the success of the reinforcements question as a vote-catching issue, and this completed the rout. Over the opposition of the parliamentary caucus, conscription became party policy for the election of 1945, all hope of success in Quebec was abandoned, and the party again fell victim to Mackenzie King.

What had happened to Conservatism, it now seems clear, was that the party's conscious efforts to establish itself as an omnibus party on the North American model had failed. Mackenzie King had been successful in moulding the Liberals into a model party of consensus. And, thought Conservatives, he had done this with nothing more than a spurious and cynical appeal for national unity. To oppose King, imitate him. Tweedledum and Tweedledee must be made as similar as possible. Principles such as support for conscription and a cautious attitude to social welfare had to be sacrificed for popularity. There was nothing wrong with these principles, progressive Conservatives believed, except that they were out of tune with the times. And they were right. Under skilful leadership, the party might have succeeded in becoming all things to all Canadians. But Bracken was no Mackenzie King; he brought with him few western votes, and he was unable to control the party's right wing, the bearer of the torch for principled Conservatism.

Of necessity, the continuing conflict within the party was thinly papered over with compromise, but the facade of unity between the opposing factions could not be maintained by ineffectual leadership. Appeased by Mackenzie King's concessions and guided by his indefatigable propagandists, the public was never allowed to forget the contradictions inherent in Progressive Conservatism.

The history of the Conservative party during the Second World War is one of almost unrelieved failure. Desperately weak in leadership, torn between adherence to principle and expediency, and wracked by internal conflicts, the party came perilously close to extinction. Ironically, Conservatism survived as a viable force only because of the C.C.F., not through any inherent strength of its own. Whatever the reason, Conservatism had played the politics of party survival and won.

APPENDIXES

Appendix 1

THE GENERAL EXECUTIVE OF THE DOMINION
CONSERVATIVE ASSOCIATION

As constituted by the Conservative caucus on May 30, 1941, the General Executive was to consist of the following persons:[1]

Presidents of Provincial Conservative Associations
Provincial Association Representatives[2]
  Ontario and Quebec—14 each
  Other provinces—8 each
Young Canada Conservative Club Representatives—4
D.C.A. National Executive—4
Dominion Acting Leader
Dominion Publicity Chairman
Provincial Conservative Leaders
Secretaries, Provincial Associations
Conservative Privy Councillors
Members of Parliament
Senators
Defeated Candidates, 1940 Election[3]
Members of Conservative Provincial Governments still in the Legislatures

Despite this elaborate structure, invitations to the November 1941 conference do not appear to have followed this plan. Table I shows the basis on which invitations were issued by province and category (acceptances indicated in brackets).[4]

[1]Meighen Papers, B. O. Hooper to Meighen, Nov. 29, 1941 (mimeographed form letter).
[2]The original caucus decision was to have 7 representatives from Ontario and Quebec and 4 from each of the other provinces. This was changed to 14 and 8. Progressive Conservative Party Files, File PEI-P-2, MacNicol to P. W. Turner, July 31, 1941 (mimeographed form letter).
[3]The inclusion of defeated candidates was a "stupid blunder" by MacNicol (Bell Papers, Vol. 1, Bell to John Lederle, Jan. 6, 1942, letter not sent.
[4]Hanson Papers, File O-160-2, "Invitation Summary," Nov. 6, 1941.

TABLE I

	Yukon	B.C.	Alta.	Sask.	Man.	Ont.	P.Q.	N.B.	N.S.	P.E.I.
D.C.A. Executive	2(2)	3	10(5)	10(6)	11(6)	21(17)	15(12)	13(6)	7(3)	10(2)
Privy Councillors*	—	—	—	—	—	9(2)	3(1)	—	1	—
Senators*	—	3(1)	2	4(2)	3(2)	8(3)	9(2)	6(2)	6(1)	—
M.P.s*	—	4(4)	—	2(2)	1(1)	23(20)	—	3(3)	1(1)	—
Defeated Candidates	—	11(1)	10	5	14(6)	53(20)	52(14)	4	11(1)	3
Prov. D.C.A. Secretaries	—	1	1	1	—	1(1)	—	2	—	1
TOTAL	2(2)	22(6)	23(5)	22(10)	29(15)	115(63)	79(29)	28(11)	26(6)	14(2)
GRAND TOTAL	360(149)									

*Not otherwise provided for in another category.

Appendix 2

This is not a platform. It is a statement of aims and beliefs subscribed to by a group of Conservatives from coast to coast in unofficial conference at Port Hope on September the 5th to 7th, 1942, in an effort to formulate a present-day political philosophy in terms of modern needs and the best traditions of the Conservative Party; we accordingly recognize that we do not speak for the Party in any official sense.

. . .

The statement following represents our views of a democratic society which we believe Canadians are prepared to fight for, and to guard and defend. We call on all thinking persons in Canada to view the plight of democratic states in the world today and to contemplate the grave dangers to Canadian democracy. These dangers lie equally in the totalitarianism of the right and the left. We suggest earnest study of our problems by citizen groups and especially by young men and women, interested as they and we are in revitalizing Canadian political thought and public life. We believe that Conservative philosophy will contribute greatly to this growth and we are interested in a revived study of its principles.

. . .

WAR

We of this conference re-affirm our loyalty to the British Commonwealth of Nations, and our earnest belief that the future of this Dominion as a free nation can best be secured as a member of the Commonwealth.

. . .

We demand immediate and complete conscription of the manpower of the Dominion for the Armed Services for duty in any part of the world.

. . .

When a country is actually committed to a war, the support of the war becomes a necessity that weighs on the whole nation. The sacrifice of a nation at war should be evenly distributed as well as privations, taxes, production, increase of work, material support and drafting of men. It is for Parliament and Government to decide as to the number of men to be enlisted, because the Parliament and Government alone have the keys to the situation. If few are required, so much the better. But at all events, those who are needed should be called automatically according to age classes, and with no favour or discrimination based on social position or other preferences. We condemn the practice, under the disguise of a voluntary system, of indirectly and deceitfully causing some classes to enlist for Overseas Service because of misfortune and by causing others to be deprived of employment or refused new work, and generally working on men through social or economic pressure. We also condemn the camouflaged calling of youth to camps, supposedly for Home Service training, but with a view to submitting them to all kinds of pressure and humiliation designed to force them to enlist for Overseas Service.

. . .

STATEMENT OF AIMS AND BELIEFS

We recall with pride and gratitude that our party rose to greatness through a fruitful partnership between two great races, French and English. We affirm our belief that the two cultures are part and parcel of our future development and that Canada's true greatness depends on sympathy and understanding between these two original races and all other races that have come to join in the building of our country.

. . .

The peace for which we fight must produce a world in which the benefits of specialized production are not destroyed by barriers to trade. We believe that the guiding principle of Canadian tariff policy should be the extent to which tariffs contribute to the assurance of gainful occupation and maintaining real standards of living.

. . .

In the field of labour relations, we advocate:

By Dominion Provincial agreement, or failing such an agreement then by appropriate legislation, that jurisdiction affecting industrial labour relations be vested in the Dominion;

Collective bargaining is desirable and necessary in the interests of labour, employers and consumers;

Workers shall have full freedom of association, self-organization and designation of representatives of their own choosing for the purpose of negotiating the terms and conditions of collective bargaining agreements;

. . .

Effective collective bargaining shall be guaranteed by making it an offence with appropriate penalties for an employer:
  (i) To attempt to interfere with or restrain any employee from taking part in trade union activities,
 (ii) To attempt to dominate or interfere with any labour organization,
(iii) To discriminate in regard to the hiring or employment of any employee with a view to encouraging or discouraging membership in any labour organization,
 (iv) To make any financial contribution to any labour organization, and
  (v) To refuse to bargain collectively with the collective bargaining agency;
. . .
For us it is an axiom that every person able and willing to work at socially useful tasks must be assured of gainful occupation with sufficient income to enable him to maintain a home and family. Full employment at fair wages and under proper and progressively improving standards is a fundamental objective of the state. The foundation stone of social and economic security is gainful occupation for all citizens, under conditions whereby they can be self-supporting through the exchange of their labour, their skills or the produce of their lands. We oppose relief as a substitute for work.
. . .
This conference for the achievement of that fundamental objective of the state—full employment at fair wages and under proper and progressively improving standards—and for the welfare and development of society strongly advocates the strengthening of the basic Canadian tradition of individual initiative and individual enterprise and opportunity and the freeing of economic activities from bureaucratic controls. Government authority, however, should be maintained and exercised wherever necessary to protect primary producers, workers and consumers from exploitation through such abuses as price-fixing combines, monopolies and patent cartels. To these ends we believe that Government should seek to create conditions under which the maximum volume of employment and the maximum national income may be assured through the initiative and enterprise of the people themselves but if, in any field, private enterprise fails or is unable to serve these national interests, government should directly or indirectly develop in that field socially useful undertakings.
. . .
We advocate a national long-range low-cost housing plan underwritten by government designed to make houses available on a lease-purchase

basis to all families, whether urban or rural, who are in the lower income brackets. Slum clearance because of its social benefits and employment possibilities should be undertaken as a governmental responsibility in order to provide housing on a less-than-cost basis for those unable to pay the full cost. The cost of slum clearance should be fully borne by the state. The plan should be a continuous one, but intensified in its operation in depression periods so as to provide employment for workers in the building trades as well as to stimulate the construction industries.
. . .

We believe that the reconstruction of post-war Canadian economy must be based upon the following principle enumerated in Section 5 of the Atlantic Charter:

"Fifth: They desire to bring about the fullest collaboration between all nations in the economic field with the object of securing, for all, improved labour standards, economic adjustment and social security."

A social security measure, the adoption of which we advocate, would include in a unified system:

(1) Unemployment insurance;
(2) Adequate payments for the maintenance of unemployables;
(3) Retirement insurance;
(4) The payment of increased old age pensions, at a reduced age, until such time as the retirement insurance scheme becomes fully operative;
(5) Adequate pensions for the blind;
(6) Adequate mothers' and widows' allowances; and
(7) A programme of medical service because we recognize the obligation of government to make available to every citizen adequate medical, dental, nursing, hospital and prenatal care so that health may be safe-guarded and preserved. To this end we advocate a national contributory and equitably financed system of medicine including the further advancement of public health and nutritional principles and their practical application.

Relief in lieu of work has been found to be the most wasteful of all forms of unemployment measures both in money and in human values, and we believe that it will not be again acceptable as a means of dealing with the problem. We believe that the encouragement of private initiative and enterprise and the undertaking of complementary development projects by the government will result in increasing gainful occupation and help to maintain the income of the people at a high level. Believing, notwithstanding the initial cost, that the result is a national gain, we advocate the various development projects and social security measures designated in this Report.

Appendix 3

EXCERPTS FROM THE WINNIPEG CONVENTION PLATFORM, DECEMBER 1942

PROGRESSIVE CONSERVATIVE CREED

Security

Freedom will be a reality when social security and human welfare become a fundamental objective of the nation. Freedom from want and freedom from fear are essential to a happy and normal family life. Want and fear must be banished and security brought within reach of all Canadians.

. . .

PROGRESSIVE CONSERVATIVE POLICY

WAR

We favour the formation of an Empire War Council in which Canada and the other Dominions shall be represented.

Recognizing that the world struggle in which Canada is engaged requires a total war effort, we believe in Compulsory National Selective Service, and that all those selected to serve in the Armed Forces should be available for service wherever required. We believe in the effective total utilization and proper allocation for war, by compulsion where necessary, of all the resources of Canada, including agriculture, industry and finance, as well as manpower, and that our aim should be at all times to bring about so far as human means can achieve it, an equality in sacrifice.

. . .

WAR VETERANS' REHABILITATION

In carrying out demobilization of Canada's Armed Forces the primary consideration should be the interest of those who have served. Demobilization should be based on the principle that members of the Armed Forces should not be discharged until their economic security is assured by placement in gainful employment or by assisted training and education to that end.

. . .

LABOUR RELATIONS

In order that free enterprise may be retained as the economic system best calculated to provide stability, prosperity and security and as a necessary part of that system that freedom of association and organization may be guaranteed to workers and in order that confidence may be restored between industry and labour and that sound labour relations may be established, this Convention recommends:

1. Uniform labour relations shall be established throughout the Dominion by Dominion-Provincial Agreements, appropriate legislation, or by vesting jurisdiction in industrial labour matters in the Dominion.

2. Collective bargaining is desirable and necessary in the interests of labour, industry and the social welfare of the people.

3. Workers shall have full freedom of association, organization and designation of representatives of their own choosing for the purpose of negotiating the terms and conditions of their employment and, when requested, employers shall be required to bargain collectively with their employees.

4. Well-defined machinery shall be established for the election and certification of the agency which is to be entitled to represent employees in collective bargaining negotiations where there is a dispute as to the collective bargaining agency.

5. Discrimination against any employee or prospective employee on account of his activities in respect of any labour organization shall be prohibited.

. . .

RECONSTRUCTION

Every person able and willing to work must be assured of gainful occupation with sufficient means to maintain a home and family. The objective is full employment at fair wages under progressively improving standards. We oppose relief as a substitute for work.

For the achievement of that objective—full employment at fair wages under progressively improving standards—and for the welfare and development of society, we strongly advocate the strengthening of the basic Canadian tradition of individual initiative and individual enterprise and opportunity, and the freeing of economic activities from bureaucratic controls. Government authority, however, should be maintained and exercised wherever necessary to protect primary producers, workers and consumers from exploitation through such abuses as price-fixing combines, monopolies and patent cartels. To those ends we believe that government should seek to create conditions under which the maximum volume of employment and the maximum national income may be assured through the initiative and enterprise of the people themselves.

It is the duty of the state:

(a) to maintain at high level the income and standard of living of the individual citizen, whose interests must always be paramount.

(b) To maintain the principle of private initiative and enterprise.

(c) To initiate, undertake and control projects of public and national benefit in those fields in which private enterprise is precluded from serving or is unable to serve the public interest.

. . .

A social security programme, the adoption of which we advocate, would include in a unified system:

(a) Unemployment insurance;

(b) Adequate payments for the maintenance of unemployables;

(c) Retirement insurance;

(d) The payment of increased Old Age pensions, at a reduced age, until such time as the retirement insurance scheme becomes fully operative;

(e) Adequate pensions for the blind;

(f) Adequate mothers' and widows' allowances.

We advocate the appointment of a Minister of Social Security and Reconstruction, charged with the administration of social security in this country.

The State's share of the cost of the social security system should be borne by the Dominion.

We recognize the obligation of government to make available to every citizen adequate medical, dental, nursing, hospital and pre-natal care, and to further advance public health and nutritional principles so that health may be safeguarded and preserved. This programme is to be financed under a contributory system supplemented by government assistance.

A Select Bibliography

There is no specialized Canadian bibliography comparable to the American Historical Association's *Guide to Historical Literature*. The best sources for contemporary works are the bibliographies regularly published in the *Canadian Historical Review* and the list of theses and dissertations in progress formerly listed in the September issue of the *CHR* and now being published by the Canadian Historical Association. Since 1948, the *Canadian Index to Periodicals* has provided a compendium of articles in Canadian magazines. Since 1951, the Public Archives of Canada has published *Canadiana*, a listing of articles and books concerning Canada and Canadians. Guides to archival materials include the *Annual Reports* and Manuscript Group catalogues published by the Public Archives and the reports of the various provincial repositories. As well, a union catalogue of manuscript sources has been prepared by the Public Archives.

PRIMARY SOURCES

Archival Collections

Bonar Law-Bennett Library, University of New Brunswick
R. B. Bennett Papers. A large, badly organized collection of limited value for the war years. The Public Archives of Canada is reorganizing the Papers.
Department of Public Records and Archives of Ontario, Prime Minister's Department
G. D. Conant Papers. A small collection of very limited value.
George A. Drew Papers. A small collection covering Drew's years as Leader of the Opposition in the legislature. There is little of value for federal politics.
Mitchell F. Hepburn Papers. A massive but well-culled collection.
Directorate of History, Canadian Forces Headquarters
General H.D.G. Crerar Papers.* The Papers are primarily of military interest but there are occasional letters of political significance.
General A. G. L. McNaughton Papers.* The Papers are of most value for the period 1944–45 and especially for the Grey North by-election of February 1945.
Military Files.* Massive holdings on all aspects of Canadian military history.

---

*Closed collection.

Douglas Library, Queen's University
  T. A. Crerar Papers. A very large collection covering the last sixty years of Canadian history. The material on World War I is better than that for World War II.
  Grant Dexter Papers.* A large collection of reporter's working files and memoranda. A large amount of the material is not in the Dafoe Papers.
  Charles Dunning Papers. A small collection stripped of most valuable material. Occasional letters of interest on the wartime anti-socialist campaign.
  Norman Lambert Papers. The Lambert Diaries are without doubt the best source for Liberal financial details.
  J. M. Macdonnell Papers. A large collection of limited value. Some correspondence relating to the Port Hope Conference.
  C. G. Powers Papers.* Large and valuable. Includes much political and military correspondence on all aspects of the war years.
  Norman McLeod Rogers Papers. The collection is of value only for the 1940 election.
  Lord Tweedsmuir Papers. Primarily literary but occasional tidbits of political information.
Franklin Delano Roosevelt Library
  F. D. Roosevelt Papers. A badly organized collection. For the purpose of this book, valuable mainly for the hundred or so letters exchanged with Mackenzie King.
Houghton Library, Harvard University
  J. Pierrepont Moffat Papers.* U.S. Minister in Canada, 1940–43. A good collection of high value for its dispassionate view of Canadian politics.
Public Archives of Canada
  Richard A. Bell Papers.* A small, extremely important collection of particular value for party organization and finance.
  John Bracken Papers. Correspondence from the Office of the Leader of the Opposition, with correspondence from 1942 to 1948. Very little of real value.
  A. Kirk Cameron Papers.* One volume of correspondence with T. A. Crerar is useful.
  Co-operative Commonwealth Federation Records.* A massive collection of some use for the York South by-election, party finance, and organization.
  John W. Dafoe Papers (microfilm). A good source on Liberal policy.
  John Graydon Papers. Correspondence of the House Leader of the Progressive Conservative Party from 1943 to 1945. Mostly routine material.
  C. D. Howe Papers. A large collection of importance for a history of war production. Very little political material.
  Ernest Lapointe Papers. A meagre collection of limited use.
  Robert J. Manion Papers. A large, very well organized collection of first rank importance for all aspects of Conservative policy, 1938–40. Some recently discovered office correspondence was added in 1968. Mostly routine materials.
  Arthur Meighen Papers. A massive collection of extraordinary value. When the Papers were examined in 1964, the important material had not yet been arranged.

---

*Closed collection.

J. Layton Ralston Papers.* A large and very important collection for all aspects of the war years.

Harry H. Stevens Papers. Stevens' Papers are most valuable for the years before 1939 and contain some useful material on the 1938 convention.

James S. Woodsworth Papers. Valuable for pre-war pacifist opinion.

Saskatchewan Provincial Archives (Regina)

G. H. Barr Papers. A Saskatchewan leader of the New Democracy, 1940. Only the correspondence with W. D. Herridge is useful.

James G. Gardiner Papers.* A huge, partially organized collection of primary importance for prairie history. Interesting material on federal elections, the rise of the C.C.F., and on Liberal organization. An excellent pamphlet collection, but very little in the way of cabinet documentation.

Sigmund Samuel Library, University of Toronto

Woodsworth Memorial Collection, C.C.F. Ontario Records. Minutes and records of the Ontario C.C.F., including some party newspapers and publications.

Private Collections

A. Rodney Adamson Papers, Port Credit, Ontario*

Occasional correspondence and yearly diaries of some importance as a record of Conservative caucuses.

Herbert A. Bruce Papers, Toronto*

A fairly large collection, including much correspondence with Meighen not found in the Meighen Papers. Mrs. Bruce's diary is also important. The collection has recently been acquired by Queen's University.

Richard B. Hanson Papers, Fredericton*

A large and valuable collection for all aspects of Conservatism during the war. The collection has been deposited at the P.A.C., except for material relating to New Brunswick politics which is now held at the University of New Brunswick.

J. Earl Lawson Scrapbooks, Cooksville, Ontario*

Two scrapbooks with some correspondence and clippings.

W. D. Herridge Papers, Toronto*

A small collection with some correspondence relating to conscription and the New Democracy.

Progressive Conservative Party Files*

A large collection recently re-organized and microfilmed by the P.A.C. Very valuable material on organization, finances, and personnel.

A Note on Additional Manuscript Sources

Many other collections would have been useful for this study. The late Hon. John Bracken's personal papers are not yet available; Gordon Graydon apparently left no personal files; the Drew Papers are in the P.A.C. but are firmly closed; Mackenzie King's Papers are still closed for the war years; George McCullagh's Papers were opened to one student in 1964, but they have since been sealed; and the Papers of the National Liberal Federation are closed pending sorting.

Other collections that might have been useful include the papers of Angus Macdonald and Ian Mackenzie. Both are closed indefinitely.

*Closed collection.

Interviews

Bell, The Hon. R. A.   Ottawa, July 15, 1964, August 24, 1964.
Bracken, The Hon. John.   Manotick, Ontario, June 1, 1963.
Crerar, The Hon. T. A.   Ottawa, July 17, 1964.
Coldwell, The Hon. M. J.   Ottawa, July 6, 1963.
Finlayson, Rod. K.   Ottawa, June 1, 1963, July 6, 1963.
Forsey, Dr. Eugene.   Ottawa, August 25, 1964.
Gardiner, F. G.   Toronto, September 8, 1964.
Golden, L. L. L.   New York City, October 5, 1965.
Green, The Hon. H. C.   Vancouver, August 23, 1966.
Jackman, H. R.   Toronto, September 8, 1964.
Jolliffe, E. B.   Toronto, June 2, 1965.
Macaulay, Leopold.   Toronto, September 17, 1964.
Macdonnell, The Hon. J. M.   Toronto, July 10, 1963, September 5, 1964.
MacRae, His Honour F. J.   Toronto, June 2, 1965.
McNaughton, The late General the Hon. A. G. L.   Ottawa, March 23, 1966.
McTague, The late Hon. C. P.   Toronto, June 1, 1965.
Price, Harry.   Toronto, September 8, 1964.
Roebuck, The Hon. Arthur.   Ottawa, July 15, 1964.
Rowe, The Hon. W. Earl.   Toronto, September 9, 1964.
Stevenson, John A.   Ottawa, July 15, 1964.

Government of Canada Documents

The Canada Gazette, LXXV (June 23, 1942).
Chief Electoral Officer, *Active Service Voting Regulations*. Ottawa, 1940.
———— *Report on By-Elections Held in 1942*. Ottawa, 1943.
———— *Report on the General Election of 1940*. Ottawa, 1941.
Dominion Bureau of Statistics. *Eighth Census of Canada, 1941*. 11 vols., Ottawa, 1944.
Parliament. House of Commons. *Debates*, 1938–45.
———— Senate. *Debates*, 1938–45.
Report on the Canadian Expeditionary Force to the Crown Colony of Hong Kong by Rt. Hon. Sir Lyman P. Duff, G.C.M.G., Royal Commissioner. Ottawa, 1942.
Secretary of State. *Report of the Committee on Election Expenses, 1966*. Ottawa, 1966.
Statutes of Canada, 4 George VI (1940). Ottawa, 1941.

Party Documents

National Conservative Party. *Resolutions Passed at the National Conservative Convention, July 5, 6, 7, 1938*. N.p., n.d.
National Liberal Committee. *Programme for Canada*. N.p., 1945.
———— *Reference Handbook, 1945*. Ottawa, 1945.
Progressive Conservative Party. *Freedom, Security, Opportunity and the British Partnership: Policy of the Progressive Conservative Party Adopted at the National Convention Held at Winnipeg, December 9th, 10th, and 11th, ·1942*. Ottawa, n.d.
———— *Progressive Conservative Speaker's Handbook, 1945*. Ottawa, 1945.

Memoirs, Autobiographies, Diaries, and Speeches
BARRETTE, ANTONIO. *Mémoires*, Montréal, 1966.

BRACKEN, JOHN. *John Bracken Says.* Toronto, 1944.

FORD, ARTHUR R. *As the World Wags On.* Toronto, 1950. Recollections of a Conservative journalist and editor. Interesting, but not always accurate in detail.

HOOKER, NANCY H., ed. *The Moffat Papers.* Cambridge, 1956. Published selections from the papers of the U.S. Minister to Canada, 1940–43.

KING, W. L. MACKENZIE. *Canada and the Fight for Freedom.* New York, 1944.

―――― *Canada at Britain's Side.* Toronto, 1941.

―――― *Mackenzie King to the People of Canada.* Ottawa, 1940. A collection of radio addresses.

MANION, ROBERT J. *Life is an Adventure.* Toronto, 1936. An exuberant autobiography written before Manion became Conservative leader.

MASSEY, VINCENT. *What's Past is Prologue: The Memoirs of the Right Honourable Vincent Massey, C.H.* Toronto, 1963. High Commissioner in the United Kingdom during the war. His contempt for Mackenzie King is made all too clear.

MEIGHEN, ARTHUR. *Unrevised and Unrepented.* Toronto, 1949. A collection of Meighen's greatest speeches.

PICKERSGILL, J. W. *The Mackenzie King Record.* I. *1939–44.* II. *1944–45.* Toronto, 1960, 1968. A very important source.

POPE, MAURICE A. *Soldiers and Politicians: The Memoirs of Lt.-Gen. Maurice A. Pope, C.B., M.C.* Toronto, 1962. The too discreet recollections of Canada's Ismay.

WARD, NORMAN, ed. *A Party Politician: The Memoirs of Chubby Power.* Toronto, 1966. The delightful—and very useful—memoirs of one of Mackenzie King's best cabinet ministers.

SECONDARY SOURCES

Dissertations and Theses

BELL, RUTH M. "Conservative Party National Conventions, 1927–56; Organization and Procedure." Unpublished M.A. thesis, Carleton University, 1965.

CAPLAN, GERALD L. "The Co-operative Commonwealth Federation in Ontario, 1932–45: A Study of Socialist and Anti-Socialist Politics." Unpublished M.A. thesis, University of Toronto, 1961.

HARRILL, EUGENE E. "The Structure of Organization and Power in Canadian Political Parties: A Study of Party Financing." Unpublished Ph.D. dissertation, University of North Carolina, 1958.

HOUGHAM, GEORGE M. "Minor Parties in Canadian National Politics, 1867–1940." Unpublished Ph.D. dissertation, University of Pennsylvania, 1954.

KOTTMAN, RICHARD. "The Diplomatic Relations of the United States and Canada, 1927–1941." Unpublished Ph.D. dissertation, Vanderbilt University, 1958.

LEDERLE, JOHN W. "The National Organization of the Liberal and Conservative Parties in Canada." Unpublished Ph.D. dissertation, University of Michigan, 1942.

NAUGLER, HAROLD A. "R. J. Manion and the Conservative Party, 1938–1940." Unpublished M.A. thesis, Queen's University, 1966.

OLIVER, MICHAEL. "The Social and Political Ideas of French Canadian Nationalists, 1920–1945." Unpublished Ph.D. thesis, McGill University, 1956.

REGENSTREIF, PETER. "The Liberal Party of Canada: A Political Analysis." Unpublished Ph.D. dissertation, Cornell University, 1963.

YOUNG, BRIAN J. "C. George McCullagh and the Leadership League." Unpublished M.A. thesis, Queen's University, 1964.

Books

ARMSTRONG, ELIZABETH. *The Crisis of Quebec, 1914–18.* New York, 1937.

BRUNET, MICHEL. *Histoire du Canada par les textes.* II. *1855–1960.* Montréal, 1963.

———— *La Présence anglaise et les Canadiens.* Montréal, 1958.

COOK, RAMSAY. *The Politics of John W. Dafoe and the Free Press.* Toronto, 1963.

DAWSON, R. MACGREGOR. *Canada in World Affairs: Two Years of War, 1939–41.* Toronto, 1943.

———— *The Conscription Crisis of 1944.* Toronto, 1961.

DEENER, DAVID, ed. *Canada-United States Treaty Relations.* Durham, N.C., 1963.

EAYRS, JAMES. *In Defence of Canada.* I. *From the Great War to the Great Depression*; II. *Rearmament and Appeasement.* 2 vols. to date. Toronto, 1964, 1965.

GRAHAM, ROGER. *Arthur Meighen.* I. *The Door of Opportunity*; II. *And Fortune Fled*; III. *No Surrender.* Toronto, 1960–65. A well-written biography marred only by the author's excessive partiality to Meighen. The period of the Second World War is most inadequately treated.

HUTCHISON, BRUCE. *The Incredible Canadian.* Toronto, 1952.

LA ROQUE, HERTEL. *Camillien Houde: le p'tit gars de Ste-Marie.* Montréal, 1961.

LAURENDEAU, ANDRÉ. *La Crise de la conscription, 1942.* Montréal, 1962.

LINGARD, C. C. and R. G. TROTTER. *Canada in World Affairs, 1941–1944.* Toronto, 1950.

MACLENNAN, HUGH. *Two Solitudes.* Toronto, 1945.

MAHEUX, ABBÉ ARTHUR. *Problems of Canadian Unity.* Quebec, 1944.

MANSERGH, NICHOLAS. *Survey of British Commonwealth Affairs: Problems of Wartime Co-operation and Post-War Change, 1939–52.* London, 1958.

PICKERSGILL, J. W. *The Liberal Party.* Toronto, 1962.

QUINN, HERBERT F. *The Union Nationale: A Study in Quebec Nationalism.* Toronto, 1963.

RUMILLY, ROBERT. *Henri Bourassa.* Montréal, 1953.

SCARROW, HOWARD A. *Canada Votes.* New Orleans, 1962.

STACEY, CHARLES P. *The Military Problems of Canada.* Toronto, 1940.

———— *The Official History of the Canadian Army in the Second World War.* I. *Six Years of War.* 3 vols. Ottawa, 1955.

URQUHART, M. C., ed. *Historical Statistics of Canada.* Toronto, 1965.

WADE, MASON. *The French Canadians, 1760–1945.* Toronto, 1956.

WILLIAMS, JOHN R. *The Conservative Party of Canada, 1920–1949*. Durham, N.C., 1956. This not altogether satisfactory work was written too early to take advantage of the availability of significant archival collections.

Articles, Papers, and Pamphlets

ARMSTRONG, ELIZABETH. "French Canadian Opinion on the War, January, 1940–June, 1941," *Contemporary Affairs*, No. 12 (Toronto, 1942).

BRUNET, MICHEL. "Coexistence Canadian Style," *Queen's Quarterly*, LXIII (autumn, 1956).

CAPLAN, GERALD L. "The Failure of Canadian Socialism: The Ontario Experience, 1932–45," *Canadian Historical Review*, XLIV (June, 1963).

FERGUSON, R. T. *We Stand on Guard*. Montreal, 1945. A typical anti-socialist polemic.

GODBOUT, ADÉLARD. "Canada, Unity in Diversity," *Foreign Affairs*, XXI (April, 1943).

GRANATSTEIN, J. L. "The Conservative Party and the Ogdensburg Agreement," *International Journal*, XXII (winter, 1966–67).

———— "Conservative Party Finances, 1939–45," in Canada, Secretary of State, Committee on Election Expenses, *Studies in Canadian Party Finance* (Ottawa, 1967).

———— "The York South By-Election of February 9, 1942: A Turning Point in Canadian Politics," *Canadian Historical Review*, XLVIII (June, 1967).

HALLETT, MARY. "The Social Credit Party and the New Democracy Movement, 1939–1940," *Canadian Historical Review*, XLVII (December, 1966).

HOROWITZ, GAD. "Conservatism, Liberalism and Socialism in Canada: An Interpretation," *Canadian Journal of Economics and Political Science*, XXXII (May, 1966).

LEDERLE, JOHN W. "National Party Conventions: Canada Shows the Way," *Southwestern Social Science Quarterly*, XXV (September, 1944).

LEFEBVRE, FLORENT. "The French-Canadian Press and the War," *Contemporary Affairs*, No. 2 (Toronto, 1940).

MACDONNELL, J. M. "Amateurs in Politics," *Queen's Quarterly*, XLIX (winter, 1942–43).

MCNAUGHT, KENNETH. "Canadian Foreign Policy and the Whig Interpretation, 1936–39," Canadian Historical Association *Report*, 1957.

PICKERSGILL, J. W. "Mackenzie King's Speeches," *Queen's Quarterly*, LVII (autumn, 1950).

Politicus [L. L. L. Golden]. "Who Did Support National Government?" *Saturday Night*, LVI (April 12, 1941).

RICHARD, JEAN D'A., s.j. "Reconstruction: The French Canadian Viewpoint," in A. R. M. LOWER and J. F. PARKINSON, ed., *War and Reconstruction* (Toronto, 1942).

PORTER, DANA. "The Future of a Conservative Party," *University of Toronto Quarterly*, XII (January, 1943).

SANDWELL, B. K. "The Federal Election," *Queen's Quarterly*, XLVII (spring, 1940).

TRESTRAIL, B. A. *Stand Up and Be Counted.* Toronto, 1944. Perhaps the most virulent anti-socialist tract printed in Canada.

TURCOTTE, EDMOND. "The Future of Unity in Canada: As Seen by a French-speaking Canadian," *University of Toronto Quarterly*, XIV (January, 1945).

———— "What Canada's War Effort Might Be," in A. R. M. LOWER and J. F. PARKINSON, eds., *War and Reconstruction* (Toronto, 1942).

WILBUR, J. R. H. "H. H. Stevens and R. B. Bennett, 1930–34," *Canadian Historical Review*, XLIII (March, 1962).

———— "H. H. Stevens and the Reconstruction Party," *Canadian Historical Review*, XLV (March, 1964).

YOUNG, BRIAN J. "C. George McCullagh and the Leadership League," *Canadian Historical Review*, XLVII (September, 1966).

Newspapers and Magazines

L'Action Nationale
Canadian Forum
Halifax Chronicle-Herald
Maclean's
Montreal *Gazette*
Montreal *La Presse*
Montreal *Le Devoir*
Montreal Star
New Commonwealth
Ottawa Citizen

Ottawa Journal
Public Opinion
Round Table
Saturday Night
Toronto Daily Star
Toronto *Evening Telegram*
Toronto *Globe and Mail*
Vancouver Sun
Winnipeg Free Press

Index